ADVANCE PRAISE FOR

Women & Everyday Uses of the Internet

"This eclectic international collection provides a needed infusion of energy into the study of gender and the Internet. The contributors use a range of theories, approaches, and research sites to collectively demonstrate how much gender matters to Internet users in their everyday lives, and how much it should matter to anyone concerned with social dimensions of the Internet."

Nancy Baym, Department of Communication Studies,
University of Kansas

"This book is a highly worthwhile collection of essays on women in new media. It avoids much of the problems of earlier work that either celebrated cyberspace as a feminine domain or vilified it as a masculine space of expanded patriarchal culture. *Women & Everyday Uses of the Internet* is refreshing by comparison in exploring the diversity of women's various practices in cyberspace as well as the differences among the women who are online. This book is warmly recommended to those interested in this important topic."

Mark Poster, Director and Professor of Film Studies,
Professor of History, University of California, Irvine

Women & Everyday
Uses of the Internet

Steve Jones
General Editor

Vol. 8

PETER LANG
New York • Washington, D.C./Baltimore • Bern
Frankfurt am Main • Berlin • Brussels • Vienna • Oxford

Women & Everyday Uses of the Internet

Agency & Identity

EDITED BY
Mia Consalvo &
Susanna Paasonen

PETER LANG
New York • Washington, D.C./Baltimore • Bern
Frankfurt am Main • Berlin • Brussels • Vienna • Oxford

Library of Congress Cataloging-in-Publication Data

Women and everyday uses of the Internet: agency and identity /
[edited by] Mia Consalvo and Susanna Paasonen.
p. cm. — (Digital formations; vol. 8)
Includes bibliographical references and index.
1. Internet and women. 2. Women—Identity. 3. Internet—
Social aspects. I. Consalvo, Mia. II. Paasonen,
Susanna. III. Digital formations; v. 8.
HQ1178 .W66   004.678′082—dc21   2002069279
ISBN 0-8204-6141-5
ISSN 1526-3169

Die Deutsche Bibliothek-CIP-Einheitsaufnahme

Women and everyday uses of the Internet: agency and identity /
Mia Consalvo and Susanna Paasonen (eds.).
−New York; Washington, D.C./Baltimore; Bern;
Frankfurt am Main; Berlin; Brussels; Vienna; Oxford: Lang.
(Digital formations; Vol. 8)
ISBN 0-8204-6141-5

Cover design by Joni Holst

The paper in this book meets the guidelines for permanence and durability
of the Committee on Production Guidelines for Book Longevity
of the Council of Library Resources.

Printed in the United States of America

Table of Contents

Part Two: Addressing Women

Part Three: Everyday Uses

Part Four: Gender, Agency, and New Media

Foreword

Steve Jones,
Editor, Digital Formations

On the continuum of identity that stretches from presence to telepresence we are constantly modulating who we are. Thanks to the work of many scholars, we have begun since the mid 1990s to determine that gender operates in the realm of online communication no matter the proclamations of "gender neutrality" to be had on the Internet, or that on the Internet, no one knows you're a (fill in the blank). Indeed, whether it is gender, race, ethnicity, or an array of different (and differentiating) factors, to ourselves we are who we are because of our bodies and our minds.

It is most important therefore that we pursue our understanding of these factors the best that we can. I am grateful to the contributors to *Women and Everyday Uses of the Internet*, and to its editors Mia Consalvo and Susanna Paasonen, for asking the "what happens next?" question concerning gender and the Internet. They show us not only that gender matters online but also that gender matters in important ways, in novel ways, and that theorizing about it can provide us with important frameworks we can use to think about the Internet's place in everyday life. Moreover, it can help us think about the ways the Internet has become internalized both in the practices of the everyday and also in everyday thinking.

It is to Consalvo's and Paasonen's great credit, and that of their collaborators on this volume, that they demonstrate that women matter and make a difference *on* and *to* the Internet. This book therefore makes a major contribution to our knowledge and understanding of life online.

On the Internet, Women Matter

Mia Consalvo and Susanna Paasonen

Introduction

It is hardly ironic that this book, about women and their uses of the Internet, was produced by two women editors largely over email. It was a practical necessity, as one is in Milwaukee and the other in Helsinki. We met at the first Association of Internet Researchers (AoIR) conference in Kansas, where we both presented papers in a panel on women and the Internet, and conceived the book idea. Meeting again at the second AoIR conference in 2001, at Minneapolis, we were able to discuss the shaping of the manuscript and see where things had gone in terms of research and theory over the past year. Susan Herring, while attending the conference's last panel addressing women and the Internet, pointed out that in all of the panels at the conference concerning gender, it seemed that feminist researchers had successfully demonstrated that gender did "matter" in studying and understanding the Internet and peoples' uses of it. The challenge, therefore, was to figure out where to go "next" as feminist Internet researchers.

We believe this book is a step in that direction, taking feminist theory and Internet studies beyond the (important) pronouncement that "gender matters" online, to determine how it matters, how other factors influence its expression and composition, and how feminist theorizing of the Internet can respond to this new challenge.

Some Directions in Studies on Women and the Internet

During the past decade, studies on gender and the Internet have been occupied with the very question, "does gender matter?" In the mid 1990s, the Internet became increasingly discussed as "cyberspace," a realm alternative to and separate from the "real world"—as formulated in John Perry Barlow's 1996 "Declaration of the Independence of Cyberspace," which argued for online identities separate from embodiment and power. While such "cyberfantasy" has been criticized as neoliberal and voluntarist (Eisenstein, 1998; Paasonen, in this volume), it has also been highly influential and operational in studies on gender and online interactions. Researchers like Allucquère Rosanne Stone (1995) and Sherry Turkle (1995) have considered how gender is a factor online, yet they have become better known for their attention to users who experiment with identity online, and they have come to stand for an approach to Internet studies where users have wider latitude than in traditional spaces to explore alternate or multiple identities. In this paradigm, the Internet becomes understood as transformative spatiality where gender categories become reconfigured.

Another highly influential theorist for feminist Internet research has been Donna J. Haraway, with her manifesto detailing the potential of the dualism-shattering, metaphorical cyborg (1985/1991). Feminist academics have embraced this figure in examining how traditional media as well as new media have reconfigured the possibilities for bodies, technologies, and gender (Balsamo, 1996; Braidotti, 1996; Kirkup et al., 2000; Lykke & Wolmark, 1999; Springer, 1996). Although not predominantly concerned with women's uses of the Internet, theorizations of cyborgs have helped develop a critical approach to conceptualizations of gender that have been articulated with new media technologies and that have been naturalized and obscured in popular discourses. Haraway's manifesto has also inspired female media artists and writers to coin, and to identify with, the term "cyberfeminism," as introduced by the artist group VNS Matrix in their 1991 "Cyberfeminist Manifesto for the Twenty-First Century"(VNS Matrix, 2002).

Perhaps the most vocal and widely read proponent of cyberfeminist research has been Sadie Plant, who reads information networks as signs of feminization, an alliance of women and machines, both tools for male culture that represent complexity beyond governance. In strongly metaphorical vein, Plant defines Net culture as a continuum of the female practice of weaving and feminization as a process that erodes and subverts the culture of masculine dominance (Plant, 1995, 1997). Other cyberfeminists have advocated a more traditionally "liberal" approach to women and technology, arguing that women need equal access to, and skills in, this new technology so that they can then empower themselves (Cherny & Weise, 1996; Spender, 1995). Yet this approach has been critiqued as a "technology neutral" or "technological determinist" position, where there is little critique of the social structures and culture surrounding new media, and women are simply urged to "plunge in" and make their own mark (Luckman, 1999; Munster, 1999). Still other researchers have looked for situated formulations of cyberfeminism that would account for historicity, for differences between women, and enable critical feminist politics, thus bringing cyberfeminist discourse into closer proximity with media studies, women's studies, and cultural studies. All in all, authors identifying and working with cyberfeminism have looked at women hacking the Net, using it as a medium for activism, as an artistic medium, and as a tool for international networking and collaboration (Braidotti, 1996; Cutting Edge, 2000; Harcourt, 1999; Hawthorne & Klein, 1999; *n. paradoxa*, 1998; Sollfrank & Old Boys Network, 1998, 1999). Research has also been done on grrrl web zines and sites, their ties to wider subcultural grrrl networks, and their unruly gender performances (Leonard, 1998; Wakeford, 1997).

Emphasis on the Everyday

While these studies have been important in establishing a base for feminist analysis centered on the Internet, which David Silver, in his presentation at the 2001 AoIR conference, referred to as the first and second wave of Internet research, *Women and Everyday Uses of the Internet: Agency and Identity* seeks to broaden this scope of investigation to the more mainstream, everyday practices of Internet use: It looks at portals and other sites designed for women; chats; personal home pages and virtual stables; web camera sites; information society projects, interactive television, and ways of popularizing the World Wide Web.

Scrutinizing popular and widespread uses is especially relevant as the Internet and the World Wide Web become more ubiquitous and more commercialized. Ever since the 1993 launching of Mosaic, the first graphical browser, the World Wide Web has become framed as the "shop window" of the Internet with its uses of colors and graphic shapes, images, sounds, animations, videos, and movie files. This has meant greater corporate interest and the presence of advertising as well as a widening user interest, resulting in the constitution of the Internet as a mass medium (Abbate, 1999). This tale is occasionally narrated as one of loss, changing from free, open cultures of hacking to increasing control, censorship, commercialization, and closure. Such narratives of loss enjoy a certain popularity, but they also risk falling back on nostalgia toward an idealized and exclusive avant-garde medium of hackers and activists. In terms of "the popular Internet" (including the spread and use of email, chat, and web sites), commercialization has been a key motivation, even precondition, for developing "user-friendly" solutions and interface designs and making the medium more accessible to users. We would like to follow a narrative path that pays attention to the ways in which popularization and commercialization of the Internet have enabled increasing access to the Internet for social groups generally excluded from hacker cultures—such as young girls and women of various ages.

At times, however, these contradictions and tensions can seem futile when attempting to understand women and the Internet, especially as usage statistics change daily, as Internet businesses and personal sites appear and disappear and female users grow more or less comfortable online, and as teenage girls take up Internet-related activities. Likewise, studies of gender and the Internet and women's use of the Internet have changed dramatically even in a few short years. The Internet has changed from a place where identities were joyfully discarded, experimented with, or reconfigured, to a medium (discussed in spatial terms) where identity seems to be a driving force for involvement, and an aspect of embodiment that few users actually want to leave behind. Likewise, common understandings of just what the Internet "is" have changed from the text-based spaces of email, listservs, and Multi-User Domanins/Dungeons (MUDs), to the graphical places of the World Wide Web and online gaming. Also, the Internet is growing as a place for commerce, and critics are questioning whether the Internet's future lies solely along the lines of other communications technologies, which in the United States and elsewhere exist mainly through commercial channels. Clearly, where we are now is not where we will stay. Nevertheless, in studying the Internet and women's current uses of it, we need to step back and consider how our theorizing has changed, or must change, in order to remain relevant.

As the Internet is increasingly used for communication, consumption, and other leisure-related uses, it is important to analyze critically the ways in which these practices have been gendered, how they are entwined into the structures of everyday life, and how women make use of them. Looking at the various areas of the "mainstream" Internet, this volume points out the multiplicity of practices involved, and argues for a need to go beyond simple—and often pejorative—dualities such as commercial versus noncommercial, mainstream versus independent, or conservative versus progressive. Instead, this volume, like *Virtual Gender* (Green & Adam, 2001), looks for critical analysis of these concepts and their reevaluation in terms of practices of media use, sig-nification, and appropriation.

Ways in Which Women Matter

The chapters in this volume investigate case studies showing the ways in which gender matters, and is made to matter, in online services and communications of various kinds. In doing this, the volume looks at the continuities and connections between cyberfeminist investigations and the tradition of feminist media studies, in which both the gendering of users and the hailing of women as consumers have been central topics of research. This approach looks at agency not only as practiced by "content producers," artists and other professionals, but also by audiences and consumers who use media for different means, derive different kinds of pleasures from it, and are addressed in specific ways by companies, services, and public projects. The contributions point to the specific features of online communications but also argue for the situated and contextual nature of these practices and their connections to other areas of media culture.

As the title of the book suggests, it addresses issues to do with agency, identity, gendered usage, and the Internet as a component of the everyday media environment. Centrally, it deals with the ways in which the category of women becomes defined, marked, and understood in relation to the popular Internet. The authors are representatives of North America and Western Europe, areas with high Internet penetration, large investments in communication technologies in general, and considerably higher percentages of female Internet users than other parts of the world. These are also regions where the Internet is most enthusiastically narrated and marketed as a mass medium. The geographic variety of the case studies has, in the course of the editing process, become narrower than initially intended, and the female users discussed in the chapters, in spite of their varying national, regional, and class locations, represent privileged access to media technology. This makes it even more crucial to discuss which women and which everyday uses of the Internet this volume addresses.

The demography of Internet use pointed, throughout the 1990s, to the dominance of white, middle-class Western males, but lately the increase in female users has led to an increased interest in addressing female users and designing services for them. This has, however, also meant that the category of female users has been assumed to be internally unified and defined against the normative "opposite gender," that of men. Addressing women, then, leads into questions concerning gender as a system of regulation, signification, and naturalization: what and who counts as "female" is by no means given but based on continuous processes of inclusion and exclusion. Quite often this implies a process of "whitewashing" where white women are positioned as points of identification for the category of women in general, and their interests become narrated in the lines of consumerist leisure activities.

Analysis of women's web sites has made visible (Sadowska, Cooks et al., and Dorer, all in this volume) the way the category of women becomes defined in very familiar terms such as domesticity, fashion and beauty, heterosexual romance and relationships, pregnancy and maternity, menstruation and fitness.

These pages' designs make use of "feminine" soft pastel colors, round shapes, and italic fonts, and the sites are often characterized as "communities"—a term which, as Jodi Dean has argued, has become something of a protean catch-phrase in online communication and is used to imply "meaningful, personal, self-organized communication," a certain longing for authenticity that is otherwise assumed lost in mainstream media (Dean, 2000, p. 12). "Woman," here, stands for feminine as communicative, sharing, and caring. Furthermore, women's interests become defined to a large degree through embodiment and practices of reproduction. Thus the category of women is defined through acts of naturalization and references to women as nurturing and reproducing creatures. Consequently, gender becomes defined, *to matter*, as a fixed and genetically determined binary structure of differences, desires, and complementarity (Butler, 1990, 1993).

While the category of women becomes, on the one hand, fixed in various acts of address, it remains, on the other, divided along the axis of ethnicity, "race," class, sexuality, nationality, age, region, and profession, which represent different marks of identity. The contributions in *Women and Everyday Uses of the Internet* illustrate the workings of such differences—acts of differentiation and community building, proximity and distance. The case studies analyze identity and agency as both textual positions produced in site design and media theory (Gustafson, O'Riordan, Sadowska, Consalvo, and Paasonen, all in this volume) and as local, lived situations (Vehviläinen, Poster, Tiernan, Oksman, Bird & Jorgenson, van Zoonen & Aalberts, all in this volume)—and, of course, as movements between the two.

Commercial Underpinnings

While the frames of women's web sites may be seen as regulative and even stereotypical, such an interpretation does not fully account for the ways these sites are used. Paraphrasing Michel de Certeau (1988), consumption can be seen as *tactics*, practices of use and interpretation that are something other, or over and above, what has been intended by the product manufacturers and advertisers. Media uses are contingent, scattered practices that cannot be reduced to implied meanings or commercial activities. Yet it is of equal importance to acknowledge the ways in which usage is conditioned and framed, the ways in which the Internet becomes narrated as a mainstream medium.

Women became targeted as a user category around the mid 1990s, as potential e-commerce customers and as an audience for online advertising. These commercial ties are hardly surprising, given that women have been addressed by various media—television, cinema, radio, magazines, and romantic fiction—as their central source of income. Female media use has, with considerable persistence, been figured as passive, escapist, and even compulsive. The passiveness often associated with consumption of television (and consumption at large) has been given a range of feminine features that become repeated in spite of redefinitions of both gender and consumption (Bowlby, 2000; Spigel & Mann, 1992).

Contrary to formulations that mark the Internet as cyberspace with a logic of its own, the analysis of gender and consumerism necessitates an approach that is both contextual and intermedial. Separated from the spaces and practices of everyday life, the Internet (as cyberspace) can be narrated as a realm of promise and rupture, while formulations within feminist media studies at large pay attention to the social contexts and conditions of media use, the different locations of media users, and the ways of reading, negotiating, and producing meanings in their everyday life. If we are to make sense of the Internet as an everyday medium, such situated case studies, along with critical conceptual analysis, are badly needed.

As Daniel Miller and Don Slater (2000, p. 1) put it: "the Internet is not a monolithic or placeless 'cyberspace'; rather, it is numerous new technologies, used by diverse people, in diverse real-world situations." And, it could be added, also numerous discourses, texts, literacies, and modes of representation. Female users may not subvert "the nature" of the Internet, as there is no fixed or unified essence or core of the Internet to subvert—and as women are hardly united in their uses of the medium. Increasing numbers of users, designers, and content producers from varying geographical, ethnic, and class backgrounds are likely to add to the diversity of mainstream Internet services and also challenge the position of English as the lingua franca of the Internet—and, perhaps, that of the USA as the hub of Internet services, terminology, and research.

The goal of this collection is thus to chronicle and theorize women's uses of the Internet as they begin to go online in greater numbers. In the early 90s the Internet was represented as a place where few women spent their time, and a place potentially hostile to them as well. During the early 1990s, less than 20% of Internet users were women, and in press accounts, their experiences were not presented as positive. The women who *were* online were portrayed as tough "settlers" of "the electronic frontier," who were unafraid of dealing with the rough-and-tumble "man's world" that comprised most of the Internet. However, we prefer this volume to focus on more recent activities, starting at the point where women have achieved parity, or near parity, online. This profile of women is also different from the first one in that a growing number are not "pioneers" settling the new space, but are instead part of a growing wave of "early" or "late" adopters of this new communications technology. These women are therefore hardly marked as "revolutionary" in their presence online, but they make up the first mass group of women users.

These female users are also using different areas of the Internet: not only preoccupied with identity play in MUDs, or the text-only talk of bulletin boards or listservs, they are creating web pages and virtual stables, being hailed as consumers by commercial sites for women, creating places of community denied to them in physical space, and negotiating the slipperiness of identity online when they are greatly invested in maintaining a certain vision (or version) of themselves. These activities may appear mundane, but they are important to study and theorize. Feminist scholars have long argued that it is too easy to denigrate women's traditional choices, activities, and interests, that we should rather understand what pleasure (and perhaps resistance) can be realized through these things. So, although women chatting on Oprah's sites may not be perceived as more "radical" than those creating lesbian separatist spaces, each can yield valuable information about how different groups of women see themselves. Further, we can investigate the role that the Internet is playing in the lives of various women, how this role is being integrated into their particular constructions of identity, and how the Internet becomes understood and defined in its usage.

Although this book addresses women and their uses of the

Internet, there is little if anything we can say about *women* and the Internet in general. As commercial sites like iVillage have learned, women are not a monolithic group to be appealed to with a ready stock of signifiers. More varied identity markers play crucial parts in women's uses: including sexual orientation, class, age, region, and educational level. Further, varying interests play a part in how the Internet is used—and how women are hailed. Still it can be argued that one component relevant to women's uses and interests is the underlying importance of embodiment and the materiality of lives lived—whether a denial of more traditional "real" spaces or the chance to find a new sort of community or commonality that is missing from "real" life.

Organization of This Book

Women and Everyday Uses of the Internet: Agency and Identity consists of 13 chapters, some of which are based on papers read at the 2000 Association of Internet Researchers conference but most of which have been attracted through an open call for manuscripts. The authors represent various disciplinary backgrounds, from communications and media studies to design, anthropology, information systems, and cinema studies, but they are united in their interest in both women's studies and Internet research. To paraphrase Miller and Slater (2000, p. 1), the following chapters do not simply ask about the "use" or "effects" of the Internet; they look at how women in specific contexts "make themselves a(t) home in a transforming communicative environment"—how women are defined and positioned, how they situate themselves in such contingent media environments, and how they appropriate these environments for their own needs.

The following chapters have been thematically divided into four interconnecting and partly overlapping parts: "Defining Gender," "Addressing Women," "Everyday Uses," and "Gender, Agency, and New Media." These parts form the basic structure of the volume, bringing together articles on the basis of their argumentation and themes rather than their choice of research material or theoretical approaches, in an attempt to make it easier for the reader to grasp connections between individual chapters.

The first part, "Defining Gender," addresses the larger issue of how gender, and particularly the category of women, is "made to matter" online through case studies of personal home pages, women as Information Technology (IT) workers, women's web camera sites, and the gendered design of web sites. The individual chapters look at how gender categories are constructed and how they work in online representations and work practices.

Chapter 1 addresses the question of "easy play" with gender online, particularly Sherry Turkle's and Sandy Stone's suggestion that the Internet allows for multiple identities that are easily shuffled by individuals and that the Internet also allows for the exploration of different identities leading to greater understandings of other people's realities. Through a focus on personal home pages, Susanna Paasonen argues for a differentiation between identities as internalized, lived locations and narratives, and textual constructs such as characters. Amateur representations are also discussed by Kate O'Riordan in chapter 2 on web camera sites that focus on representations of the female body. Outlining a topography of such sites, O'Riordan studies the organization of look and gaze in the web camera medium, and the ways their representations build on the conventions of commercial (visual) erotica and porn on the one hand, and alter these conventions and modalities on the other. Web camera sites are discussed as sites of gender performativity that may open up ways for questioning the naturalness of gender and desire.

Johanna Dorer shifts the focus into the realm of IT professionals, expertise, and the making of gender in chapter 3. Through qualitative research on women in IT professions, Dorer analyzes internal hierarchies of the field, women's views on their own work, agency, and technical competence. Contrary to some cyberfeminist arguments, gender hierarchies and divisions are hardly erased in the context of the Internet, and neither are the categories of professionalism. This focus on design practices is expanded in Noemi Sadowska's study of the design tactics of the British women's web site BEME.com. In chapter 4 she analyzes the influence that the print magazine industry, its representational conventions, and its gendered assumptions have on web design, and how these unspoken practices can be better articulated and explored. Furthermore, Sadowska explores the possibilities of alternative design strategies that would challenge the structuring of information through increased interactivity and engagement of female users.

Part two, "Addressing Women," analyzes how women have been positioned as consumers on the World Wide Web as they have increased their numbers online. Case studies focus especially on women's web sites, their publicity, codes of interaction, and community construction. In chapter 5, Mia Consalvo looks at older media's representations of the Internet during the 1990s and how women were constructed in this discourse. Drawing historical parallels with other media technologies, the telephone and radio in particular, Consalvo looks at the interconnections between female media users, metaphors, and commerce, as well as how definitions of the Internet as "safe" for women translate as safe economic transactions.

In chapter 6, Leda Cooks, Mari Castañeda Paredes, and Erica Scharrer analyze one of the largest commercial women's web sites, Oprah.com, focusing on how the site shapes and maintains a sense of community among users. The multiple meanings and forms of such community are studied in relation to Oprah Winfrey's public image, the corporate underpinnings of the site, the discourse of mutual support and nurturing, and users' reflections on the significance of such spaces of communication and interaction. Community has become a key component in women's web sites such as Oprah.com, yet these communities are often more about discourse and marketing strategies—selling the Internet to women—than about a sense of community or connection between returning users. Karen Gustafson provides a highly interesting analysis of the physical coding of community in iVillage, Oxygen, and Women.com in chapter 7. Gustafson looks at the norms and conditions involved in joining commercial online communities and the means of controlling and governing them. All in all, the authors question how well the sites analyzed serve women, whether they can ever fulfill the promises they make of providing community, and how they are faring in the current Internet economy downturn.

Part three, "Everyday Uses," considers how women occupy multiple roles (beyond simply "as women") when they venture online, and how these roles structure their actions and opportunities. Writers in this section consider how women view the Internet and its promises (occasionally, its empty promises) as lesbians, as war veterans, and as girls engaged in play. The game industry, for example, has tended to cater mainly to boys, while girls' games, such as Mattel's Barbie Fashion Designer and Purple Moon's Rockett series, have been accused of stereotyping. Against the backdrop of gaming culture and young people's uses of Information and Communication Technology (ICT), Virpi Oksman analyzes the practices of young girls setting up and maintaining virtual horse stables on the World Wide Web in chapter 8. Girls' networking and creation of a breeders' union illustrate a field of Internet gaming culture so far overlooked in media studies, and points to possibilities for content production scripted not by corporations but by young users themselves.

Quite a different case of female networking is presented by Jennifer Tiernan in chapter 9 on female Vietnam veterans and their use of the Internet in reconnecting and establishing spaces for reflecting on their experiences of war and the ways their identities have been marked by it. Their listserv, web site, and occasional face-to-face meetings enable these marginalized women to maintain a community that would not be possible using other media. Themes of marginalization, identity, and exclusion of outsiders in online communities are also addressed by Jamie Poster in chapter 10, which focuses on the lesbian chat room "#LesChat." Poster analyzes the definitions and boundaries of sexual identity, as well as the forms of agency that the chat rooms, as community, enable. Contrary to theories of online communities as sites of identity play, Poster outlines quite a different understanding of identity politics in establishing spaces for marginalized articulations of sexuality and desire. Together, these authors make the case that gender, as a general category, is not sufficient when studying how women make use of the Internet. Instead, we must consider other aspects of "identity" and also how individuals within more specific groups are still not monolithic in their interests or desires.

Part four, "Gender, Agency, and New Media," addresses different forms of female agency in information society programs and experiments, as marked by class and regional differences. The section also looks at how practices of media use are, or may become, reconfigured with the establishment of Internet use as daily practices.

Information society agendas and publicly funded programs

remain highly influential in introducing information technology to underserved groups. In chapter 11, S. Elizabeth Bird and Jane Jorgenson look at the gender dynamics that have been at play in low-income, working-class families in Florida with the introduction of the Internet-based "Family-Net" program. Aimed at "extending the school day," the program has brought computer technology into low-income homes with children designated as academically "at risk." Bird and Jorgenson analyze how mothers in particular receive and reflect on the educational experiment, the Internet, and technical competence in general. In chapter 12, Marja Vehviläinen discusses rural information society experiments in Finland with special attention to the definitions of gendered agency and citizenship. Without paying more attention to the differences within the category of "citizen," and without encouraging women's own initiative and interests in uses of ICT, the results and significance of such programs are likely to be limited. In addition to a contextual understanding of situated citizenship, Vehviläinen argues for the introduction of computers and the Internet as media used in and for practices of everyday life.

The Internet is also increasingly becoming an everyday medium through its projected convergence with television—that is, interactive television. In chapter 13, Liesbet van Zoonen and Chris Aalberts look at the potential disruptions and contradictions this new technology may introduce into household use. Through a study of young heterosexual couples' uses of television and the Internet, van Zoonen and Aalberts analyze the gendered patterns of television and Internet usage and expectations concerning the emerging medium.

All in all, this volume aims to contribute to the diversification of Internet studies, in terms of gender as well as other identity positions and markers of difference, in the context of everyday life (among other recent enterprises are Green & Adam, 2001; Kolko et al., 2000). This requires interdisciplinary as well as international networking, and a desire to think through the situatedness of Internet use in various social, cultural, economic, and political contexts. *Women and Everyday Uses of the Internet: Agency and Identity* addresses such contexts in areas of comparative privilege, but without claiming a universality of experiences or uses. It is only through case studies and focused textual close reading that we can discuss the Internet other than in terms of technical standards—or by postulating entities such as "Internet culture" as ephemeral points of reference.

In conclusion, it seems difficult to pin down, analyze, and theorize women's uses of the Internet, as the technology, women, and individual practices all change daily. Even as we were engaged in creating this volume, some sites being analyzed shut down, while others experienced financial crises. Listservs and home pages may come and go, and newer possibilities for engagement and communication on the Internet may appear. Yet, the work done here provides outlines for understanding contemporary practices and situates them in expanding social and cultural contexts. As editors, we hope that this volume will expand and refine theorization on women and the Internet, thus providing a springboard for future investigations.

References

Abbate, J. (1999). *Inventing the Internet*. Cambridge: MIT Press.

Balsamo, A. (1996). *Technologies of the Gendered Body: Reading CyborgWomen*. Durham, NC: Duke University Press.

Barlow, J. P. (1996). A Declaration of the Independence of Cyberspace. Electronic document at http://www.eff.org/~barlow/Declaration-Final.html.

Bowlby, R. (2000). *Carried Away: The Invention of Modern Shopping*. London: Faber and Faber.

Braidotti, R. (1996). Cyberfeminism With a Difference. Electronic document at http://www.let.ruu.nl/womens_studies/rosi/cyberfem.htm.

Butler, J. (1990). *Gender Trouble: Feminism and the Subversion of Identity*. New York: Routledge.

Butler, J. (1993). *Bodies That Matter: On the Discursive Limits of "Sex."* New York: Routledge.

Cherny, L., & Weise, E. R., eds. (1996). *Wired Women: Gender and New Realities in Cyberspace*. Seattle: Seal Press.

Cutting Edge, eds. (2000). *Digital Desires: Language, Identity and New Technologies*. London: I. B. Tauris.

Dean, J. (2000). Community. In T. Swiss (ed.), *Unspun: Key Concepts for Understanding the World Wide Web*. New York: New York University Press, 4–16.

De Certeau, M. (1988). *The Practice of Everyday Life*. Berkeley: University of California Press (1984).

Eisenstein, Z. (1998). *Global Obscenities: Patriarchy, Capitalism, and the Lure of Cyberfantasy*. New York: New York University Press.

Green, E., & Adam, A., eds. (2001). *Virtual Gender: Technology, Consumption and Identity*. London: Routledge.

Haraway, D. (1985/1991). *Simians, Cyborgs and Women*. New York: Routledge.

Harcourt, W., ed. (1999). *Women@Internet: Creating New Cultures in Cyberspace*. London: Zed Books.

Hawthorne, S., & Klein, R., eds. (1999). *CyberFeminism: Connectivity, Critique and Creativity*. Melbourne: Spinifex.

Kirkup, G., Janes, L., Woodward, K., & Hovenden, F., eds. (2000). *The Gendered Cyborg: A Reader*. London: Routledge.

Kolko, B. E., Nakamura, L., & Rodman, G. B., eds. (2000). *Race in Cyberspace*. New York: Routledge.

Leonard, M. (1998). Paper Planes: Travelling the New Grrrl Geographies. In T. Skelton & G. Valentine (eds.). *Cool Places: Geographies of Youth Cultures*. London: Routledge, 101–118.

Luckman, S. (1999). *(En) gendering the Digital Body: Feminism and the Internet*. Hecate, 25(2), 36–48.

Lykke, N., & Braidotti, R., eds. (1996). *Between Monsters, Goddesses and Cyborgs: Feminist Confrontations with Science, Medicine and Cyberspace*. London: Zed Books.

Miller, D., & Slater, D. (2000). *The Internet: An Ethnographic Approach*. Oxford: Berg.

Munster, A. (1999). Is There Postlife After Postfeminism? Tropes of Technics and Life in Cyberfeminism. *Australian Feminist Studies*, 14(29), 119–131.

n. paradoxa: *International Feminist Art Journal*, 2 (1998) (Volume title: Women and New Media).

Plant, S. (1995). The Future Looms: Weaving Women and Cybernetics. In M. Featherstone & R. Burrows (eds.), *Cyberspace, Cyberbodies, Cyberpunk*. London: Sage, 45–64.

Plant, S. (1997). *Zeros + Ones: Digital Women and the New Technoculture*. London: Fourth Estate.

Silver, D. (2001). Evolving Digital Discourses: Community Rhetoric and Commercial Practice. Presentation at the annual conference of the Association of Internet Researchers, Minneapolis-St.Paul, Minnesota.

Sollfrank, C., & Old Boys Network, eds. (1998). *First Cyberfeminist International*. Hamburg: OBN.

Sollfrank, C., & Old Boys Network, eds. (1999). *Next Cyberfeminist International*. Hamburg: OBN.

Spender, D. (1995). *Nattering on the Net: Women, Power and Cyberspace*. Melbourne: Spinifex.

Spigel, L., & Mann, D. (1992). Introduction. In L. Spigel & D. Mann (eds.), *Private Screenings: Television and the Female Consumer*. Minneapolis: University of

Minnesota Press, vii–xiii.

Springer, C. (1996). *Electronic Eros: Bodies and Desire in the Postindustrial age.* Austin: University of Texas Press.

Stone, A. R. (1995). *The War of Desire and Technology at the Close of the Mechanical Age.* Cambridge: MIT Press.

Turkle, S. (1995). *Life on the Screen: Identity in the Age of the Internet.* New York: Simon and Schuster.

VNS Matrix. (2002). Manifesto. Accessed at http://sysx.org/vns/manifesto.html.

Wakeford, N. (1997). Networking Women and Grrrls with Information/ Communication Technology: Surfing Tales on the World Wide Web. In J. Terry & M. Calvert (eds.), *Processed Lives: Gender & Technology in Everyday Life.* London: Routledge, 51–66.

Wolmark, J., ed. (1999). *Cybersexualities: A Reader on Feminist Theory, Cyborgs and Cyberspace.* Edinburgh: Edinburgh University Press.

Part One

Defining Gender

Chapter 1

Gender, Identity, and (the Limits of) Play on the Internet

Susanna Paasonen

Since the early 1990s, discussions on gender and the Internet have had a strong focus on the possibilities of play and experimentation. The Net is said to enable gender blending and bending, the taking up of different identities, and the exploration of the limits of "the self." As the medium has become invested with a general aura of possibility and subversion, these notions of freedom and play have become truisms. This has particularly been the case with gender-swapping: in MUDs (multi-user domains/ dungeons), MOOs (object-oriented MUDs), and chats one's body cannot be seen, and text-based self-representations (or the use of avatars of some kind) are all scenarios that other participants can interact with; this has been translated as freedom to "be whatever."

This chapter looks at the writings of Sherry Turkle and Allucquère Rosanne (Sandy) Stone on gender and identity, which have become canonized as pioneering studies on identity in online environments. As Beth E. Kolko, Lisa Nakamura, and Gilbert E. Rodman (2000, p. 5) argue, the work of Turkle, Stone, and Mark Poster, among others, has established "an intellectual center for cyberspace theory."[1] The figure of an Internet user who creates parallel identities and crosses categories of gender, sexuality, and race, as introduced in these studies, has often been taken as a starting point for studying social relations on the Internet (Bolter, 2000, pp. 24–25; Danet, 1998; Fuchs, 2000, p. 35; Hayles, 1999, pp.

27–28). In this framework, users are seen to take up and build "virtual selves" that blur common understandings of identity. However, such scenarios are often different from everyday uses of the Internet (Wynn & Katz, 1997), and the discourse of freedom and play easily leads into a twist in perspective that makes it difficult to analyze, or even acknowledge, many mainstream uses of the medium.

This chapter, then, concerns "the limits of the performance, the rules of the game" (Bell & Valentine, 1995, p. 144). It looks at the discourse of gender play and the kinds of questions concerning power and everyday Internet use that it leaves untouched, focusing especially on personal home pages. Home pages have been used in arguing against the discourse of online gender play, yet they have also been studied as sites for identity construction and self-invention. Rather than simply presenting personal home pages as the "antidote" to enthusiastic writings on "online" gender and identity, I suggest that the norms and conventions of self-representation on home pages can be used in studying other forms of Internet-based communication, such as chats and virtual communities.

So Many of Me: Identity, Performativity, and Play

Sherry Turkle (1995, pp. 9–10) sees both computers and information networks as basically identity-transforming, as they erode the boundaries of real and virtual, human and machine, and enable constant self-invention. This is especially the case with virtual communities like MUDs, which, according to Turkle, "make possible the creation of an identity so fluid and multiple that it strains the limits of the notion. Identity, after all, refers to the sameness between two qualities, in this case between a person and his or her persona. But in MUDs, one can be many" (Turkle, 1995, p. 12). In a similar rhetorical move, Stone (1996, p. 42) discusses "cyberspace" as a spatiality "irruptively constituting identities that are simultaneously technological and social, a catastrophic emergence of the lucid and the unpredictable ... [T]he technosocial, the social mode of the computer nets, evokes unruly multiplicity as an integral part of social identity." Both Turkle and Stone frame the Internet and virtual communities as alternative social configurations where the rules of "making the self" are subverted. Spaces of media use become understood as mere terminals from which one sets out to "travel in cyberspace," leaving behind the confines of embodiment, along with the markers of identity and difference (Nakamura, 2000c).

For Turkle (1995, p. 9), computers and especially the Internet are "changing the way we think, the nature of our sexuality, the forms of our communities, our very identities." In this process, the self becomes understood as multiple and fluid, and is able to perform several characters (p. 15). Turkle (p. 18) thus reads computers as illustrations of poststructural theories on dispersed identities and also as means of bringing these theories "down to earth." This, however, seems to translate as downplaying issues to do with power: If computer-mediated selves are textual, multiple, and constituted in interaction, it does not follow that they equal poststructural critiques of the autonomous and unitary self. Play with multiple identities—inventing, taking up, living, and discarding different personae online—can be seen as illustrations of voluntarism, belief in the possibilities of intentional identity-formation. Such a formulation may work to support understandings of the self as a private, more than social or cultural, construction project.

Stone (1996, pp. 2–3) sees the Internet as a site for floating identities that are independent from what she calls a "root identity," the conventional assumption of the self as coherent. According to Stone, the Net is a space in which "the transgender is the natural body. The nets are spaces of transformation, identity factories in which bodies are meaning machines, and transgender—identity as performance, as play, as wrench in the smooth gears of the social apparatus of vision—is the ground state" (pp. 180–181). This is to say that different crossings from one gender and identity position to another are so common online that gender identity, identifiable as either female or male, is no longer a viable category. Stone, like Turkle, emphasizes the fluidity of the self and sees the Internet as a site where this multiplicity may flourish: "I tend to see myself as an entity that has chosen to make its life career out of playing with identity. It sometimes seems as though everything in my past has been a kind of extended excuse for experiments with subject positions and interaction. After all, what material is better to experiment with than one's self?" (Stone, 1996, pp. 1–2). In Stone's formulation, power is repressive rather than productive, and the Internet is a sphere where spatial forms of power do not apply. Identities are about play and masks, and authenticating them through references to one's embodied location translates as both an anachronistic longing for a coherent self and a misconception of what identities are about (pp. 2–3, 171–172).

According to Turkle (1995, p. 14), as "people can play at having different genders and different lives, it isn't surprising that for some this play has became as real as what we conventionally think of as their lives, although for them this is no longer a valid distinction." If gender is thought of as something one has, rather than something one is constituted by, this may be a logical outcome. Ideas of "real life" as merely another level of self-performance, and not necessarily the prioritized one, are discussed throughout her book, *Life on the Screen*. These widely embraced assumptions are based on rather simplified understandings of what it means to live, and perform, as an embodied, gendered, classed, and raced individual. To pose the question of fragmented identity as one of constant self-invention and conscious construction leads to voluntarist views of subjectivation that can be quite efficient in downplaying the role of power in the "making of the self."

In their discussions on performativity, both Turkle and Stone are "informed" by Judith Butler's research (Stone, 1996, pp. 40–41; Turkle, 1995, p. 313n). However, in their texts, as in some other readings of Butler's *Gender Trouble* (1990), gender performativity tends to be equated with play, free and intentional activity where different subject positions can be tried out. This is the case in Turkle's chapter titled "TinySex and Gender Trouble." A similar stance is shared by Jay David Bolter and Richard Grusin in a section from their *Remediation* (1999) titled "Gender Trouble in MUD's," where they quite rightly argue that, for Butler, gender is "always a performance rather than an essential quality." For them, however, it follows that "an individual can fluctuate between male and female identities, just as a MUD player can change avatars with a few keystrokes" (Bolter & Grusin, 1999, p. 264).

Arguing against such readings, Judith Butler (1993, p. x) refuses humanist understandings of a free-choosing subject "who decides *on* its gender," "is not its gender from the start and fails to realize that its existence is already decided *by* gender." On the contrary, "gender is part of what decides the subject." For Butler, gender (as well as the category thought of as "sex") is constituted as the ritualized reiteration of norms that govern cultural intelligibility, as compulsive repetition. This "doing-gender" is far from voluntary activity, it is performativity that concerns the very sense of the self. For Butler, individual intelligibility—and thus identity—assumes a prior reference to the status of subject. There is no identity unmarked or "free from" the matrix of power, by which the subject is made (Butler, 1997, pp. 10–11; Hall, 1997, p. 56). However, identity positions are subject to change and re-signification: Subjects are not simply locked in mechanisms of power, since agency cannot be derived from, or reduced to, its conditions but enables purposes unintended by them (Butler, 1997, pp. 12–15). So, even if identity is the performative product of iteration, and even if ruptures in what counts as identity can be created by repetitions with a difference (such as Stone's transgender performances), spaces for intentional engineering of the self are hardly limitless. Since being gendered (raced, classed) is a precondition for thinking, living, and making sense of the world, the individual cannot take up any identity position s/he pleases. In this context, notions of "free play" and "choice" appear as "not only foreign, but unthinkable and sometimes even cruel" (Butler, 1993, p. 93).

There is a kind of willful misreading of gender performativity in Turkle's, Bolter's, and Grusin's uses of Butler's work, where conscious performances are equated with performatives and constitutive utterances. These takes on performativity, like those of Stone, owe more to sociologist Ervin Goffman's *Presentation of the Self in Everyday Life*. Butler, unlike Goffman, detaches gender performativity from choice, will, and intention, and discusses it as effects of discourse rather than individual acts. But Goffman also believes identity is an outcome of constant production, continuous sets of performances that are never done but are being done in various presentations of the self. Individuals aim to impress others and show themselves in the best possible light, to be presentable (Goffman, 1990, p. 14). In presentations of the self, a certain character is created or various characters are created; these in turn shape what is known as identity. The self is produced in interaction with others, marked by others' actions and reactions, since it is the presence of an audience that forces us to keep our "act together" (pp. 63–64).

The "performers," for Goffman (p. 87), are not simply autonomous, but have internalized social norms, standards, and expectations, deviation from which would lead to potential embarrassment. There is, however, a certain distance between the norm and the individual, and social interaction is based on calculated performances and self-presentations. One is familiar with the norms to the degree that some of them are internalized, yet these norms are not seen as constitutive of the subject. Social interaction shapes one's identity, but Goffman's theory does not discuss how this identity has come into being. To a degree, then, the gendered, raced, classed, and nationed subject is a given.

When criticizing the discourse of identity play, several researchers have turned to Goffman's work and argued for the usefulness of his concepts, particularly when studying impression management and self-presentation on personal home pages (Chan, 2000; Chandler, 1998; Cheung, 2000; Kibby, 1997; Miller, 1995; Paasonen, 2000; Wynn & Katz, 1997). Home pages and online communications are both about creating characters, (re)presentations of the self that others can be "impressed about" (Miller, 1995), and in many instances Goffman's suggestions are productive when applied to online communications. Yet Goffman's theoretical framework is insufficient for discussing the norms, limits, and conventions of identity construction, for conceptualizing gender, power, and performativity, online or offline. Goffman's agents are intentional and apparently unconditioned by power relations or desire.

Although Turkle and Stone, like Goffman, discuss the self as split, this self can intentionally "do" identities, create parallel lives, play around with genders and sexualities, and choose which ones to embrace and prioritize. Especially in Turkle's *Life on the Screen*, there is surprisingly little emphasis on the social conditions of subjectivation, on the self as a product of various social technologies. That is, the particular social location of the performers is not seen as formative of the possible selves performed (Turkle, 1995, pp. 184–186). In fact, parallel virtual lives are presented as "ways out" from an unsatisfactory life.

Freedom and Cyberdiscourse

The interest in play with gender and identity can be understood in the wider context of *cyberdiscourse,* which depicts the Internet as a dimension, a parallel reality, a "cyberspace," a term coined in William Gibson's 1984 novel, *Neuromancer,* and further popularized by authors like John Perry Barlow (1996). Barlow argues that in cyberspace, identities do not have bodies and all users are free to enter this world of the mind on equal terms and express themselves without limitations. As the Internet is depicted in this vein as "free for all" and users as equally free to "be whoever they like," the workings of power and conditions of access are bypassed. Cyberdiscourse is, for Zillah Eisenstein (1998, pp. 31, 94–95) deeply tied to American neoliberalism in its emphasis on freedom over equality: Discussions center on the possibilities to practice the First Amendment rather than on responsibility, equality, or the conditions of free speech.

For Eisenstein, cyberdiscourse is a double-movement of sorts, which involves promises of overcoming the limitations of time, space, or embodiment, but is nevertheless deeply rooted in the reproduction and enforcement of economic and political power structures and structured privilege. Eisenstein (1998, pp. 70–71) calls it cyberfantasy, an imaginary that masks relations of power in uses of the Internet. According to her, "cyberspace functions as a new imaginary location of escape, promise, and profit. Cyberspace becomes a whole new arena to conquer where privatization openly seduces some, but silently punishes those who are excluded" (Eisenstein, 1998, p. 74).

In contemporary media studies, the user/viewer of television, cinema, radio, and other media is generally seen as social and situated, and media usage is seen as equally situated and contextual. In "cyberstudies," this has not been the case, as Internet usage has been defined as "travel," "surfing," "visiting," and "being online" (Nakamura, 2000b, p. 714; Paasonen, 1998). The Internet is postulated as a disembodied cyberspace, a parallel reality, as in, for example, Turkle's often quoted analysis of identity and Internet: "when we read our electronic mail or send postings to an electronic bulletin board or make an airline reservation over a computer network, we are in cyberspace. In cyberspace, we can talk, exchange ideas, and assume personae of our own creation" (Turkle, 1995, p. 9).

This rhetoric of freedom and mobility can be seen as an ideological choice that enables us to overlook issues of power, gender, race, and class (Sloop, 2000). As Lisa Nakamura argues, the maxim of optimistic libertarian rhetoric (as found on the pages of *Wired* magazine) is that "information wants to be free." This, again, assumes that "making information available on the Internet will liberate users from their bodies and hence from those inconvenient markers attached to the body such as racism and sexism. The equation seems simple: if nobody is visible while they are in cyberspace, racism and bigotry cannot exist at that time and place" (Nakamura, 2000a, p. 43). The positions of Internet users are defined in the libertarian rhetoric (cyberdiscourse) as unmarked, as illustrated in the often quoted pun, "on the Internet, nobody knows if you are a dog."[2]

But although bodies may not be *visible* in text-based communications, identity categories matter. Social, economic, or political power relations do not disappear in "cyberspace," although the discourse of freedom and possibility tries to render them invisible. Rather, these very power relations regulate and structure access and participation. Gender, race, and class (and age, nationality, sexuality, and religion) are not to be rendered insignificant for the reason that there is no Internet user not conditioned through these very categories. Identity presupposes embodiment—and this embodiment, again, is socially and culturally situated and signified. As Sara Ahmed puts it: "in assuming a different sexual identity in cyberspace one is not suddenly freed from constraints. Subjects are already constituted as embodied before they enter such a space, however much that already-ness does not lead to a fixed and fully determined identification. This negative model of freedom (freedom from constraint) in such theories of liberation-from-identity-through-technology provides ideological support for neo-liberalism, where self-making becomes the obligatory expression of the new 'ethics' of consumerism" (Ahmed, 1998, p. 112).

Research on virtual communities represents somewhat limited, selective, and even elitist understandings of online interaction and self-performance, which are nevertheless easily taken as illustrative of Internet usage in general. Eleanor Wynn and James E. Katz (1997) state that the data used in Turkle's and

Stone's work, "come from within the target community of computer users that most exemplify the extremes of behavior upheld as social trends. Without social theory and more grounded methods, the Internet is plausibly portrayed as fantastic and unreal rather than practical, effective and socially constructed" (p. 4). Cyberdiscourse relies on cyberpunk-influenced fantasies that are circulated in fiction, popular media, and media studies alike, and through which the "new" revolutionary potential and attraction of the Internet has been articulated (Adam, 1997). What kinds of Internet use does the rhetoric of travel and freedom, then, relate to? And what is its relation to widespread, mainstream uses of the Internet?

Going Mainstream

Thinking of the experience of Internet use—doing one's email, browsing web pages, clicking from one hyperlink to another—"travel in cyberspace" is not the first description I would resort to. On the Web, "cyberspace" opens up as flat surfaces with flickering icons, wallpapers, and bright colors, and great amounts of text: Portals and search engines function as nodes from which users start their "explorations" and to which they return. And, as Lisa Nakamura (2000a, p. 41) points out, the "multiple self" celebrated by Turkle is often totally absent from mainstream web services, which tend to be firmly raced, gendered, and classed.

In addition to web sites and other online services, public memoranda, popular guidebooks, and magazine and newspaper articles about the Internet often operate on a naturalized gender difference that can be based on genes, behavioral differences, evolution, hormones, or combinations of these factors. Women's web sites and other online services targeted at women rarely promote deconstructive approaches to gender with their horoscopes and tips on relationships, home, and food. The use of soft pastel colors, italic fonts, and images of smiling women mark these sites as "feminine," adding to the gendering of the implied users as female, feminine, and, predominantly, heterosexual (Paasonen, forthcoming; Consalvo, Gustafson, Sadowska, Cooks, et al., all in this volume). In such cases, gender is something already known, common knowledge that requires no further explanation. Like stereotypes, binary gender categories acquire their consistency and self-evident status through constant repetition and reiteration (Bhabha, 1994, pp. 66–67, 77–79). Female users are addressed by Internet service providers and content producers as representatives of the "category of women," defined in terms of embodied difference (menstruation, pregnancy, maintenance of femininity), the gendered division of labor (child care, housework, home decoration, cooking) or interests (relationships, fashion, beauty, romantic fiction). In these instances, gender categories are hardly subverted.

Personal home pages, which have become one of the most popular web page formats (Cheung, 2000, pp. 45–46), are centrally about representing one's embodied social locations. Home pages are introductions to one's domestic or private self, the hobbyist self, the subcultural and/or professional self. They include information on one's interests, hobbies, studies/ profession, friends and family, and place of residence, and are often illustrated with personal photos, small animations, and clip art files. Sites can include links to friends' pages or photo archives to be shared by friends and family, and online diaries and dream diaries are increasingly common. Home page practices are less about fantasies of transgressing one's corporeality and social location, than about manifesting one's presence online.

Through updates, home page "guests" and "visitors" are informed of the latest activities and events in one's life. Daniel Chandler (1998) and Hugh Miller (1995) have argued that representing one's identity on home pages means producing that identity through narration. Discussing home pages in this vein as performative utterances in which one's identity is called into existence as a coherent entity can easily lead into a reading of performativity as identity exploration and production where the individual can consciously rework, or construct, her/his (sense of the) self. Such a formulation downplays the role of power which creates the illusion of a stable identity (Butler, 1993, pp. 122, 129). In fact, personal home pages have been discussed as a sort of haven for individual identity work on the Web, separate from frameworks of commerce and power. Jay David Bolter (2000, pp. 20–21), for example, defines personal home pages as sites where users are not only consumers, but able to "talk back," "project their identity on the Web," and engage in identity construction.

Sherry Turkle (1995, pp. 258–259), again, defines home pages as a "dramatic illustration of new notions of identity as multiple yet coherent," as postmodern bricolage. Optimistic views on home pages as counter-discourse play or postmodern identity work pay little attention to the representational norms and conventions, or the consumerist ties and underpinnings, of personal home pages.

Like domestic photography and video, personal home page production is linked with the marketing of technical equipment and guidebooks to homes. Computers, scanners, software, server space, digital cameras, fonts, animations, guidebooks, and special interest magazines build on already-existing markets of domestic photography and imaging (Slater, 1995). These products are advertised for the creation of home pages, but also as suitable for making digital family albums, cards, illustrated calendars, or even T-shirts. In terms of authorship, it is important to see individual home page practices as influenced by commercial frameworks and generic formats. Home pages are highly generic media products that are based on home pages seen before and illustrated in guidebooks and manuals, on software for producing home pages, models presented in html courses, and so on. Gif-animations, Java-applets, and clip art files are used on one home page after another, and home pages tend to rely on a similar basic structure and modes of address. With home page templates, the activity of the author equals that of filling out forms.

Personal home pages have been studied as identity construction (Chan, 2000; Chandler, 1998; Turkle, 1995) but less as representations governed by different patterns, conventions, genres, and norms. As already said, home pages and discussion groups are sites for representing and thus producing different aspects of the self. How are these representations encouraged? How are they structured and composed? How is gender articulated and performed as different textualities? There is a need to look not only at the individual agents who maintain home pages but also at the frameworks for understanding these agents and their textual productions.

Personal home pages rely on codes of interpretation, such as amateurism and authenticity, referentiality, and conventions of representing the self, body, gender, and identity. The representations of the self on home pages are taken as signs or reflections of the person in question. The use of photographs helps in depicting the self as integrated and authorial, as located in embodiment, place, and time (Rugg, 1997, p. 2). Like auto-biographical representations in general, the somewhat lighter—even flat (Chan, 2000, p. 283)—home page representations are about exerting control over self-image. In brief, in these representations one is the author of one's own biographical narrative and persona (Rugg, 1997, p. 4; Chandler, 1998). Yet home pages are limited forums for "making the self," as the possibilities of making one's self are not, for the most part, dependent on one's intentions and interests. Home pages are sites for "doing" gender identity, but this "doing" is hardly constitutive of the individual in the sense that it could change and challenge the forms of subjectivation.

Like Lisa-Jane McGerty (2000, p. 899) and Renate Klein (1999, p. 209), I argue that online and offline communications are not separate forms of existence, experience, or identity work. Sherry Turkle may, then, have a point in claiming that online play and the life offline are equally real, for they are basically the same—the agent is, in both cases, a product of social technologies, embodied experiences, and desires.

Identities and Characters

In spite of all the writing and discussion on identity, the category of "identity" has been surprisingly little analyzed or used as synonymous with those of "role," "persona," or "character" in writings on personal home pages and online communications. Yet the differentiation between the terms "identity" and "character" is nothing short of crucial: Whereas identity traditionally refers to the specificity of a person, of her/his personality and even inner substance, the word "character" has a double meaning as the unique personality and the inner strength that define an individual, and centrally also as a constructed representation of a person. It is the latter sense of the word that I would like to apply, while paying attention to the ways in which the term carries connotations of individuality and interiority. Character is a constructed representation, and in fiction the characters standing in for the author are called personae (also implying a personality trait and thus individual uniqueness). Sherry Turkle discusses "the selves" performed online as personae, yet occasionally conflates them with the category of identity: "In traditional theater and in role-playing games that take place in physical space, one steps in and out of character; MUDs, in contrast, offer parallel identities, parallel lives. ... MUDs are dramatic examples of how computer-mediated communication can serve as a place for the construction and reconstruction of identity" (Turkle, 1995, p. 14).

Building on cyberspace imagery and discourse, Turkle depicts the Internet as a parallel universe where characters become identities. This is a suggestive argument, for if identity and representation are seen as intimately interlinked, extensive character construction would seem to function as in-depth identity work that questions the category of "self." Nevertheless, such a tendency to depict identity as both disembodied and a product of voluntary choice is highly problematic. Understanding the self as split does not make it a puzzle that individuals may construct at will.

As textual and visual self-presentations, home pages produce narratives of an individual's past and present, as well as a sense of identity, and they involve characters constructed roughly according to the same principles as those in literary or cinematic fictions (Plummer, 1995, p. 172). According to Richard Dyer, contemporary individualist (and humanist) understandings of personhood, as a basis for character construction, assume an individual's separateness from others. The invisible but coherent core of personhood is "supposed to consist of certain peculiar, unique qualities that remain constant and give a sense to the person's actions and reactions. However much the person's circumstances and behavior may change, 'inside' they are still the same individual; even if 'inside' she or he has changed, it is through an evolution that has not altered the fundamental reality of that irreducible core that makes her or him a unique individual" (Dyer, 1986, p. 8). Individualist identity assumes uniqueness and internal depth, which give continuity to one's actions in changing situations and contexts, keeping the individual self-identical (Hall, 1999, p. 249).

It may well be, as Dyer (1992, p. 23) argues, that "there is increasing anxiety about the validity of ... autonomous, separate identity—we may be our 'performance,' the way in which we take our various socially defined roles of behavior that our culture makes available." However, this is not enough to shake the assumption of a self who masters her/his own performance. On the contrary, the concept of individuality can provide these performances with a coherence—given that the category of an individual is central for the intelligibility of home pages. Identities are to a large degree narrative in form, given shape and continuity in the stories we tell about ourselves, and conditioned by conventions and narrative formulae (Plummer, 1995). However, these narrative rules are not up to the narrator to make.

For Jay David Bolter (2000, p. 17), "The World Wide Web ... permits us to construct our identities in and through the sites that we create as well as those we visit." Following Teresa de Lauretis (1987), again, media usage can be defined as a constant (re)production of identity and desire through identification and dis-identification with different representations of subject positions. Whereas for Bolter, the user literally uses media to construct and define her/his identity, de Lauretis conceptualizes identity construction as an outcome of the subject's positioning in different, mutually contradicting discourses and forms of social knowledge. I believe that the latter formulation ought to be more prevalent in discussions on identity constructions on the Internet than it tends to be currently.

Home pages enable an objectification of the self, a reflection of sorts, where one can compare and negotiate one's self-representation to cultural ideals and norms, and define oneself through categories such as age, gender, nationality, religion, locality, professionalism, or sexual orientation. Similar categorizations are also applied in online personals ads, user profiles, chat rooms, and bulletin boards. Paraphrasing Judith Butler, this can be seen as an indication of how subjects seek recognition of their own existence in categories, terms, and names that are not of their own making (Butler, 1997, pp. 20–22). For Butler, social categories signify subjectivation and existence at the same time: Self-reflection and objectification have to do with consciousness as "the means by which a subject becomes an object for itself, reflecting on itself, establishing itself as reflective and reflexive." Objectification, then, enables self-consciousness (pp. 20–22). In this sense, home page representations are not merely playful, or at least this play is conditioned.

Imagination at Its Limits

Why is it assumed that people represent themselves in chat rooms or on home pages "as they are," instead of taking up and playing with alternative identity categories and representations? Sharon Y. M. Chan (2000, p. 279), for example, argues that "It does not really matter who you really are: We are the symbols that we display on our home pages." Although gender play is common in online communities and chats, I find it problematic to assume that play with different characters, constantly "being someone else," would be a norm in all online communications. For example, in chats, users are often looking for sex partners or more permanent lovers, while personal home pages and personal ads function as advertisements or portfolios of sorts. Furthermore, it has too infrequently been pointed out that creating online characters easily leads into reproduction and recycling of stereotypes. Characters are outlined through easily recognizable categories such as gender, age, locality/nationality, race, ethnicity, general looks, and sexual preference. Taking up the categories of a "14-year-old gay schoolboy from Kansas City," a "33-year-old female secretary from Kiev," or a "69-year-old pensioner and widower from Liverpool," if one is identifiable as, say, a "27-year-old white female Ph.D. student from Helsinki," one is left with little else to work with than common knowledge. Imagining these "others" and building their characters may result in a process of reflection and redefinition, but this does not necessarily happen. For, as Lisa Nakamura argues, "far from becoming sensitized to what it feels like to be of another race in cyberspace, many users masquerading as racial minorities in chat spaces tended to depict themselves in ways that simply repeat and reenact old stereotypes." Often such play "reveals more about users' fantasies and desires," than it does about what it "feels like" to be a representative of another race (Adam, 1997, p. 24; Nakamura, 2000a, p. 44; Sloop, 2000, p. 90).

A similar presence of projected fantasies and desires is pervasive in various examples of online gender-crossing, as illustrated in Sherry Turkle's discussion of the experience of a man, Garrett, passing as a female frog character, Ribbitt, for a year in a MUD. His passing was motivated by a wish to "experiment with the other side," to see "what the difference" feels like, and is compared to the anthropological practice in which "one leaves one's own culture to face something unfamiliar" (Turkle, 1995, pp. 216–218). Here gender becomes understood as a structure that consists of two categories (m/f) alien to each other. Being a woman was, after the initial strangeness, like another nature to Garrett: "OK, so I log in and now I'm a woman. And it really didn't seem odd anymore" (Turkle, 1995, p. 218). Garrett was able to jump from male to female experience, from being male to being female, by the force of his decision, and these visits to "the other side" helped him to rethink his masculinity and integrate some of the "feminine" helpfulness of Ribbitt into his life offline.

In the example of Ribbitt, play with gender is less about blurring gender categories than about imaginary gender tourism, "visits to the other side" (Nakamura, 2000b). Seeing this as an example of subversive gender performance is perhaps besides the point, as this "doing gender" is based on a rather shallow—and disembodied—understanding of gendered identity and experience. The experiences of Garrett worked to naturalize assumptions of a given gender difference: He felt at ease with what he called "the canonically female way of communicating" as opposed to the male communication culture based on aggression and competition. After his online experiment, Garrett got together with a woman who lent him books on the differences in male and female communication styles. However, gender identity, as I understand it, is not merely a conscious imitation of stereo-typically "female" or "male" forms of interaction, but the product of a series of different body technologies, identifications, and ways of looking and being looked at, addressed, and categorized.

Caroline Bassett (1999, p. 13) argues that "much of the gender-twisting on the net was defensive, or even normative ... you slipped out of one stereotype into another. It marked you, in de Lauretis's terms, even when the performance was your own." Bassett argues that identity play may be intentional and voluntary, but not something one can totally master—after all, performances are also about audiences and interaction with other performers, about how others come to understand, situate, define, and classify one's self (or one's character). The performer is not the source or master/mistress of these meanings, which derive from social categories and cultural norms.

Ultimately, the performer is not the source of one's character, which is based on cultural representations and stereotypes concerning different identity categories. As "already familiar" and "already known," these features provide the performance with credibility. The marking discussed by Bassett is, according to Teresa de Lauretis (1987, p. 12), a "process whereby a social representation is accepted and absorbed by an individual as her (or his) own representation, and so becomes, for that individual, real, even though it is in fact imaginary." This imaginary nature of social representation as self-representation is quite clear in the case of "made-up" characters and gender-swapping, since social representations are really all one has access to in creating these disembodied characters. The two become one with little negotiation or "filling in." Often, although not necessarily, this involves the use of stereotypical characterizations.

There are limits to one's imagination with regard to gender, race, sexuality, identity, and these limits are conditioned, and reproduced by the ways that one has become, and constantly becomes, situated as a subject. Patricia Wallace (1999, p. 88) points to this, writing (stylistically in line with cyberdiscourse) that "we enter the virtual world laden with the psychological baggage of a lifetime and certainly don't abandon our suitcases in the entrance lobby." Furthermore, as pointed out by Sara Ahmed (2000, p. 132), the desire to both know and *be* the other, central to the discourse of play online, implies privilege, "the ability to be anywhere, at any time." Such theatrical acts mark difference safely as "a style that the white … body can put on and take off" (pp. 132–133), and this kind of identity tourism may work to reinforce, rather than to dismantle, categories construed as "other" to one's self.

Different Kinds of Freedom

In chats and other "communities," users with female handles or screen names are likely to encounter intimidation and harassment, and in order to avoid this, many take up names that do not clearly indicate gender. Taking up a male handle, and thus the "neutral" position of a user, is another solution to the problem (Wallace, 1999, p. 47). Gender-swapping and gender-bending are not necessarily about fun and play; they are also tactics of preserving one's integrity. This, again, leads to questions of privilege, and different kinds of freedom.

The discourse of freedom is concerned with the right to speak, write, and read online uncensored, while relatively little interest has been paid to the very conditions of access and reading— namely, who has access, and what kind of access it is; to whom and in what language are reading, writing, and communication available; and what forms of implicit censorship and silencing are at play against those who "do not fit in" (Eisenstein, 1998). Feminist research has made visible the occasionally aggressive tactics of silencing of women in mailing lists, chat rooms, and MUDs (Spender, 1996, pp. 193–225; Wallace, 1999, pp. 219–222). It has been argued that "free speech often amounts to free speech for the white man ... women and people of color, for example, have always had to watch what they say" (Spender, 1996, p. 225; Sloop, 2000, p. 91). Given this, a great deal remains to be written about power relations and the limits and conditions of "play," also on a more international, class, and race sensitive level that looks into the differences and power relations among and between women.

Cyberdiscourse, in its emphasis on freedom and play, helps to render invisible the constitutive role of power, systems of sig- nification, and conditions of intelligibility. As stated previously, identity should not be conflated with character. Characters may influence one's perception of the self, and communication with others may help in understanding different social locations. But even if some may like to think of their online characters as more "true" than their everyday self-presentations, this is only half the story. Identities are not only what we "decide" or desire them to be; they are, to a high degree, decided for us.

Notes

1. This chapter is structured around a critique of some aspects of Turkle's and Stone's work. Lumping the two very different writers together is an artificial move that may lead into a caricature of their theoretical frameworks. My criticism here addresses sections from Turkle's *Life on the Screen: Identity in the Age of the Internet* (1995) and, to a lesser degree, Stone's equally popular *War of Desire and Technology at the Close of the Mechanical Age* (1995/1996), which, I argue, have been influential in producing "common knowledge" about online gender performativity. This criticism is by no means targeted against their wider *oeuvres*, because both writers have done important work on human-machine relations.

2. The cartoon is a recurrent example of identity play in Internet guidebooks as well as academic texts. Nakamura discusses the cartoon in an earlier version of her article "Race in/for Cyberspace" (Nakamura, 2000c), accessible at http://www.humanities.uci.edu/mposter/syllabi/readings/nakamura.html.

References

Adam, A. (1997). What Should We Do With Cyberfeminism? In Rachel Lander & Alison Adam (eds.), *Women in Computing*. Exeter, UK: Intellect Books, 17–27.

Ahmed, S. (1998). *Differences That Matter: Feminist Theory and Postmodernism*. Cambridge: Cambridge University Press.

Ahmed, S. (2000). *Strange Encounters: Embodied Others in Post-Coloniality*. London: Routledge.

Barlow, J. P. (1996). A Declaration of the Independence of Cyberspace. Electronic document at http://www.eff.org/~barlow/Declaration-Final.html, accessed December 17, 2001.

Bassett, C. (1999). A Manifesto Against Manifestos? In Cornelia Sollfrank & Old Boys Network (eds.), *Next Cyberfeminist International*. Hamburg: OBN, 13–16.

Bell, D., & Valentine, G. (1995). The Sexed Self: Strategies of Performance, Sites of Resistance. In Steve Pile & Nigel Thrift (eds.), *Mapping the Subject: Geographies of Cultural Transformation*. London: Routledge, 143–157.

Bhabha, H. K. (1994). *The Location of Culture*. London: Routledge.

Bolter, J. D. (2000). Identity. In Thomas Swiss (ed.), *Unspun: Key Concepts for Understanding the World Wide Web*. New York: New York University Press, 17–29.

Bolter, J. D., & Grusin, R. (1999). *Remediation: Understanding New Media*. Cambridge: MIT Press.

Butler, J. (1990). *Gender Trouble: Feminism and the Subversion of Identity*. London: Routledge.

Butler, J. (1993). *Bodies That Matter: On the Discursive Limits of "Sex."* London: Routledge.

Butler, J. (1997). *The Psychic Life of Power: Theories in Subjection*. Stanford: Stanford University Press.

Chan, S. Y. M. (2000). Wired_Selves: From Artifact to Performance. *Cyber-Psychology & Behavior*, Vol. 3, No. 2, 271–285.

Chandler, D. (1998). Personal Home Pages and the Construction of Identities on the Web. Electronic document at http://www.aber.ac.uk/media/Documents/short/webident.html, accessed May 2, 2001.

Cheung, C. (2000). A Home on the Web: Presentations of the Self on Personal

Homepages. In David Gauntlett (ed.), *Web Studies: Rewiring Media Studies for the Digital Age*. London: Arnold, 43–51.

Danet, B. (1998). Text as Mask: Gender, Play, and Performance on the Internet. In Steve Jones (ed.), *Cybersociety 2.0: Revisiting Computer-Mediated Communication and Community*. London: Sage, 129–158.

De Lauretis, T. (1987). *Technologies of Gender: Essays on Theory, Film, and Fiction*. Bloomington: Indiana University Press.

Dyer, R. (1986). *Heavenly Bodies: Film Stars and Society*. New York: St. Martin's Press.

Dyer, R. (1979/1992). *Stars*. London: BFI.

Eisenstein, Z. (1998). *Global Obscenities: Patriarchy, Capitalism, and the Lure of Cyberfantasy*, New York: New York University Press.

Fuchs, C. (2000). Gender. In Thomas Swiss (ed.), *Unspun: Key Concepts for Understanding the World Wide Web*. New York: New York University Press, 30–38.

Goffman, E. (1959/1990). *The Presentation of the Self in Everyday Life*. London: Penguin Books.

Hall, S. (1997). The Work of Representation. In Stuart Hall (ed.), *Representation: Cultural Representations and Signifying Practices*. London: Sage and Open University, 15–64.

Hall, S. (1999). *Identiteetti*. Mikko Lehtonen & Juha Herkman (eds. & trans.). Tampere, Finland: Vastapaino.

Hayles, N. K. (1999). *How We Became Posthuman: Virtual Bodies in Cybernetics, Literature, and Informatics*. Chicago: University of Chicago Press.

Kibby, M. (1997). Babes on the Web: Sex, Identity and the Home Page. Electronic document at htttp://www.newcastle.edu.au/department/so/babes.htm, accessed February 5, 2001.

Klein, R. (1999). If I'm a Cyborg Rather Than a Goddess Will Patriarchy Go Away? In Renate Klein & Susan Hawthorne (eds.), *CyberFeminism: Connectivity, Critique and Creativity*. Melbourne: Spinifex, 185–212.

Kolko, B. E., Nakamura, L., & Rodman, G. E. (2000). Race in Cyberspace: An Introduction. In Beth E. Kolko, Lisa Nakamura, & Gilbert E. Rodman (eds.), *Race in Cyberspace*. New York: Routledge, 1–14.

McGerty, L. J. (2000). "Nobody Lives Only in Cyberspace": Gendered

Subjectivities and Domestic Uses of the Internet. *CyberPsychology & Behavior*, 3(5), 895–899.

Miller, H. (1995). The Presentation of Self in Electronic Life: Goffman on the Internet. Paper presented at Embodied Knowledge and Virtual Space Conference, Goldsmiths' College, University of London, June 1995. Electronic document at http://www.ntu.ac.uk/soc/psych/miller/goffman.htm, accessed February 5, 2001.

Nakamura, L. (2000a). Race. In Thomas Swiss (ed.), *Unspun: Key Concepts for Understanding the World Wide Web*. New York: New York University Press, 39–50.

Nakamura, L. (2000b). Race in/for Cyberspace: Identity Tourism and Racial Passing on the Internet (1995). In David Bell and Barbara M. Kennedy (eds.), *The Cybercultures Reader*. London: Routledge, 712–720.

Nakamura, L. (2000c). "Where Do You Want to Go Today?" Cybernetic Tourism, the Internet and Transnationality. In Beth E. Kolko, Lisa Nakamura, & Gilbert B. Rodman (eds.), *Race in Cyberspace*. New York: Routledge, 15–26.

Paasonen, S. (1998). Living Room Wonderlands: Gendered Spaces of Media Use. In Anu Koivunen & Astrid Söderbergh Widding (eds.), *Cinema Studies Into Visual Theory?* Turku, Finland: University of Turku, 192–211.

Paasonen, S. (2000). Making Oneself a(t) Home: Internet Home Pages and Domestic Metaphors. In Kris Knauer (ed.), *On the Move: The Net, the Street, and the Community*. Writers Online, 2000. Online publication at http://128.241.130.127/nonfiction.htm.

Paasonen, S. (forthcoming). The Woman Question: Addressing Women as Internet Users. In Maria Fernandez, Faith Wilding, & Michelle Wright (eds.), *Domain Errors: Cyberfeminist Tactics, Subversions, Embodiments*. New York: Autono-media.

Plummer, K. (1995). *Telling Sexual Stories: Power, Change and Social Worlds*. London: Routledge.

Rugg, L. H. (1997). *Picturing Ourselves: Photography & Autobiography*. Chicago: Chicago University Press.

Slater, D. (1995). Domestic Photography and Digital Culture. In Martin Lister (ed.), *The Photographic Image in Digital Culture*. London: Routledge, 129–146.

Sloop, J. M. (2000). Ideology. In Thomas Swiss (ed.), *Unspun: Key Concepts for Understanding the World Wide Web*. New York: New York University Press, 88–99.

Spender, D. (1995). *Nattering on the Net: Women, Power and Cyberspace*. Melbourne: Spinifex.

Stone, A. R. (1995/1996). *The War of Desire and Technology at the Close of the Mechanical Age*. First paperback edition. Cambridge: MIT Press.

Turkle, S. (1995). *Life on the Screen: Identity in the Age of the Internet*. First Touchstone edition. New York: Simon & Schuster.

Wallace, P. (1999). *The Psychology of the Internet*. Cambridge: Cambridge University Press.

Wynn, E., & Katz, J. E. (1997). Hyperbole Over Cyberspace: Self-presentation & Social Boundaries in Internet Home Pages and Discourse. *The Information Society*, 3(4), 297–328. Electronic document at http://www.slis.indiana.edu/TIS/articles/hyperbole.html, accessed May 2, 2001.

Chapter 2

Windows on the Web:
The Female Body and the
Web Camera

Kate O'Riordan

Introduction

This chapter will frame the uses of the web camera in terms of both technological development/convergence and discourses of gender and sexuality. It will offer an interpretation of these practices pointing toward new modalities of perception in relation to gender and sexuality. Research indicates that web cameras are integrated with the sex industry but there are also categories of sites that cannot be formulated in this way. The web camera presents a "window on the world" model of mediation. I will explore the way this model is constructed through a high-tech form of mediation. This includes an analysis of the dynamics of public/private space and notions of naturalness, performance, and connectivity.

Web site consumption is often isolated, the audience is fragmented, and reception often occurs in the home. There are differences according to whether reception occurs through a desktop computer or through a television screen, which can be more communal than a computer. The fragmentation of the audience and consumption within the domestic sphere have been connected to decreased inhibition in some users in relation to the consumption of erotica or activities such as online gambling

(King, 2000). These factors also contribute to the idea that the viewer can have a personal relationship with the site owner. The more explicitly commercial sites use language that frames the images as performed especially for "you" the viewer, with the individualization of the audience played upon again to create the idea of further intimacy. Sites which have similarities to mainstream erotica or pornography become increasingly formally similar to traditional media forms with staged orgies, their own porn stars, and filmed scenes which are simply video clips of material indistinguishable from offline hardcore erotica. The establishing of intimacy becomes more problematic the closer to mainstream erotica the site is, because the codes and conventions of erotica become more explicit and exceed the conventions of intimacy exploited by the web camera. These dynamics of form and content, and intimacy and distance, provide the central themes here.

The Technology

In terms of form, web cameras can provide photographs, time-lapse photography, and live streaming or recorded video clips. Thus, although a new technology, they are embedded in the practices of much older forms that predate film. In terms of content the sites range from nonsexual images of the routines of everyday life to explicitly sexual images, which are associated with erotica or pornography. However, even the apparently routine images of everyday life exceed those which are conventionally documented through the media. The similarity to the dominant genre of "reality TV" is significant and I discuss this below. "Private" bodily activities like sleeping are of course dramatized in the media but are only available to us as "real" in our own private sphere of family and friends. Now the private domain of strangers is available to viewers through the web camera.

Personal web camera sites are related to the home page genre and often use the same format with the addition of the web camera as an extra feature. Other sites revolve entirely around the web camera. The cameras referred to here are moving image cameras and the output sometimes requires streaming to be presented on the Web. Most sites operate through the far less sophisticated "update" system where photos are transmitted and updated in anywhere between 5 and 35 seconds. Web camera sites thus refer to much older technologies which predate film, such as slide shows or moving picture-grams where stills are rotated so quickly that they appear to represent motion. Occasionally sites update only daily or even monthly but these tend to be on the "for fun" sites or home pages where the camera is a peripheral novelty. Some sites which present themselves as web cameras actually provide stills from cameras rather than live or prerecorded access, and the effect is the same as the use of a conventional photograph. These sites can be loosely grouped as follows:

1. "For fun" sites which are free, largely nonsexual, and often contain photos or occasional updates. Home pages also fall into this grouping. These are distinct from "my life" sites because the central focus is not the image of the owner but a more general representation of their views, interests, family, and work.

2. "My life" sites which frame a representation of everyday life. These are similar to home pages but it is the image of the site owner that provides the central structure.

Figure 2.1 © 2000, All American Girl, used with permission.

An example is "All American Girl" (Figure 2.1). This web camera page appears to represent All American Girl's bedroom. It is generally active between 11 p.m. and 2 a.m. The web site is a-typical in the sense that it offers a web camera without requiring a subscription fee. The site is similar to the home page format with an introduction, including a picture of the owner, and a list of links to other pages in the site including the camera and off-site links to sites of interest. This site is more interactive than many of the home pages observed previously. Web camera pages in general incorporate more functions of interactivity.[1] This one has a message board and mailing list as well as the camera. There is also a Frequently Asked Questions (FAQs) page, which is typical of a communications page such as a bulletin board or mailing list.

All American Girl constructs her camera as a window on her life: "I'm just trying to share my life in a small way, online. I don't sit and pose for the camera like some people do, I just let it watch me in my day-to-day life" (FAQs page). The agency granted to the camera in this statement relates to my earlier statement about the camera as actor. The camera is regarded as an automated eye. The protagonist, who is simultaneously an actor in front of the camera, drives it. The collapse in production terms of the camera operator into the camera presents a new formulation where the camera is restaged as actor, a place it held in much earlier discourses of film. Walter Benjamin, for example, described the process of film as active in itself. "Then came the film and burst this prison world asunder by the dynamite of the tenth of a second" (Benjamin, 1936, p. 78). As well as positioning the camera as actor, this discourse also reconstructs the female body as object to the gaze. However, while the camera is constructed as "watching," the statement, "I let it watch me," reconfigures the body as active agent. The subject (I) enables (lets) the object (camera/it) to be active (watch) over the subject/object (me). Far from reasserting the active/passive paradigm suggested by Mulvey and Berger, this actor network sets up a new configuration of subject/object, which is notable in its complexity. The camera operator frames herself and uses the conventions of the gaze to attract site traffic. She uses the slogan "100% pure" (playing on the conventional "100%" descriptor used to package sexually explicit images) which maximizes the site's appearance in search results. This active and knowing use of the conventions of representation suggests a subjectivity which reworks the notion of subject as constrained to a notion of the subject as simultaneously subject to and in control of her social representation.

3. "My Life" sites include nudity and sexual imagery in their representation of the everyday. These are slightly different from the first category in that they often require subscription and they are more explicit in what is considered to be "everyday." These sites begin to expand the concept of private by including a more explicit content than the second category.

An example is the "HollyBear" site, a partly subscription and partly free access site. You pay $6.95 a month or a one-time $50 payment, for the following:

♦ A 30-second refresh rate on (usually) four cameras and live streaming video.

♦ Access to the thousands of pictures I took back when my site was adult.

♦ Access to other live camgirl adult streaming video feeds (I personally no longer do adult shows though).

♦ My private journal.

♦ Silly members-only galleries and themed shows once in awhile.

This site shares many similarities with the home page format but is also more interactive with mailing lists and chat. In a spectrum from "fun" to commercial sex site this site is closer to the "for fun" genre and many of the themes are playful. These themes include icons of popular culture such as science fiction and cartoon characters. Much of the site is related to HollyBear's journal and she also presents her material as a "window" on her life with occasional silliness. The front page of the site shows a montage of images of HollyBear and pictures from popular science fiction. There is a warning on the front page: "my site shows real life and therefore may not be appropriate for younger viewers." HollyBear's "real life" is made up of many components, and science fiction, films, and cartoons are all part of that reality. Although HollyBear's site warning implies a relative lack of explicit material, the site acts as a portal to a selection of overtly explicit sites.

4. "Cam Girl" sites which focus specifically on sexual imagery or the promise of it revolve around notions of the sexual and require subscription. They rework definitions of "everyday life" further by emphasizing sexual imagery as the central focus.

An example is "CoyCam." In contrast to the semi-naturalness represented by the real life emphasis of the two previous cameras, CoyCam is highly staged. The previous sites state that the camera watches them, while Coy overtly plays to the camera. This site has a large component of free material but again has a member's level at $5.95 a month. Payment is for access to "live" shows and archives. The rest of the site promotes the live section and is mainly composed of samples and stills from the live camera show archive. This site is not presented as a "window" on Coy's life; conversely, the show factor is emphasized. There is also an "evil twin" section that involves the same protagonist but is presented pseudonymously with more of a "hard-core" persona. The twin is a dramatic plot device. This allows a limited story to unfold about the twin having sex with Coy's alleged "husband" as well as performing less normative sexual practices such as bondage. This allows Coy to remain coy while also catering to as wide a range of tastes as possible. This device emphasizes the performative aspect of presenting the self through a camera. This is an explicitly sexual site and all the material on it is themed in relation to this. This site dramatizes the conventions of the web camera as a window by providing a self-consciously staged performance of intimacy. The archived camera shots show Coy at her computer keyboard, apparently working at home. She simultaneously plays to the camera, with performances of strip tease and masturbation.

5. "Cam Girl" sites which share a high level of formal and/or content values with commercial sex sites, and are indistinguishable from commercial sex sites but use the amateur and volitional status of the web camera to represent self-presentation.

An example is "Bianca's Club," which is sexually explicit and also has the least free access. Bianca represents herself as an amateur porn star and charges for all material except a "taster" tour of stills. This site is linked to other sex sites and to Sex Cam Central, which is a portal to web sites that are both explicitly sexual and commercial. This site represents the images as "hard core." The literature on the site separates it from what is described as "tame" material on other sites and a list of attractions similar to much mid-range, explicit erotica is detailed:

> These are 100% HARDCORE!!! You'll see me doing everything from getting fucked in the ass, sucking dick and getting a faceful of cum, fucking my beautiful girlfriends, sucking my tits, playing with my toys, and much more!

This kind of material is toward the "hard core" end of the spectrum in terms of publicly available UK print literature, which is highly regulated. In international terms the material is toward the center of a spectrum from soft to hard core. The content and marketing strategy bear close similarities to European and American hardcore erotica as described by McNair (1996). Although the sexual practices displayed here are mainly hetero-sexual, non-normative heterosexual practices such as anal sex and lesbian sex acts are added to widen the potential audience. As both Rimm (1995) and Amis (2001) point out, visual erotica is rarely themed around vaginal intercourse. Scenes of anal sex and fellatio are more popular and are more widely distributed among male consumers for online photo exchange systems (Rimm, 1995) and on offline film and video (Amis, 2001). Similar observations can be made in relation to online sites. As already noted, much online content is borrowed directly from offline materials.

Methodology

This chapter provides a qualitative analysis of 12 web sites, which range from the mediation of everyday life to a mediation of sex. At one end of this spectrum are the "for fun" sites that are similar to traditional home pages and at the other are commercial sex sites. The majority of web cameras that offer free access involve time-lapse photography where the image refreshes itself every few seconds. These are the usual form of the free site, interest site, or home page that is set up for the use and grat-ification of the web site creator. Live streaming or video clips are much more prevalent on the explicitly sexual web camera sites, which are often set up for the use and gratification of the con-sumer. Some of these sites frame themselves as being for the pleasure of the creator and the language used is intended to "invite" the consumer in and so add to the idea of intimacy and personalization.

I used search engines to find and access these sites. I used the key words "web cams" and "live cams," which led both to individual sites and a variety of portals. Visiting these sites also led to web rings, and award and review sites, which turned up further data. These portals contained all of the types of sites described previously, from the home page with an added web camera or stills to the commercial sex site orientated around a "live" camera. Thus, the portals themselves did not often distinguish between the home page camera and the commercial sex site although some portals were at pains to exclude the latter category. Portals which provided a mixed list were Peeping Moe Cam Girl Exchange, CamGirlsRing, and Webcam Top 100. The majority of these camera sites appeared to be based on US servers, although New Zealand, Finland, and Australia were also represented, but many had their own domain names, making it hard to ascertain a definite geographical location. The sites were also, almost exclusively, representations of the female body. The only portals which offered representations of anyone other than young females were the "for fun" portals which were apparently unrelated to sexual expression. Male bodies also appeared in some camera sites in tandem with the female protagonist. One such site provided images of a heterosexual couple having sex, but the title left no doubt as to whose body was on display: Jen's Exposed. Other sites provided images of the protagonist acting out scenes with a variety of different partners. However, these sites were most often representations of female bodies, often with their "friends," simulating lesbian sex scenes, in which case the protagonists described themselves as bisexual.

Once acquired, the sites were analyzed in terms of their content, images, and text. Levels of interactivity and points of cost and income were also factored into the analysis. As well as the immediate site content, the mailing lists attached to the sites were considered and in some cases the site owners agreed to respond to me directly through email. I also used press coverage of the sites. Many of them have appeared in print media, especially JenniCam. "About.com" has also interviewed All American Girl for "The Human Internet" online catalog. The sample cannot be considered representative but displays examples of web camera activity by women from 1999 to 2001.

The sites described in this chapter are representative of the complete data set although, as mentioned, I have not taken commercial sites into full consideration and these would be a dominant category. The grouping of sites into a spectrum from "for fun" to commercial sex correlates with a spectrum of cost to access. This is not a straightforward linear trajectory and these categories only work as an approximate model. It is also important to note that categories 3 and 4 can be conflated into "my life cam girls"; I separate them here to draw a distinction between overtly commercial production and more interest-driven, independent sites. Web camera sites range across two spectrums of taxonomy, one previously discussed is form and the other is content. In terms of content the sites range from nonsexual images of the routines of everyday life to explicitly sexual images, which are associated with the sexually explicit, erotica, or pornography.

Many of the sites, which have fast updates or streaming, require a subscription for access to the "live" web camera. Live cameras are a distinct category in terms of what they present or purport to present to the viewer. These media forms are expensive to set up and this is given as the primary reason that the viewer is asked to subscribe. The subscription is usually presented as a form of "support" from the viewer for the site owner. Many of the owners stress that these are not commercial ventures and that the subscription subsidizes the cost of the technology but does not profit the owner. Many of these sites, which invite the viewer to see into the life of the owner, do not guarantee sexually explicit images but also state that the intimate nature of the material makes it unsuitable for "family" viewing.

Category 5 sites are often linked to portals, which are evidently a commercial service. These cameras are very similar in format to the commercial sex site but claim "amateur" status.[2] Less explicitly positioned as sex sites than the commercial hard-core sites, these encourage the reader to believe that the owner has created the site for her own pleasure but is also happy to offer a service to subscribers. These sites all offer "tasters" of the subscription material in the form of stills from cameras and have both nonpaying "guests'" and paying "members'" sections. Very few of these web cameras offer an entire site that does not require payment. These sites can be conceptualized in design terms as multilayered with a surface-level free access area and a deeper-level "members" section. This is a structure identical to that of commercial sex sites and in some cases the content is very similar. The differences are largely in the way the sites are marketed and framed as the product of the exhibitional desires of the owners. They are also presented as not-for-profit and host less overt or invasive advertising than the commercial pay-per-view sites.

Everyday Life and Reality as Genre

This study leaves the category of commercial sex sites for further research, and attends to the genres which fall between this category and the "for fun" page. The "for fun" sites are not a focus here as they are not substantially different from the home pages already considered in other work. An example of a "for fun" site is "Silly Mum," which displays the kitchen and the study of a "mum" engaged in activities such as typing and baking. The most famous web camera sites to date are "Big Brother" and the streaming of a Madonna concert in December 2000 (UK). These sites differ from the sites I am looking at in many ways; most obviously these are web cameras displaying public performances already disseminated through other media forms. Of the types that I am looking at, the most famous is probably "JenniCam," whose live 24/7 production of her own life has been extensively covered in the offline media.[3] JenniCam presents the everyday and a point of discussion in this study is the repackaging of everyday, intimate, and domestic life as a media product.

In focusing on the nonsexual images of everyday life, I refer to activities carried out in the course of conventional routines in the home or workplace. The persons presented are clothed to a level conventionally acceptable in the public domain and the activities do not far exceed conventional notions of publicly acceptable behavior. However, even these apparently mundane images exceed those usually seen in what is perceived, by regulators, as the public domain. As mentioned, the significant exception is "reality TV" such as *Big Brother*. Activities shown, both in the "reality TV" genre and in web cameras, go beyond the normative conventions of the public domain by drawing the viewer into a more intimate sphere where the images show the protagonists sleeping, half-awake, and washing. Such private bodily activities are dramatized in the media but are only available to us as "real" in our own private sphere of family and friends. Now the private sphere of strangers is available to users through the web camera. The viewing pleasures and fascination involved are both culturally and historically specific. In other temporal and spatial zones the conventions of public/private and everyday/dramatic are structured differently. Thus, almost regardless of the type of content, the form of the web camera itself draws the viewer into a more intimate viewing position.

Big Brother, used here as an example of reality TV, has many dynamics similar to these types of web camera use. Like the web camera, the product, *Big Brother*, is presented as unpredictable, unscripted, and about "real" people, so it is also permanently there to watch. The environment is portrayed as "natural," technology-free, and thus vulnerable to the viewer. Like the measures taken by a magician to prove there is nothing up her sleeve, the program is presented as free from possible sources of illusion and outside communication. The promise is made, through the construction of a technology-free state, that this is real, unmediated life. The setting is also personal life that the viewer will not have seen before because the environment is constructed as the personal and private sphere of the house. Thus elements on and off camera contribute to the representation of a reality aesthetic, produced through a high level of mediation.

The simulation of everyday life through digitized images and networked computers has much resonance with mainstream mass media production. Some of the parallels with *Big Brother* have already been drawn; another example is *Survivor*. *The Truman Show* (1998) also fictionalizes "reality TV" in film. I would argue that both the desire to see into others' lives and the desire to perceive one's own life as spectacle are based in the social preoccupation with meaningful social intelligibility. The meaning signaled by mediation has become a condition of social intelligibility.

The sites all describe themselves as "real" or "genuine." Factors such as the lack of editing and the movement of camera angles create this appearance. A potentially significant point is that the camera is not driven by a cameraperson but operates for the most part as another actor in this scenario. Web cameras refer to techniques such as CCTV, also automated, which are credited with an ability to record life rather than to construct a selected view of it. Although this attributed capacity has been criticized, CCTV is used as legal testimony in the USA and UK.[4] The web camera, thus, provides an apparently unmediated view of the body. This construction of an "unmediated" view is a complex new modality of perception. It raises the question of how a highly media-literate audience can be persuaded to perceive a media product produced through a new technologies platform as a reflection of reality. Historically, visual representations were thought to reflect and document reality, and the use of police photography is an example of this.[5] However, contemporary media representations are generally recognized to be highly constructed representations of very specific viewpoints. With the advent of new technologies such as CCTV, the web camera, and video streaming on the Internet, a resurgence of the perception that mediation can represent the real seems to be emerging.[6]

As noted earlier there is a tension between the intimacy engendered by the use of the web camera and the mass production/consumption of sexually explicit commercial products. Language is used to overcome this conflict between commercial and private, and is deployed to reaffirm the virtual intimacy of the form. As is also noted by Rimm (1995), the visual is framed through language and this often gives it its meaning. An example is the following introduction to a commercial site that is attempting to exploit the intimacy of the web camera. The extract is from AnotherNaked-CamGirl.com:

> Come in. I want to share something with you. If you listen closely you can hear me breathe ... I like to be watched ... Do you like ... To watch? I can be your ... Mistress or your Kinky Little Girl ;) or your Fuck Toy Come inside; Want to know what else i like?? (Isabella's Ass My Ass) My Boy Toy —Won't you join me? I live a fantasy you can be part of it. =) The world of Grace awaits ...

This extract shows the narrative construction of the viewer as voyeur, and any number of images could accompany this text, because it is expressions of intent and desire that project meaning into the images and anchor them (Barthes, 1977). The language also reconstructs voyeurism as a two-way process with excitement on both sides. The senses are drawn on to invoke both a sense of the real and a sense of the intimate and sensuous (breathing and hearing). At the same time as it offers a range of visual services the site invokes the discourses of intimacy, presence, and interactivity: "You can be a part of it." Thus the commercial end of the spectrum uses language to recreate the intimacy implied by the other end of the spectrum, which offers a "window on everyday life" through a noncommercial frame.

The filming of everyday life, now including life with the camera, as well as providing a window on the life of the protagonist also includes the camera as an actor in the network of relations. This includes the creator looking into the camera and performing for the camera, putting on small-scale shows and more generally considering the presence of the camera as actor. In other words "everyday life" and mediation become integrated and metonymic. The camera is credited with the ability to both watch and show. I do not wish to have recourse to actor network theory entirely, although borrowing from its terminology; the relational network here is better described in relation to Haraway's formulation of the cyborg. The element that Haraway's formulation brings to the discussion is that not all actors are equal in the network. The human agent who works with the technology is determining the use of the camera here (within the constraints of distribution); the camera is not equally an actor in these relationships of viewing but is another optical dimension through which these relationships of representation and consumption are played out. An important economic aspect of the web camera is that the companies that supply web cameras have pushed the technology. Demand has been partially generated through display and the suppliers of the product host the camera exchanges and "communities," which have also generated user groups. The use of this technology is, however, industry-led. The demand-development relationship is a complex one but the web camera is a largely USA-based phenomenon because bandwidth access is much more open in the USA, and users are not (at present) charged for being online in the same way that they are in the UK.

Within these sites the idea of naturalness is set up against that of performance. Discourses of naturalness are used to establish that these are "real life" representations (HollyBear). Performance is used to establish that the product is tailored to the desires of the spectator (AnotherNakedCamGirl). Both discourses position the viewer as the voyeur, but they complicate this notion to allow voyeurism to be implicated as an active relationship where the subject wants/desires to be viewed. This is set up by the fact that the site owner is assumed to have initiated the camera in the first place and thus invites the gaze of the spectator to make their activities "real." The desire of the subject on the camera to be viewed is then reinforced, to differing degrees, by the text accompanying the camera. This argument is not sustainable in relation to the erotic pay-per-view web cameras where the agency of the protagonists cannot be assessed. These latter sights conform to the political economy of the body as commodity exchange, which does not imply voluntariness or a desire to be viewed on the part of the protagonists but a need to position their bodies as commodities. The motivation of the less commercial site producers is therefore less transparent than is the case with the commercial ones.

However, even the web cameras that are entirely integrated with the sex industry also open up new modalities of perception and different performances of gender. There is a phenomenological difference between consumption of a magazine, video, film, phone sex, live shows, physical encounters, and a web camera. The web camera shares modes of consumption with these activities: it can be consumed in the home, it is purchased, it is used in relation to desire, fantasy, power, and it is marginalized/stigmatized as a social activity. It is further constructed as an "adult" behavior. The web camera also shares formal commonalities with these other modes of consumption. It is a mediated representation and shares this element with the other media forms. It is also a form of communication: the viewer can email the protagonist or use other forms of communication such as chat and messaging. Some sites invite the consumer to relay fantasies or requests that can be responded to through the camera. They therefore seem to position the viewer as a virtual participant, virtual because this is still mediated and not a physical encounter but a symbolic mediation of physical activity. What the web camera appears to do is to reduce the level of mediation to a "virtual" mediation where "virtual" is recast to mean "only partial." This construction presents a network of mediation where the web camera appears, like the camera in the nineteenth century, to enhance the reality value of visual culture by showing viewers what they would not otherwise have been able to see. Like Walter Benjamin's claim that in terms of visual culture, film "burst these prison walls asunder," the web camera is used to explode perceptions of the binaries of public/private and natural/artificial through the adoption of the technology as intimate. This configuration simultaneously reworks what is socially intelligible as "intimate" and what is intelligible as "mediated" in a new network where the use of the web camera comes to stand as a sign for both connectivity and reality.

The web camera also signals a form of cultural understanding about representation. It is deployed in ways which suggest that mediation is not seen as unnatural or unreal, and that technologies are not only theorized in terms of integration with the body but are used in this way in everyday practice. This can be seen, for example, in the way that arguments in media theory (and popular culture) about "effects" often presuppose that there is a form of communication that is unmediated and thus "natural." Within these discourses, mediated signals are "unnatural" and a prior "natural" state is presumed. The use of the web camera can be read as an acknowledgment that communication is always about mediation. The current "novelty" of the web camera allows it to be used as a tool with which to think about mediation, and its usage suggests that mediation is being positioned as integral and prior to communication.

Conclusion

The web camera, as a modality of representation, both conforms to the conventions of commercial image production and opens up new modalities. The convention of representing the female body as a sexualized object is one of the ways that the web camera replicates conventional media production. However, as noted above, the cyborgian actor network utilized and the degree of volition occasionally apparent in this form of voyeurism reveal a departure from conventions such as photography and filmmaking. The example of All American Girl is evidence of a dynamic of performativity where a subject becomes intelligible through the repetition of existing conventions but, once intelligible, can rework those conventions to her own ends.

The web camera also represents a way of thinking about the categories of "natural" and "performed" as a dynamic rather than a binary opposition. This makes them phenomena that can be used to think through the gendering and sexualization of the body. Various claims about cyberspatial practice have already been made around the performance of gender, such as the myth that the Internet is gender free or that computer-mediated communication is somehow disembodied. While I have little sympathy for these myths, the web camera seems to occupy a space that has already been claimed for textual forums; that denaturalized practice enables a paradigm shift in relation to dominant discourses of gender determinism. The evocative (although sometimes boring) images of the web camera frame gendered sexualities as always already performed, through the contextualization of the web camera as a ritual of everyday life.

Notes

I extend my grateful thanks to all participants for their time and interest and to Julie Doyle and Susanna Paasonen for their editorial comments.

1. See Aoki (2000) for taxonomies of web site interactivity. These categorizations include such factors as whether the user can email the owner or if chat and other two-way communication channels are included. The higher taxonomies include the question of whether the user can modify the site.

2. They can be compared to the "readers' wives" or other "amateur" interventions into the commercial production of sexual imagery.

3. JenniCam was set up in 1996 as the web camera transmission of the "real life" of Jennifer Ringley. See Brockes (1999).

4. See Fiske (1996).

5. See Barthes (1977), Tagg (1988), and Fiske (1996).

6. A parallel argument has been made in relation to the nature documentary form elsewhere.

References

Amis, Martin (2001). American Hardcore. *The Guardian*, March 17, 2001.

Aoki, Kumiko (2000). Taxonomies of Interactivity on the Web. Conference paper, Internet Research 1.0: The State of the Interdiscipline. University of Kansas. September 14–17, 2000.

Barthes, Roland (1977). *Image, Music, Text*. New York: Hill and Wang.

Benjamin, Walter (1936). The Work of Art in the Age of Mechanical Reproduction." In Evans, J. & Hall, S. (eds) (1999) *Visual Culture: The Reader*. London: Sage.

Brockes, Emma (1999). Welcome to Me TV. *The Guardian*, December 10, 1999.

Cornell, Drucilla (ed.) (2000). *Feminism and Pornography*. New York: Oxford University Press.

Fiske, John (1996). *Media Matters: Race and Gender In U.S. Politics*. Minneapolis: University of Minnesota Press.

Flowers, Amy (1998). *The Fantasy Factory: An Insider's View of the Phone Sex Industry*. Philadelphia: University of Pennsylvania Press.

King, Storm (2000). Internet Enabled Pathology. Conference paper, Internet Research 1.0: The State of the Interdiscipline. University of Kansas. Sept 14–17 2000.

McNair, Brian (1996). *Mediated Sex, Pornography and Postmodern Culture*. London: Arnold.

O'Toole, Laurence (1998). *Pornocopia: Porn, Sex, Technology and Desire*. London: Serpent's Tail.

Petkovich, Anthony (1997). *The X Factory: Inside the American Hardcore Film Industry*. Stockport, UK: Critical Vision.

Rimm, Marty (1995). Marketing Pornography on the Information Superhighway: A Survey of 917,410 Images, Descriptions, Short Stories, and Animations Downloaded 8.5 Million Times by Consumers in Over 2000 Cities in Forty Countries, Provinces, and Territories. *Georgetown Law Journal*, 83 (June), 1849–1934.

Tagg, John (1988). *The Burden Of Representation: Essays On Photographies And Histories*. Basingstoke, UK: Macmillan.

Weir, Peter (dir.) (1998). *The Truman Show*. Paramount Pictures.

Web Sites

All American Girl	http://organizedanarchy.com/lilith/index.html
CoyCam	http://coycam.com
AnotherNakedCamGirl	http://www.anothernakedcamgirl.com
Bianca's Club	http://www.biancasclub.com/main.htm
CamGirlsRing	http://www.camgirlsring.com/
Holly Bear	http://iloveholly.com
Jen's Exposed	http://www.jensex.com
Peeping Moe Cam	http://www.peepingmoe.com/
Sex Cam Central	http://www.sexcamcentral.com/
Webcam Top 100	http://webcamworld.com/top100/

Chapter 3

Internet and the Construction of Gender: Female Professionals and the Process of Doing Gender

Johanna Dorer

Introduction

As recently as the early 1990s, the Internet was considered a purely male domain. Women's access to the new communication technology was limited, the share of women on the Internet being just over 10% (Dorer, 1997, p. 20). The situation has changed considerably, however: in the USA, the distribution of male and female Internet users reached a balance in mid 2000, while in Austria the share of women users was 38% in 2000, compared with 35% in Germany in 1999 (ARD/ZDF Arbeitsgruppe Multimedia, 1999; N.N., 2000; ORF, 2000). Extrapolating from current rates of development, most European countries should have equal Internet access rates for men and women within the next four years.

Nevertheless, this does not mean that the gendered order has lost its power. As a social and cultural construct, gender influences the images and expectations concerning masculinity and femininity held within a particular society. Gender is not a social role but the result of multiple representations, on the one hand, and discursive practices, on the other. As de Lauretis writes (1987, p. 9), "the construction of gender is the product and the process of both representation and self-representation." This means that gender, as a socially agreed construction, is produced and reproduced through an everyday practice of "doing gender," in which the positionings or representations of the self as masculine or feminine always also include the appropriation of the relevant meaning constructions.

These *self-positionings/self-representations* are influenced by a battery of symbolic representations. Discourses on gender in the form of symbolic representations are constituted not only by media and advertising images which produce stereotypical models of masculinity and femininity, but also in connection with social institutions such as families, schools, courts, and the entire range of social, political, and economic processes (Cockburn & Ormrod, 1993). But in the construction of cultural conceptions of masculinity and femininity, the media play an increasingly important role. As the media are omnipresent, and it becomes increasingly impossible to evade them, their relevance to societies' institutions as well as economic and political processes increases. Politics without media are unthinkable today, as are education and socialization in the home without media. Based on the assumption that the gender discourse has constant validity, that there is no gender-neutral space, then it becomes clear that the media hold a prominent place in the construction and transmission of gender discourse. Viewed thus, the media introduce the most important symbolic gender representations. Peoples' behavior in certain situations, their gender positioning, is increasingly influenced by the media's construction and transmission of gender stereotypes.

This chapter focuses on the ways the Internet as a new technology contributes to gender on three levels: media representations, societal conditions, and the everyday practice of doing gender, which are each examined in turn. All three levels are currently characterized by a strong linkage between "masculinity and the Internet." The coding of the Internet as a male domain is strongly linked to the interpretation of the Internet as male-coded technology. The gender marking of technology has been unconditionally transferred to the Internet. Beginning with the stage of research and development, the Internet is construed as a male (-dominated) area. The Internet's origins as part of war technology are commonly acknowledged in its written histories, as is the knowledge that the pioneers of the Internet were almost exclusively male. The resulting values, norms, and myths correspond to societies' value system for masculinity.

Societies' practice of linking the Internet and masculinity functions not only because the Internet's research and development phases are ascribed to male action, but also and mainly because the Internet is defined as a "technical field," and this type of field already has a long tradition of male domination and exclusion of women. Instead of defining the Internet as technology, it is equally possible to define it as a net, a braiding, a weaving, therefore a female coding, as proved by Plant (1997). Turkle (1995, 1996) also views the linkage "Internet-technology-masculinity" as unnecessary and reductive, as it eliminates other ways of imagining the Internet and uses of it.

For example, the reinscription of the Internet as a field of hypertext programming leads to an entirely different research and development context, which reveals the presence of female coding on several levels. Ada A. Byron, of Lovelace (1815–1852), for instance, is considered to have been the first programmer (Plant, 1997). The programming language COBOL was developed in 1944 by Grace Murray Hopper, and during World War II programming was almost exclusively carried out by women. However, once information technology became economically vital as it did in recent decades, the rapid displacement of women in this field became evident (Herner, 2000; Hoffmann, 1987).

So the apparently random articulations in the associational linkage of Internet and masculinity become clear once again. The connection "Internet-technology-masculinity" is therefore not self-evident but supported by societies' gender and technology discourse, and it is still developing in various ways on different levels. It is based on historical processes, such as the traditional male coding of development, invention, and science. It is also founded on the practice of exclusion, women having been denied these male-coded domains for long periods of time, and being kept away from technological and scientific knowledge today. It is based on daily social practices in which this connection is continually reproduced, most particularly in the symbolic system of representation that the media, advertising, and other social institutions use to communicate these gender binaries and linked values.

The points of departure for this chapter, then, are a three-phase model of media representations of gender with respect to the new technology and reflections on gendered social conditions in the use of the Internet. Based on the results of a qualitative study of female Internet professionals, the mechanisms of constructing and doing gender are outlined. The study examines how female Internet professionals position themselves with respect to a media technology coded as masculine in a male-dominated field and how their activities are inscribed in the discursive construction of gender.

Development of the Web and Media
Representations of Gender and the Internet

The media play a crucial role in supporting dominant discourse and in maintaining structures of hegemony, so that the media, especially the popular (mainstream) media, are always viewed in the context of power and power relations. After all, the media are societies' institutions of popular knowledge, because they produce and transmit the social knowledge that circulates as social "truth" (in the sense of Foucault) for a certain time. This is particularly valid for societies' knowledge of cultural concepts of masculinity and femininity.

Media representations of gender and the Internet continue to follow traditional gender lines. Nevertheless, an increasing differentiation can be observed in mediated constructions of masculine and feminine stereotypes. This development can be traced by examining the genealogy of the Web in terms of a three-phase model.

Lovink and Schultz (1999, pp. 299–310) distinguish three different phases in the development of the Web:

1. The *first phase* (1969–1989) occurs when the large mainframe computers in the military, in research institutions, and in large corporations are connected to communicate with each other. During this period, "hackers" and "cyberpunks"—young people who have acquired the "secret" technical know-how—fight for an open web. The idea of a virtual community is realized in a multitude of networks. It is in this phase that concepts such as disembodiment, immortality, body-machine hybrids, the cyborg, cybersex—the Internet "mysteries"—emerge and meet with an enthusiastic response by scientists, including cyberfeminists.

2. The *second phase* (1990–1995) is the period of myth formation, of rumors and rising expectations. The (old) media are busily spreading the myth of the Internet and its universal opportunities, announcing the "digital revolution." It is a time of quick profits, web-based utopias, web critique, and media arts, allowing a new "virtual class" to emerge based on these divergent interests (Kroker & Weinstein, 1994).

3. During the *third phase* the Internet develops into a mass medium. More and more users log on to the Web, while the traces their mouse clicks leave in user statistics and log files are tracked for commercial exploitation. Increased digital networking accelerates concentration and globalization processes; it changes the way the money and stock markets operate and makes the new economy the most important growth sector. Debates over control, regulation, and censorship on the one hand, versus freedom of expression and media freedom on the other (with respect to child pornography, for instance) demonstrate the struggle for political influence and control. Standardization is the arena in which much of the struggle for hegemony is fought, since different user groups have developed their own standards and rules of engagement, which are inscribed by the Web.

This chronological systematization of web development (Lovink & Schultz, 1999) can be extended into a three-phase model of media representations of gender and the Internet. The following model is based on the author's long-term observation of the mainstream media, specifically in the German-speaking world. To evaluate this model, extensive content analyses of mainstream media must be done in the future. Thus, the model has the status of informed but not systematized observation.

During the *first phase*, corresponding to the early stages of web development, the general public remained largely unaware of the newly emerging technology. It was not until the *second phase* that the hype surrounding the Internet, particularly in the popular media, familiarized a wider public with the myth of the Internet. Media representations during this period show that the mainstream of meaning production concerning the Internet is linked predominantly to masculinity.

Thus, the themes explored in public discourse are exclusively coded as masculine: technology, cybersex, cyber-Nazism, cyber-criminality, hacker cultures. The link between the new technology and masculinity is reinforced by the fact that only men appear as active agents in the public discourse whether as inhabitants of the cyberworld or as experts and professionals. The construction of the Internet in the media as a male-dominated (male-governed) space further articulates the existing construction of technology as masculine. This connection between the Internet and technology not only serves to activate male fantasies of hegemony and control but also, on the level of meaning production, to construct and to exclude the feminine as "the other."

The exclusion of women is manifested not only in the topics debated in public discourse (technology/expertise, sex/violence, hegemony/control), in the historical origins of the Web (military, scientific), and in Internet jargon, but also in the failure to mention the contributions of women to hardware and particularly software development.[1] In this process, the (old) media build on the powerful connection between the Web and technology, invoking notions of masculinity as implying an interest and competence in technology and of femininity as implying reluctance, fear, rejection, and even incompetence.[2] Thus, the two central images of masculinity in the media, constructed around the meaning-fields of technology and expertise on the one hand, and sex and violence on the other, correspond closely to conservative conceptions of masculinity.

In the *third phase*, characterized by the commercialization of the Internet, the media cease to address themselves specifically to male Internet users and they pay increasing attention to female users. Media representations of gender and the Internet have changed and give rise to more and more differentiated images of masculinity, while at the same time introducing a conservative stereotype of women circumscribed by the private sphere and with supposedly "natural, feminine" characteristics. The stereotype of women constructed by the media is limited to women as mothers, cooks, and consumers and is thus even more conservative than the stereotype espoused by TV soaps. According to this stereotype, child care, recipes, and mail order shopping form the domain of female surfers. This conservative representation of women and the Internet is still dominant in media reporting today.

Only rarely are new stereotypes of women, such as the low-skilled female tele-worker or the high-powered female multimedia expert, constructed in the media. Female multimedia professionals are acclaimed as "Internet queens" in *Mona Lisa*, a women's magazine and TV program (Makivic, 2000), but they are presented as exceptions. Hard work and childlessness are named as the prerequisites for their success (Pfeiffer, 2000).

Thus, it can be assumed that the media construction of gender and the Internet will develop primarily along the lines of two gendered binaries: technical competence versus incompetence on the one hand, and public versus private space on the other. This enables the following differentiations, among others:

♦ male technology freak ("hacker") versus female Internet avoider

♦ male professional user versus female private surfer

♦ male Internet (multimedia, information technology) expert versus female tele-worker

♦ male chat room and Multi-User Dungeon (MUD) player versus female email writer.

In this way, then, the (old) media play a key role in the social construction of gender differences and gender differentiation with regard to the Internet.

Internet and Gender-Specific Coded Social Conditions

The Internet as a new communication technology engages in multiple and varied ways with gender-coded societal conditions, which in turn affect the gendering of technology. Thus, in the early 1990s, use of the Internet and Intranets spread rapidly into some areas of business and work. As a result, members of the working population became familiar with the new technology earlier than nonworkers, and higher-skilled professionals earlier than lower-skilled staff. Gendered employment options thus produce gender-different access to the Internet.

Connected to this is the fact that the gendered spaces and boundaries existing within society affect everyday use of the Internet. Within these societal conditions, the process of doing gender takes place as a discursive practice that allows, at least potentially, for different subject and gender positionings. This process of self-positioning is not entirely predetermined but is negotiated in everyday practice. In this, the subject is confronted with specific divisions and oppositions.

First, while the Internet was initially constituted as linked to a code of masculinity, this has been changing as a result of commercialization, with a more user-friendly surface opening up applications linked to a code of femininity. Thus, independent of actual gendered use, the gendered construction of the Internet is maintained by the changed attribution practice.

Second, the exploitation of the Internet as a means of communication predominantly used in work or professional contexts creates a dividing line between the working and the nonworking population, that is, between the gendered public/professional and private spheres. At the same time, however, the different uses contribute to a blurring of gender boundaries.

Third, the early Internet created a division between jobs requiring higher and lower qualifications. Thus, the new technology intersects with a gendered job market that exhibits both horizontal and vertical segmentation.

We are at the intersection, then, of partially conflicting sets of circumstances and conditions that form the arena for gendered action. In the process of everyday practice, attributions of discursive gendered meaning can be confirmed or contested. It was this process of gender positioning that formed the subject of a qualitative study, part of which, based on interviews of female multimedia professionals, is discussed below.[3]

The Internet as a Profession:
A Study of Female Internet Professionals

Method and Sample

In order to gain an adequate perspective on the process of gender positioning in everyday work contexts, qualitative interviews were carried out with female Internet professionals (Internet workers). The goal of the interviews was less to survey the already well-documented discriminating factors affecting women's access to the Internet (including time, income, class, ethnicity, and age) than to make visible the process by which the relationship of gender and the Internet is continually and systematically reproduced as a hierarchical gendered polarity and invested with gendered myths in the practice of Internet adoption and use.

Twenty-three female Internet professionals working in Austria were interviewed for the study. Apart from sex, the selection was based on membership in the core or the first or second peripheries of the multimedia sector.[4] Selection was then further limited to the production process of the Internet (web surface production and programming). The purpose was to confine the study to web production (and exclude Internet users), while also including media publishers and large corporations, in order to obtain a differentiated view of doing gender in the everyday Internet practice of Internet workers. Respondents worked as programmers, web designers, project managers, or concept developers for Internet projects, or as system managers. Snowball sampling was used to identify subjects. This seemed an appropriate procedure inasmuch as the Internet sector was still quite compact, especially for women, and people working in this sector were acquainted with one another. In addition, this field was familiar to the author.[5]

The interviews were carried out between October 1998 and January 1999 based on a partially standardized format. The interviews, which lasted roughly one hour each, were recorded and transcribed.[6] Following transcription, the qualitative material was analyzed both for specific response categories and for language as one of the key factors involved in constituting gender. Language is thus seen as an expression of individuals' self-representation in terms of being linked to a gender discourse within which interviewees position themselves with respect to gender and the Internet. Given this deconstructionist standpoint, linguistic discourse is analyzed not primarily with respect to its individuality but mainly with regard to its positioning within the social context. In other words, individual narratives are seen as parts of social discourses, which individuals perceive in differing ways and construct meanings for, integrating them into everyday practice (Haug, 1995, 1999).

With respect to age, a broad range of respondents was sought. It became apparent, however, that the Internet represents a relatively youthful sphere of employment. Interviewees' ages range from 23 to 43, with 32.5 as the average age. Most of the women interviewed were childless; only 5 had child care responsibilities. Of the total sample of 23, 6 ran their own Internet/multimedia business, 6 worked for online magazines or publishers, 5 were involved in Internet projects sponsored by near-governmental agencies, and 3 each worked for national/multinational corporations or smaller Internet companies.

Education and Training

All of the professionals interviewed for the study possessed above-average qualifications. Ten had completed university degrees, eight were in the process of obtaining their degrees, while two had dropped out of their degree programs. The final three persons interviewed had completed general or technical secondary education up to a level qualifying them for university entrance. Most had a background in the arts or the social sciences, with only six having received a technical education.

Although their own background was mostly nontechnical, interviewees considered a technical qualification a bonus in the Internet/multimedia field. The obstacles to women obtaining a technical qualification continue to be the time required for training as well as their experiences in male-dominated sectors of the educational system at secondary and tertiary level educational environments that do not allow women to forget their status as different and outside the norm.

All of the women interviewed who had a technology-oriented education reported negative experiences. As they described it, they repeatedly had to explain and justify their interest in a "masculine field," having to endure more or less aggressive attacks by fellow students and teachers. Thus, formal education and its particular culture in the male-dominated space of technology functions as a sanctioning mechanism that reinforces the gendered norms of what are acceptable "masculine" and "feminine" pursuits. In breaking the gendered norm concerning acceptable interests, female students in technical education invariably experience themselves as transgressing boundaries and violating norms, for as "the other" they are outside the norm. While this experience, as well as the norm itself, is discursively produced, its effects are nonetheless real. Thus, although the experiences of exclusion, otherness, and difference are socially produced, female students often do not see themselves as actors, as involved in the production of this social interaction, but as victims.

In this educational context, where the social norm defines an interest in technology as "masculine," women are forced to oscillate between masculine and feminine subject positions. In many cases this situation, which usually continues for several years, is handled chiefly through projections (remembering instances of discrimination experienced by female colleagues), while respondents' own subject positions are described as predominantly masculine, citing personal staying power and refusal to give up.

In addition to thus restating and confirming the existing norm, interviewees repeatedly sought to shift the boundaries associated with the norm. An example of this can be seen when one of the interviewees first adopts the gendered distinction between "hard" and "soft" educational subjects, only to differentiate and qualify it later:

> Electrical engineering, well, that's different again. Even more masculine ... IT, they say, is not so totally masculine. But electrical engineering, that's high voltage; information technology would be low-voltage. That's a little different. But electrical engineering—.(P.K.)

This differentiation reminds us of similar gendered reworking of technology. Cockburn and Ormrod (1993) discovered that "male" technology received a "female" component as soon as women became consumers of it.

Thus, the gendered meaning of technology as a masculine field is constantly reworked. In choosing a technical education, some women break or at least question the gendered link between technology and masculinity. Also, on the one hand there are many points at which the female professionals actively contribute to strengthening this link and the dividing line, while on the other hand some of them lay the ground for a potential shift in meaning as well as gender boundaries by adding new differentiations to the discursive construction of technology.

Employment Situation

The competencies necessary for their Internet professions were acquired by respondents in the course of their careers and mainly outside mainstream education, through specialized courses, learning by doing, or working in electronic data processing (EDP) departments, computer centers, or other such places. In most cases, strong personal interest and involvement drove the acquisition of the new skills. Those holding a technical qualification, especially, had systematically shaped their careers in the direction of multimedia and the Internet.

When analyzing interviewees' career paths, three main routes can be distinguished, which are found in the sample with a relative frequency of 3 : 3 : 1.

The most important entry profession is journalism in a broad sense, including classic journalism as well as public relations, graphic design, and publishing. The practice of working on a computer soon led many of the women into jobs like online journalism or online communication.

Equally important starting points are the EDP field and EDP training. Thus we find not only technology-oriented activities, such as programming and hardware or software development, but also computer training and, later, Internet-related training.

The third important entry point is business, especially marketing, advertising, and finance. Web-based advertising and sales are seen as a future growth area (Zimmer, 1998, p. 501), and many of the women who started out in this sector saw the move into web-based activities as a logical extension of their profession.

Although the women Internet experts interviewed for this study were highly educated and possessed relevant additional qualifications, a clear bias was observed in terms of the type of jobs held by respondents at the time of the study. Thus, the highest concentrations were found in jobs that are not considered technical. Even those with a technical-education background did not necessarily work in programming, software development, or system administration. Many find it taxing, continuously having to prove their technical competence in a male-dominated professional field. Some voluntarily alter their focus to html programming, others utilize their technical know-how to further feminist goals. Particularly noticeable in these interviews are the ways in which societies' connection between "competence" and "masculinity" are developed, first in education and then in the professional arena.

The three main areas of responsibility identified in the study are the *creation and maintenance of web pages, project management,* and *education and training.* Project management is understood to include responsibility for the management, coordination, and control of the entire process from design to production, as proposed by Michel and Goertz (1999, p. 20). Areas of responsibility such as *technology support and system administration, programming,* and *software development* are named far less frequently. *Customer support and consulting,* while also mentioned, are still underrepresented on the Web but can be expected to gain in importance as competition grows. *Chat room administration* figures rarely among responses; it includes mainly content-related tasks such as the moderation of discussions and monitoring of compliance with chat room rules rather than technical tasks.

Table 3.1 Areas of Responsibility of Internet Professionals (Multiple Responses)

	Task	Number of Responses
1.	Creation and design of web pages	15
2.	Project management	12
3.	Education and training	11
4.	Technology support and system administration	5
5.	Consulting, acquisition, and customer support	4
6.	Programming and software development	2
7.	Chat room administration	2

A closer analysis of the career paths and current areas of responsibility of the women Internet professionals in the study reveals three key points, when seen in conjunction with the views expressed by respondents concerning the future development of multimedia and the Web.

First, employment in the multimedia sector seems to be undergoing a process of segmentation. Thus, most of the women interviewed were active not in technical support or programming but in web surface design. Web surface design and html programming are the domains assigned to women in the multimedia sector today, whereas hardware and other forms of programming are constituted as masculine domains that continue to be more prestigious.

Second, responses show that advanced technical qualifications are not necessarily translated into positions with commensurate responsibilities. On the contrary, women can be seen in many cases to take on socially and economically less prestigious tasks.

Third, women employed in the web and multimedia sectors are themselves significantly involved in IT education and training, specifically for women. Some of the women interviewed were active in European Union-funded projects under the New Opportunities for Women (NOW) initiative seeing their role as providing female role models and training other women for this expanding professional sector.

With respect to income, the study found considerable variation between the women web professionals studied (salaries from 1,100 to 3,200 EUR before tax, paid 14 times a year).[7] The overall pay levels must be considered low, given the respondents' high level of education. Most of the women interviewed, especially those with long professional experience and thus a better understanding of pay levels in the field, saw themselves clearly as underpaid. Generally, income seems to be higher in large corporations, whether national or multinational, whereas publishers, feminist-inspired Internet projects, and multimedia firms pay less well. Self-employed women also draw lower pay.

First Internet Experience and Self-Representations

Only five of the women interviewed can be considered "pioneers," that is, already working with the Internet in the early 1990s (based on a definition proposed by Eimerer et al., 1998, p. 425). The majority of professionals in the study were not pioneers but what might be called "early adopters." They moved into the Net at a time when, first, new software offered a user-friendly surface to web users (Netscape, Internet Explorer) and, second, Internet use became more widespread in professional and business contexts.

Most of the professionals interviewed had their first Internet experiences in a professional context, sometimes conjointly with others. Recalling their first contacts with the Internet, women usually refer to some form of male involvement: male colleagues at the office, young male staffers, and male course participants. Interestingly, closer scrutiny usually reveals that other women also played an important role in respondents' initial Internet experiences. In other words, what we are seeing are women reproducing the discursive omission of women themselves. Only two of the respondents explicitly referred to another woman as their partner during their first Internet trials. Irrespective of the actual circumstances of their Internet start, it appears that respondents' memories of the situation are characterized by a mental link between "technology and masculinity." The entry scenarios as remembered by respondents are illustrative of the subtle workings of the connection between gender and technology, since the associative chain of "masculinity-technology-help/support" is all too easily constructed. It is an association that serves as both representation and confirmation of the prevalent view that women are dependent on male support in acquiring the new media technologies.

Crucially, although their self-representations emphasized their interest and initiative in appropriating the new technology, the female Internet professionals did not manage without the aforementioned associative chain of "masculinity-technology-help/support." In the example below, the respondent relates her first Internet experiences at the office where she was then working, in a very confident manner and from a male subject position, as it were (although this is not mentioned by the respondent, both women and men were employed at the office). But this self-positioning is called into question when the respondent's boyfriend is brought into the narrative as the driving force behind the woman's interest in computers. The contradictory nature of the construction of self is evident in the way in which the boyfriend is introduced into the account. As the woman's phrasing illustrates ("Well, in a way—I guess—partly"), this ambivalent construction of self is not entirely free of inner conflict.

> Well, it was here at the office, where we had Internet access … I've always had an affinity for computers, I like them and—well, I got more and more interested in what's on offer, and at some point I learned how to make web pages. Well, in a way—I guess—partly it was also the relationship with my boyfriend that was responsible, because he's studying informatics and he was terribly happy that finally he had a girlfriend who's interested in that sort of thing. (Z.A.)

On the other hand, some self-positionings focus specifically on respondents' own interest in and enthusiasm for the new technology. Five of the narratives contain accounts of initial Internet exploration that occurred exclusively on the women's own initiative and without outside support.

> I don't remember so well but I was working in the computer centre then … I just went through all the programs, tried out everything and then, at some point, there was Mosaic, that was the precursor of Netscape. … And then it was just this intuitive thing, you just go ahead and click on it. (V.B.)

Overall, the narratives of respondents' own entry experiences correspond more or less closely to prevailing discourses on gender. The link between not necessarily but seemingly naturally connected areas—the "articulation" as defined by cultural studies (Hall, 1996a, p. 141; Hall, 1996b, p. 33) between "technology and masculinity"—is rarely questioned when respondents recall their Internet start. However, this link or articulation no longer works fully, as indicated by the ambivalence found in respondents' statements: in their insistence on their own motivation, for instance, or the way in which the articulation between "masculinity and technology" is remembered and expressed. Thus, even these female professionals, who, if only by virtue of their profession, exhibit a stronger affinity for the new technology, contribute in different ways to the discursive construction and maintenance of the myth linking technology with masculinity.

Self-Representations in the Professional Context

With respect to self-representations in a professional context, there is no single, unified feminine subject position taken by respondents. Instead, various ways of either affirming or attempting to shift the boundary lines within the gendered discourse on technology can be observed.

As women increasingly take up Internet and multimedia professions, the result seems not so much a breaking open of gender binaries with regard to technology but, rather, increasing differentiation within the prevailing discourse on technology. Web surface design and html programming appear to be the new

domains assigned to women, whereas hardware and other programming still figure as masculine, and thus more highly valued,
domains. The close connection between the more highly valued
technical domains and the less-highly-valued web surface jobs is
expressed in passing by one of the respondents.

> This [html-programming] was something I could understand. For
> me—well, in html programming I can figure out what's going on. For
> hardcore programmers, I suppose, html is something like—like child's
> play, I guess. (Q.J.)

The matter-of-fact, offhand way in which the connection
between "technology-masculinity-hardcore" is established is
amazing. Likewise, the link between "woman-html programming-
child's play" serves not only to highlight the difference but also to
increase the distance between what is valued and what is not. It
thus becomes apparent how routinely such dichotomization takes
place and how strongly it is inscribed in societal attributions of
gender. Rather than interpreting their entry into a "non-feminine"
domain as a proud act defying existing gender norms,
respondents react by shifting the boundaries, marking html programming as feminine and inappropriately undermining its
value. By constructing a new dividing line between "real" programming and html programming while attaching differential
value to each, they reinvest "masculine" technology with the
value that has traditionally been ascribed to it.

Contrary to the assumption that female pioneers in the new
technologies might break open men's domains, it seems that
gender boundaries are redrawn in ways that do not differ
substantially from traditional ways of assigning gendered
domains and attendant value, such as high and low prestige. So
what is important for the assigning of gender difference is not
only the historical, socially produced structures but also the
concrete situations in which men and women affirm the gendered
norm through the ways in which their involvement with the new
technologies is enacted in everyday social practice. What we
observe is not a smooth, contradiction-free positioning of
gendered subjectivities; rather, the self-representations display a
degree of ambivalence that precludes their clear gender positioning. Specifically, both "masculine" and "feminine" coded
characteristics can be seen to coexist within individual self-

representations, with prevalent social norms concerning feminine subject-positioning serving as the general guideline for respondents' gendered self-positioning.

However, alongside this typically "feminine" form of self-positioning, evidenced by women downgrading or belittling their professional responsibilities, there are also many self-representations characterized by a confident recognition of professional contributions and an unselfconscious approach to technology and technical concerns that are not usually associated with women.

> My business partner and I called on some clients recently and just imagine the scene: he—he's the communicative type, heavily into soft skills, zilch computer know-how. Me, I'm the computer lady. There we are, sitting across from these two people discussing our offer. They ask him the technical questions and me about social competence, and then we cross-deliver the answers. At first, we're getting odd looks but after a while they get it. ... Oh, well, I do wish sometimes I could do my job just like normal. (X. C.)

Being confronted with gender stereotypes time and again is clearly frustrating. Irritation is felt by those who, through their communication or their behavior, call into question one's self-positioning with respect to gender. The above example shows how difficult it is to deviate from fixed gender positions, since women professionals cannot demonstrate "masculine" professional competencies without first having to contest the gender attributions that are made. Professionalism and competency in multimedia professions are thus gendered, since they are equated with masculinity. Women are not expected to exhibit these attributes and are held to social expectations of femininity.

Given the need to continually clarify and assert one's professionalism and competence in the face of gendered expectations, the shift back and forth between binary gendered positions turns into a laborious process of identity construction. The choice, then, is between recurrent confrontation and clarification and, alternatively, abandonment of boundary-transgressing gender positions in favor of socially approved positions.

Career Plans and Future Visions

Both the view that women willingly forego a career for the

sake of their families and the widely held belief that women do not really care for career advancement are social expectations they customarily faced. The fact that these views seem to be borne out by empirical data serves to conceal the gendered structures creating an invisible barrier to women's career advancement. These gendered structures are expressed in the metaphor of the "glass ceiling." This social dimension is especially relevant in a field such as multimedia production, which is still considered a masculine domain. Only a few of the Internet professionals stated that they were not interested in a top career; as they saw it, their priority was to continue in their profession as long as they found their work enjoyable. These women also mentioned family planning in discussing their career visions. The subject positions taken up by these respondents reflect a shift in social discourses on femininity inasmuch as the desire for meaningful and pleasurable professional involvement is placed above the needs of family life. Although self-limitation thus gives way to positive expansion, respondents' statements can nevertheless be seen as belonging to a discourse on femininity that has probably changed in terms more of rhetoric than of substance.

What is notable in interviewees' answers concerning their future careers is the way they begin their responses, using phrases such as "Hm, I really don't know yet"; "I don't know—I'm thinking about that"; "I can't really say"; "Well, I don't really have a clear idea of where I'm headed." These sentence openings are illustrative of the discursive elements involved in the link between women and the lower rungs of the social hierarchy. They are expressions of generalized social expectations and do not necessarily represent individuals' own points of view. Thus, as the conversation unfolds, most women do express definite and concrete career goals and plans. The majority of respondents have their careers clearly mapped out, and are explicit about not wanting to leave their professional futures to chance. The indefinite opening phrases, then, are in direct contradiction to what follows in the conversation; this illustrates clearly the difficulty of breaking down the linguistic patterns associated with the feminine.

With respect to the plans and visions expressed, great diversity can be observed. Many discuss the future of the Internet and the new technologies in their answers, cautioning that this sector may not meet the expectations placed on it in terms of job creation and income generation. There is also the realization that the distribution of jobs in multimedia is likely to be gendered and that home page creation and web page design are unlikely to be among the best-paid jobs.

> I took on html production because I thought I would be earning more and have more of a say, but that was an illusion. (O.L.)

Others are anxious to work with larger organizations, to move from specific tasks to more integrated assignments involving both content and technology.

> I have an education in technology. And one of the things I like is that I'm not only working with the technology, I'm not only a technological "idiot savant." ... Basically, I want to continue in the same direction I have done until now, where I use my technical education to connect this knowledge with feminist projects. (S.H.)

Another interesting aspect is the way that female Internet professionals devalue "masculine" technology, which usually is linked with social attributions such as "meaningful," "significant," "prestigious," and "high-income." This devaluation of technology not only expresses a lack of esteem for technology but, more importantly, a general critique of the high social status technology is commonly accorded. This critical attitude to technology is not limited to Internet professionals whose background is in technology.

Many of the women professionals interviewed are planning to set up their own companies or expand already existing businesses. This is in keeping with developments in the multimedia sector. Currently, there is a boom in new business creation, with many new companies being founded. In a few years' time, a process of market restructuring can be expected to take place, which only the larger firms are likely to survive.

Experiences of Male Dominance In and Around the Net

Subjective experience and memories of such experience always imply an element of social perception. This social perception, formed in a historical process and therefore subject to change, can be said to provide a dispositif for perception that manifests itself both in public speech and in private narratives. Thus, when asking people about their personal experiences, the experiences recalled will inscribe social discourses. Experiences are thus never solely determined by social discourses nor by an individual's subjective actions but are always the result of both. According to Haug (1995, p. 9), in order to find out something about an individual's subjective experiences, it is always necessary to consider also the societal experiences involved, how they are perceived, how meanings are constructed by the individual, and how these experiences are integrated into everyday practice.

Almost all of the persons interviewed recounted experiences of male domination on the Internet. Reports were mainly of sexual harassment and come-ons in the form of anonymous email messages and sexual innuendo in newsgroups or chats.

The ready availability of sex and pornographic pages on the Web was also mentioned as an unpleasant feature of the Internet, but interviewees seemed to speak of it as something that just had to be endured. The connection between the Internet, masculinity, and sex and pornography is one that is often made in public discourse in Austria and Germany. During the phase of web commercialization the popular media in German-speaking countries, in particular, focused, and still focus today, on primarily masculine subjects such as cybersex and child pornography, thus contributing in essential ways to the positioning of the Internet with respect to gender hierarchies. When respondents speak about their experiences, therefore, these appear as mere examples of a known and widely discussed fact, providing further evidence of what everyone "already knows."

Here, discursively produced knowledge intersects with personal experience, which is then no longer new or surprising, as it would be, were it not for the media staging and public debate. This "articulation" (Hall, 1996a, 1996b), that is, a preexisting connection that is seemingly "natural," albeit not necessary, is thus reproduced or reconstituted as one carrying sexual connotations. It is for this reason that sexual harassment does not consciously register or, in the case of the Internet, is regarded as "natural" and "inevitable" and often passed over without comment. At the same time, exactly how such events are perceived is dependent on the social contexts in which respondents live and work. Thus, female Internet professionals involved in feminist projects or with a feminist background are far more explicit and reflective in discussing the connection between the Web and sexual harassment.

A similar effect can be observed in respondents' narratives about their experiences of working in the male-dominated sphere of the Internet. In this case, it is the connection between technology-Internet-masculinity that is reproduced time and again. At issue are different dispositifs for perception and different ways of dealing with experiences of discrimination. These range from ignoring the offending acts to accepting them as inevitable to keeping a reflective critical distance and, finally, to resisting assertively. A number of different behavioral strategies can be distinguished. Some women have gotten used to male domination and discrimination, accepting them as the norm. Others have developed the assertiveness and authority of the lone fighter, while still others refuse to accept the status quo, demanding social change. However, all are faced with the need to continually prove their professionalism and competence, as these are attributes traditionally associated with masculinity.

Thus, respondents' own experiences combine with a discursive knowledge that serves to invest the male domain of technology still further with attributes specifically associated with the masculine. The resulting overdetermination creates what are known as typical discourses on femininity. These include the victim discourse, on the one hand, which leaves women in a distinctly feminine subject position, where prevailing conditions are accepted as the norm and passively endured. On the other hand, there is the lone fighter, the strong and independent woman who confidently transgresses gender boundaries and moves offensively and aggressively from a masculine subject position. And finally, there is the feminist discourse seeking in a variety of ways to effect social change in matters affecting gender.

Conclusion

Where the Internet is concerned, the cultural constructions of masculinity and femininity offered by the gender system as a symbolic or meaning-producing system are binary categories.

Both societal (mediated) representations and self-representations provide evidence of the fact that socially constructed gender positioning disappears less easily than the early theories of cyberfeminists had envisaged. Nevertheless, the potential for repositioning and shifting existing boundaries should be recognized, although current representations in the popular media continue to deploy conservative constructions of gender differences or differentiations.

As the present qualitative study shows, the myth that the Internet is to do with technology exerts a strong influence on discursive practices of doing gender, although alternative conceptions are beginning to emerge.

Women still represent a minority in the multimedia field. The social context of education plays a large part, such that women's experiences in male-dominated technical schools and universities confront them with the situation of being different, outside the norm.

Women students and scholars react to this differently: to them it represents a constant shift between male and female positioning of subjectivity. Self-confident demeanor and male-coded self-consciousness alternate with the female-coded victim role. Even a high level of education does not guarantee equality: Many professionals work in less esteemed html programming or in training, and not in other programming or systems administration. This is also due to the ambivalence of the interviewees self-positioning in a male-dominated professional environment. The constant need to justify oneself and the fact that one is not simply evaluated on the strength of achievement and qualification are stressful for many, and pave the way for a female subject positioning.

This is, however, not necessarily definitive, as for some it leads to the assumption of a decidedly feminist subject position. For the most part, however, women professionals collaborate not only on the structural level (distribution of work, salary) but also on the level of self-positioning in the gender-specific-coding of "technology and the Internet," thereby differentiating the technological terminology into male- and female-coded parts. Although an alternation between differing male and female subject-positioning could be observed among the interviewees, it was proven that women actively participate in the articulation of "Internet-technology-masculinity." They force a gender differentiation in technical terminology, by verbally producing and evaluating, for instance, the connection between "woman-html programming-child's play." On the other hand, new positionings are evolving, which reject this connection and renegotiate feminist education options in an exemplary fashion.

Creating spaces for reflection, rewriting cultural narratives, and developing new perspectives are best achieved when the tensions and contradictions inherent in one's own self-positioning are clearly perceived. Involvement in feminist contexts, or the experience of a technically orientated education, appears to offer such critical vantage points.

Notes

1. There are many ways in which women have contributed to developing the basis for today's Internet technology, especially in the context of computer technology and software. See, for example, Plant (1997), Haraway (1990), Hoffmann (1987), and Herner (2000).

2. The connection between technology, the Internet, and masculinity has been described by the author in more detail in another publication (Dorer, 2001).

3. The study was carried out as part of a larger research project funded by the Austrian Ministry for Science and Transport. For further results of the study "Construction of Gender and the Internet" (Geschlechterkonstruktion und Internet), see Dorer, 2000, 2001.

4. Members of the multimedia core include, according to Michel and Goertz (1999, pp. 20, 110), producers of multimedia products working in agencies while the first periphery includes producers and users in media companies, and the second periphery includes users in all sectors of the economy.

5. A first study conducted in this area indicates that in 1997 there were 90 multimedia production firms operating in Austria. These were small or tiny organizations rarely with more than five staff members. Only men were interviewed for this study of the multimedia profession (Hummel & Götzenbrucker, 1997, p. 195). Since there are no representative data available for Austria, the share of women in this sector is not known. For Germany, Michel and Goertz (1999, p. 122) found women to have a 21% share in the multimedia core sector. Half of the female multimedia professionals were active in project management, the other half in design and conception. None of the women interviewed worked as a programmer.

6. Gertraud Kohlbacher conducted the interviews. During data analysis all personal references to individuals were removed and the qualitative material was subjected to systematic categorization based on coding guidelines. The following transcription rules apply to the excerpts reprinted in this chapter: a dash stands for a pause in the interviewee's speech flow, whereas ellipsis points indicate deletions made by the author.

7. The incomes reported are clearly lower than in Germany, where Michel and Goertz (1999, p. 123) found monthly pretax incomes between DEM 750 and DEM 15,000. In Germany, the gender gap in monthly pretax incomes is around DEM 1,000. There are no comparable figures available for the multimedia sector in Austria. According to the most recent survey by the Central Statistical Office, conducted in 1999, the average income difference across all branches of employment was 35%.

References

ARD/ZDF Arbeitsgruppe Multimedia. (1999). Internet—(k)eine Männerdomäne [ARD/ZDF Working Group on Multimedia (1999), The Internet—(Not) a Masculine Domain]. *Media Perspektiven, 8*, 423–429.

Cockburn, Cynthia & Ormrod, Susan. (1993). *Gender and Technology in the Making*. London: Sage.

De Lauretis, Teresa. (1987). *Technologies of Gender. Essays on Theory, Film, and Fiction*. Bloomington: Indiana University Press.

Dorer, Johanna. (1997). Gendered Net. Ein Forschungsüberblick über den geschlechtsspezifischen Umgang mit neuen Kommunikationstechnologien [The Gendered Net. A Survey of Research on the Gendered Use of the New Communication Technologies]. *Rundfunk und Fernsehen, 45*(1), 18–19.

Dorer, Johanna. (2000). Geschlechterkonstruktionen in der Aneignung und Anwendung des Internet. Ergebnisse einer qualitativen Studie [Constructions of Gender in the Appropriation and Use of the Internet. Results of a Qualitative study]. *Medien und Zeit. 15*(2), 40–51.

Dorer, Johanna. (2001). Internet und Geschlecht. Berufliche und private Anwendungspraxen der neuen Technologie [Internet and Gender. Professional and Private Practices of Use of the New Technologies]. In Klaus, Elisabeth, Röser, Jutta & Wischermann, Ulla (Eds.), *Gender Studies und Kommunikationswissenschaft [Gender Studies and Communication Studies]*. Wiesbaden: Westdeutscher Verlag, pp. 241–266.

Eimerer, Birgit, Gerhard, Heinz, Oemichen, Ekkehardt & Schröter, Christian. (1998). Onlinemedium gewinnt an Bedeutung. Nutzung von Internet und Onlineangeboten elektronischer Medien in Deutschland. ARD/ZDF-Online-Studie 1998. [Online Medium Gains in Significance. Use of Web-Based and Online Services Offered by the Electronic Media in Germany. ARD/ZDF Online study 1998]. *Media Perspektiven 8*, 423–435.

Hall, Stuart. (1996a). On Postmodernism and Articulation. In Morley, David & Chen, Kuan-Hsing (Eds.), *Stuart Hall. Critical Dialogues in Cultural Studies*. London: Routledge, pp. 131–150.

Hall, Stuart. (1996b). Signification, Representation, Ideology: Althusser and the Post-Structural Debates. In Curran, James, Morley, David & Walkerdine, Valerie (Eds.), *Cultural Studies and Communication*. London: Arnold, pp. 11–34.

Haraway, Donna. (1985/1990). A Manifesto for Cyborgs. Science, Technology, and Socialist Feminism in the 1980s. In Nicholson, Linda (Ed.), *Feminism/Postmodernism*. London: Routledge, pp.190–233.

Haug, Frigga. (1995). Das Projekt [The Project]. In Haug, Frigga & Hipfl, Brigitte (Eds.), *Sündiger Genuss? Filmerfahrungen von Frauen [Sinful Pleasures? Women Experiencing Film].* Hamburg: Argument, pp. 7–14.

Haug, Frigga. (1999). *Vorlesungen zur Einführung in die Erinnerungsarbeit [Lectures on Memory Work and How to Approach it].* Hamburg: Argument.

Herner, Christine. (July 14–15, 2000). Die Töchter der Madam Curie [Madame Curie's Daughters]. *Wiener Zeitung Extra,* p. 12.

Hoffmann, Ute. (1987). *Welchen Anteil haben Frauen an der Computergeschichte und –arbeit? [Women's Contribution to Computing History and Computer-Based Work].* Munich: Hampp Verlag.

Hummel, Roman & Götzenbrucker, Gerit. (1997). Wenig lernen-alles können. Empirische Ergebnisse zur Entwicklung von Multimediaberufen in Österreich [Learn a Little—Know It All. Empirical Data Concerning the Development of Multimedia Professions in Austria]. *SWS-Rundschau, 37*(2) 91–104.

Kroker, Arthur & Weinstein, Michael. (1994). *Data Trash. The Theory of the Virtual Class.* New York: St. Martin´s Press.

Lovink, Geert & Schultz, Pit. (1999). Aus der Schatzkammer der Netzkritik [From the Treasure Trove of Web Critique]. In: Maresch, Rudolf & Weber, Niels (Eds.), *Kommunikation—Medien—Macht [Communication, the Media, and Power].* Frankfurt: Suhrkamp, pp. 299–328.

Makivic, Svetlana. (2000). Die Internetqueens. http://www.zdf.de/ratgeber/aktuell/monalisa/39331/index.html

Michel, Lutz & Goertz, Lutz. (1999). *Arbeitsmarkt und Multimedia: Trends und Chancen. Qualifikationsprofile und Karrierewege in einer Zukunftsbranche [The Job Market and Multimedia: Trends and Opportunities. Competence Profiles and Career Paths in an Expanding Sector].* Berlin: Vistas. Also http://www.mmbmichel.de /mmquali99_kurz.doc

N.N. (August 10, 2000). Amerikas Frauen holen auf [American Women are Catching up]. *Online-Spiegel.*

ORF. (2000). Strukturvergleich-2. Quartal 2000 [Austrian Broadcasting Corporation, A Structural Comparison—Second Quarter of 2000]. http://media research.orf.at/inter_05.htm

Pfeiffer, Carola. (2000). Die Schattenseiten der IT-Branche [The Darker Sides of the IT Sector]. http://www.zdf.de/ratgeber/aktuell/monalisa/39332/index.htm

Plant, Sadie. (1997). *Zeros and Ones.* London: Fourth Estate.

Turkle, Sherry. (1995). *Life on the Screen. Identity in the Age of the Internet.* New York: Simon & Schuster.

Turkle, Sherry. (1996). Parallel Lives: Working on Identity Space. In Grodin, Debra & Lindlof, Thomas (Eds.), *Constructing the Self in a Mediated World.* London: Sage, pp. 156–178.

Zimmer, Jochen. (1998). Werbemedium World Wide Web. Entwicklungsstand und Perspektiven von Onlinewerbung in Deutschland [The World Wide Web as an Advertising Medium. Present State and Future Prospects of Online Advertising in Germany]. *Media Perspektiven, 10,* 498–507.

Chapter 4

Women's Internet Sites: A Search for Design Strategies to Engage the Female Viewer

Noemi Sadowska

The dramatic commercial growth of the Internet has resulted in women emerging as the new and promising consumers. However, this sudden interest does not come as a result of rising social awareness and reformulation of gender meanings; rather, this development is driven by the recognition of the independent spending power women have achieved in recent decades. Under such circumstances, the relationship female users have developed with the Internet as communication technology spans a spectrum of issues from physical access through notions of consumption to ideals of empowerment (Hawthorne & Klein, 1999). This chapter focuses in particular on the issue of commercial Internet consumption. It examines the different design metaphors that are used to communicate content to online users in the form of visual language. The purpose of this discussion is to establish and draw attention to the need for an alternative set of design strategies that invite female users to more actively engage with the Internet.

With the recognition of new means of communication comes the responsibility of their development, shared by both men and women. This chapter, therefore, looks at the relationship that female users, within the Western world, have engaged in and are negotiating, between the Internet as a communication technology and design as the practical implementation of that communication in the gendered context of the Internet.[1] In particular, it focuses on design as a set of strategies that communicate different gendered messages embedded in women's Internet portals. The chapter examines a specific site (BEME.com) as a case study to evaluate existing design strategies as a starting point in a search for alternative design approaches. Such a method, I believe, leads to a broader search for ways in which female users, engaging with alternative design strategies, can develop new approaches that give them a stronger voice in shaping this communication technology. The underlying question is whether this approach will open up broader social, cultural, and political opportunities for empowerment or reify existing static commercial structures.

In order to approach this question, a more concrete definition of "design" is required. Here, design represents different visual elements such as text and images that are used to communicate various meanings within women's sites. Design, therefore, is defined as a purposefully embedded set of communication tools that are physically visualized in a text or image. In practical terms design can include page layout, font, color, and photography. It is the process of creating a visual language that forms a meaning-carrying relationship specified by the client like the publisher and executed by the designer.

Consequently, design tools are the means or elements that the designer has at his/her disposal to communicate the intended meaning. These range from the visual elements that define the image or text to the specific ways in which they are arranged on the page. The key to understanding these concepts is purposefulness. Each element and the way it is visualized goes through an endless process of design editorial decision-making. This activity engages the designer in two different but parallel processes based on professional expertise and intuitive decision-making. These processes combine and feed off each other to arrive at the best visual solution. The participating designer, in order to judge accurately the framework of communication as well as the necessary tools and strategies, will have undergone a rigorous process of training within the design profession. Therefore, the discussed context of design is seen as a combination of various independent agents (designers, visual tools, messages, intent, and interaction context) that come together in the process of visual, practice-embedded communication—in this case BEME.com.

In order to fully engage with the analysis of the case study, it is crucial to gain a deeper understanding of BEME.com. The key to selecting this site is its development directly out of the paper women's magazine industry. BEME.com is a product of the magazine publishing company IPC Media (UK). It is a women's magazine portal established in 1999, and IPC Media's response to the economic boom in the dot.com online industries. This particular publishing house specializes in what are generally termed traditional women's magazines: *Marie Claire, Woman, Woman's Own*, and so on. BEME.com represents an electronic version of a women's magazine strongly positioned within the traditional women's publishing industry and the associated understanding of women's gendered social status within Western culture. According to IPC Media the brand profile of BEME.com is as follows:

> BEME.com's proposition is to be the first choice place for women on the web. Building on IPC Media's unique position within the women's market, BEME.com aims to provide users with compelling content that satisfies key information needs, across a broad range of life stages. BEME.com aims to weave branded content right through the site, driving two-way traffic between BEME.com and IPC's other women's brands. (IPC Media, 2001)

However, the process does not exist in a vacuum. The visual language used by BEME.com is intended for users, predominantly female ones. These female users may be passive or active, reading, scanning, viewing, "dipping in" for diversion or relaxation, or may be searching with a very concrete purpose in mind. However, their predesigned role is to encounter the visual language and engage with its consumption prompting meanings.

The Internet Context—Political Empowerment Alongside the Commercial Imperative

In describing the general environment of women's Internet portals, I will clarify the context that defines sites like BEME.com and allows them to exist and thrive. There are two main forms of publishing directed to women online; these coexist but are very different in their focus on gender. In the context of current feminist/women's activism, the Internet as a publishing medium is seen as a medium of empowerment. Through its communication innovations it offers enormous potential for political organization on both the local and the global level (Hawthorne & Klein, 1999). A number of feminist activists are excited about this communication medium, seeing its potential to combat gender inequalities (Pattanaik, 1999).

On the other hand, the Internet's market potential in terms of new consumers is explored through commercial publishing. As argued in the February 2001 issue of *Metro* (a London, UK-based newspaper), "the web has been a male domain, an exciting new playground for geeks and chancers, but this has changed as it has matured into mainstream medium ... business has spent billions attracting women online" ("Websites Fork Out," 2001). However, it is crucial to note that these new products are part of a powerful tradition of paper publishing. Especially in the case of the women's online publishing industry, this tradition has prevailed in the new medium. Its ideologies are firmly grounded in the belief that its products promote "a collective social 'reality,' the 'world of women'" (Shevelow, 1989, p. 19). In opposition to men's sites that concentrate on particular interests, women's magazine sites specialize in gender itself. Their focus is fixed on the readers—women—carried forward from traditional magazine publishing. As Shevelow (1989) reveals, the bond that develops between women and women's magazines is reinforced by a secondary connection based on women's reading of these sites. However, first and most important, women's magazines (paper or digital) are designed as commodities. As Beetham (1996, p. 2) suggests, they are "products of the print industry ... [and] ... a crucial site for the advertising and sale of other commodities." Furthermore, she argues that they are "deeply involved in the capitalist production and consumption as well as circulating in the cultural economy of collective meanings and constructing an identity for the individual reader as gendered and sexual being" (p. 2). Beetham concludes that women's magazines are ultimately positioned as products, perched at the crossroads of various agendas including capital, public discourse, and individual desire (Beetham, 1996). Through these agendas, women's magazines or portals acquire their gendered meanings, which they then communicate through design as the desirable feminine identity.

By making products accessible at home via the Internet, the magazine publishing industry tries to reach new markets that might not have been previously available. Weale (2000) observes that this is "one of the key differences in the way women are targeted. They are seen first and foremost as shoppers; everything is dictated by the commercial imperative" (Weale, 2000). According to Internet surveys, women generally go online with a purpose in contrast to men who tend to surf randomly (Tran, 2001). It is this purposefulness that the magazine publishing industry wants to tap into. The big magazine publishing houses, such as IPC Media, base their experience on the paper tradition and demographic surveys, and so use long-established design strategies to engage users with their magazine-like Internet portals. This approach reinforces the conclusion that Internet sites are seen as static magazine pages, where room for manipulation in terms of imagery in relation to text is still dictated by the publishing industry, rather than the users.

Figure 4.1 BEME.com targeted its content at women at "different stages of their lives." Yet its visual communication propagated the old gendered stereotypes. Used with permission of IPC Media Ltd.

Female users of BEME.com are described by IPC Media as a heterogeneous set of women at various stages of their lives (IPC Media, 2001), with a geographic focus on the Western hemisphere. However, as often noted by feminist researchers, this understanding represents a particular, homogenized, and stereotyped view of women strongly rooted within patriarchal social structures. The users of BEME.com are seen as professional women with financial stability and constant access to the Internet. They are in a privileged position, and these instances of negotiated use should be viewed in light of that fact. At the same time, it is important to recognize that Western female Internet users live in a culture with strong ties to the tradition of reading women's magazines. This traditional practice has engendered a level of product loyalty that also transfers from paper publishing into e-commerce.[2] Consequently, the BEME.com female users have an insider's knowledge of the communication codes and design tools that they have learned and absorbed from the paper magazine industry. I will support these observations with a closer look at BEME.com, considering what the female users encounter and the gendered discourse in which this interaction occurs.

BEME.com—An Interactive Environment

The environment that IPC Media attempts to create is one of total trust between the publishing house and its readers. With great confidence IPC Media announces to potential advertisers:

> You'll either read them or you'll know a woman who does. It's an enviable position. A position built on a breadth and depth of consumer understanding no other media company can rival. It's about having the power to communicate, entertain, and advise. It's about freedom. Women don't want to be dictated to, and neither do our brands. (IPC Media, 2001)

In terms of design, strategies do not stray far from paper industry design specifications in the use of images and text to create company-approved sets of meanings. Due to technological limitations the site is largely text based, but the content changes mostly on a daily basis. Although the corporate vision for the site states that "BEME.com is able to connect women everywhere, appealing to those in different stages of their lives and reflecting their diversity in age, lifestyle, socio-economic and ethnic groups" (IPC Media, 2001), the design strategies stray from these commendable corporate ideals.

To substantiate my analysis I will use the taxonomy established by Aitchison and Jordan (2001) in their research on discourses of tourism and the body. They have conducted extensive research into the notions of how cultural constructions of the body are mediated through different leisure activities.

> Tourism is generally influenced by image and, as an expanding international phenomenon, itself plays a significant role in shaping the

identities of places and of people. Thus, the marketing of tourism through association with particular images of women potentially exerts an important influence over women as consumers of tourism. (Aitchison & Jordan, 2001, p. 32)

I would argue that this association is also very relevant to other cultural/consumer industries including the Internet. Such an approach allows for an informed view of how female online users are shaped and/or taught by the medium itself to become consumers of the women's magazine portals. Aitchison and Jordan looked at a number of women's magazines between January and June 2001. Their investigation led them to establish five categories (homogenized, sexualized, disciplined, scrutinized, and invisible) that best represented their collected data sample in the form of women's body images.[3] These categories are equally relevant to the design strategies used by BEME.com on the Internet. This clearly points to the fact that the Internet environment is not free from traditional discourses of women's representation, which are deeply rooted in the women's magazine industry and are perpetuated through design strategies.

A closer look at the structure of the site in question is needed. An edition of BEME.com comprises the following elements. The site is divided into six interest channels: entertainment; love, sex, and friendship; fashion and beauty; health, body, and soul; travel; and news. Each has its own content and color-coding. Each page consists of several feature articles that include an image, a headline, and a thematic introduction. Content deemed less important is represented only by a headline and a thematic introduction. To access a complete article one has to click on a headline that leads to another page with the entire text, images, and other related links. Often one of the links will offer the possibility of voicing an opinion in the form of a vote. Each of the six channels can be accessed simultaneously alongside a menu bar that provides thematic shortcuts to the features considered most interesting. Articles that include images mostly portray women with "beautifully toned bodies" or photographs of the latest celebrities. The images of women that are employed on the site fall within the approved and acceptable boundaries of contemporary social expectations of feminine attractiveness. Although they are polysemic, the photographs aim to provide a model of comparison for female users. In terms of design processes, one difference between

BEME.com and paper magazines is the speed of delivery. The tone of the site also differs from paper editions, being more straightforward and factual in approach, as is characteristic of many web publications. The visual language is much more austere then in the luscious paper editions; however, it still clearly and effortlessly communicates the design strategies discussed below.

Figure 4.2 BEME.com was divided into six interest channels, each with its own content and color-coding. Used with permission of IPC Media Ltd.

Illustrating the use of the "sexualized" category, the edition of BEME.com dated July 26, 2001, includes various articles supported by images of highly sexualized women. These images present women's bodies as if they are ready and possibly available for a sexual encounter. This is achieved by the pose, the facial expression of the photographed subject, or a stereotypical setting. Associated headlines support the sexualized meanings of images, which range in their degree of explicitness. The use of this design strategy is very strongly embedded in the paper magazine tradition, which promotes a patriarchal understanding of women's social position. By taking on the role of providing "social guidance" for women, the women's magazines have created a normalized system for teaching women how to become socially accepted gendered individuals. This system skillfully employs design in its visual language of gender. The visual codes embedded in the language, therefore, range from the very subtle to the more explicit, but they never have to be obvious in their connotations.

As with many sites dedicated to female audiences, BEME.com includes several articles that focus on control of the users' bodies through professionalized strategies of personal discipline. This approach falls under the "disciplined" category. The channels dedicated to fashion, beauty, or health contain titles such as, "Get Expert Diet Advice" or "Personal Trainer: When Toning Turns to Moaning" (BEME.com, 2001b; Freeland, 2001a, 2001b). Here the supporting images portray the disciplining experts, who voice their commentaries or tips and encouragements on how to achieve socially accepted bodily norms. Such articles are accompanied by images of bodies that have already achieved their goal, functioning as testimonials to the experts' advice. This particular design strategy employs carefully selected images of "beautifully toned bodies" and clever, catchy headlines, to make social beauty norms appear easily achievable. Through careful, conscious design the visuals become the justification as well as proof of the exhortations of the text. Without this interplay of text/image components, the discourse of "achievable discipline" would quickly collapse.

To entice customers and evoke their loyalty, BEME.com creates and positions itself at the center of a female social community. Through the use of the "scrutinized" category, BEME.com positions its content in a certain relation to the community it claims to represent. The tone of the site and the numerous opportunities offered for users to "voice their opinion" allow BEME.com to take on the role of a best friend or confidante, the one with important contacts in the larger social circle. These "contacts" also allow the user access to "exclusive" information, as BEME.com reports on the lives of celebrities. Through the use of articles giving intimate details of celebrities' lives, BEME.com brings the "extraordinary" into the realm of the "ordinary." These designed meanings are an invitation to female users to believe that the "extraordinary" lives of the "rich and famous" are easily emulated by BEME.com users, who lead "ordinary" lives. This strategy attempts to make normal (or accessible) the privilege of a few by visually producing celebrities and making their lives seem as "mundane" as those of the "normal" user. At the same time, it positions the represented celebrities as role models, showing both celebrities and the "everyday" female users under the scrutiny of others. Images of Emma Bunton (Baby Spice of the UK's Spice Girls) crown the article entitled "Celebrity Fashion Blunder: Emma Bunton" (BEME.com, 2001a), followed by a survey on the prettiness or ugliness of Angelina Jolie (the actress who plays Lara Croft in the movie *Tomb Raider*) under the title "Ugly or Pretty: Angelina Jolie" (BEME.com, 2001d). In both cases, an appropriate photograph to illustrate the story or allow the user to make a judgment accompanies the textual narrative. The documentary-like look of the images and the "honest" tone of the text make this design strategy a powerful carrier of social meanings and norms. The "reality" element functions as an authoritative force in creating interest and loyalty in the female users. Again, it is the design tools that provide the visual language from which female users extract pertinent meanings.

The final category, the "invisible," seems to be just that at BEME.com. Editorial decisions reinforce ideals and values that treat body shapes outside of the norm as the invisible "other." Carefully designed images and headlines leave out references to ages, body shapes, or ethnic backgrounds that do not fit the Western norm, and so all "deviations" remain invisible. Although the brand profile claims to reflect a multiplicity of ages, lifestyles, and ethnicities (IPC Media, 2001), after a quick browse it becomes apparent that the focus is on the stereotyped norms of the "Western woman." The previously described design strategies are used to filter out "other" bodies, rendering them invisible. In addition, the use of design tools that alter the digital images themselves, through the use of sophisticated imaging software, narrow even further the range of the "ideal." Images representing the achievable feminine norm have been designed to filter out that which is not "beautiful," clean, or of a certain shape. The site does not cater to female users who are not sophisticated, cool, and "collected" or at least those who are not doing their best to get there. In the best traditions of women's periodicals, BEME.com positions itself as a perfect example of a guidebook on how to become that "ultimate feminine norm," immaculately dressed and a perfect size 8–10 on the UK fashion scale. The users of BEME.com are very well versed in the right steps on the journey to become "feminine" (Ferguson, 1983). In this case it is the visual language that reveals and communicates these steps.

The BEME.com example shows that particular design strategies have social meanings embedded in their practical uses, and are caught up in gender politics. Using these design strategies to develop articles like "Turn Your Office From Sweatshop to Style Oasis With Our Do and Don't Guide for Summer in the City" (BEME.com, 2001c), the portal has the answer to any problem posed. However, there seems to be very little use of design tools in acknowledgment of the socially defined "other."

These design strategies reflect a particular set of feminine norms. Thus, developed normative systems become particular sets of values that society tries to impose on individuals and their sense of self. The world of women's magazines or Internet sites can be viewed as a space for a "rite of initiation" or a guide to gaining access to society.[4] In these spaces, individuals (women) make specific changes to achieve "true" personhood (in particular womanhood), which then defines them in our social context. Design strategies contribute to this process alongside "other social institutions such as the family, the school, the church and the other media ... [which contribute] to the wider cultural processes which define the position of women in a given society at a given point in time" (Ferguson, 1983, p. 1). Here, I agree with Ferguson that through exchanges within the larger context of social structure, design strategies are part of the process that shapes women's notions of themselves and society's notions of them (Ferguson, 1983).

Closely examining a site like BEME.com makes it quite apparent that female users are not given a real opportunity to interact with the environment in which they view the content. Rather, as in the paper magazines, they are positioned as receivers of various items of information. The design strategies function as a dictatorship of meanings, creating an environment where female users do not necessarily explore their full potential as self-aware individuals but are seen as "unadulterated shopaholics" (Weale, 2000).

Women's negative or ambivalent attitudes toward commercial sites such as BEME.com are likely due in part to the sites' visual grammar or design.[5] That is why I would like to open up this discussion to a consideration of alternative design strategies that invite users to engage in "authoring" sites at the same time as they interact with them. I believe the notion of interactivity offers a number of interesting and innovative solutions. Placing the focus on interactivity as a design strategy allows users to engage with web sites in a manner different from that of traditional mass media. Participation between users and site creators can be negotiated in a much more fluid way.

An Issue of Empowerment—Online Female Users as Authors/Audiences

An understanding of the gendered context of Internet technologies is important when exploring empowerment issues that female users might better negotiate as authors. The gendering of the Internet as masculine space is strongly located in the overall historical relationship between gender and technology. As Stewart Millar (1998, p. 15) argues, "in contemporary western culture, men are assumed to make the machines, and, if culturally appropriate, women may use them." She goes on to explain such thinking as grounded in "traditional images of masculinity ... [representing] ... the technological 'Progress of Man' from so called barbarism to civilization. ... Such an identification is reinforced by millennia of historically constituted gender constructions that have come to define our very notions of what it is to be male and female" (p. 15). However, women did get involved with technology and its innovations. When we extend the meaning of what constitutes technology to embrace traditionally feminine areas, like the domestic sphere, we see numerous examples of women's preoccupation with technology and contributions to innovations (Plant, 1997). Therefore, the gendering of technology does not occur primarily because of lack of access for women to the object in question. It rather stems from ongoing social, cultural, and political control over the technological discourse that sees women as inferior (Hawthorne & Klein, 1999; Plant, 1997; Scott, 1998; Stewart Millar, 1998).

Perhaps not surprisingly, female Internet users are subjected to very similar gendered attitudes in the realm of the Web as they are when encountering technology generally. Although female users are increasingly engaging with the Net to satisfy their information and communication needs, many quickly find what they are looking for and move on. Their different initial aims, the unwelcoming environment of the technological discourse (Stewart

Millar, 1998), and/or technophobia all result in the type of interaction that can lead to rejection of the medium and/or refusal to share in its ownership. When interacting with sites like BEME.com where design strategies are deeply grounded in patriarchal social norms, female users can become discouraged from participation. Therefore I would like to propose a new approach to visual design.

My proposal is to conceptualize design strategies as interactive processes where female users take an active part in designing the meanings involved during use of the site. Authorship in Internet publishing already has a strong appeal because of its relative ease and its cost benefits. Many female users have claimed this medium to make themselves visible through the creation of diary-like sites. In such cases, the Internet allows women agency over authorship in order to quickly convey information and bring them together with others.

> Women online are participants rather than consumers. Information flow is interactive. Problem-solving in online groups ranges from the personal to the technological. This enables women to speak for themselves and develop strategies with others who are supportive or have had the same experience. (Pollock & Sutton, 1999, p. 35)

Many women's sites include the opportunity to participate in chat rooms, email exchanges, or online forums. Here the interactivity is not understood in design terms, but as participation, a way to keep female users interested in the content provided. However, what is lacking is the consideration (and exploration) of interactivity as a design strategy. There are already sites on the Internet that encourage users to personalize online pages. A good example is Yahoo.com, which allows its users to customize the amount of content the site displays as well as the order of importance of that content. Unfortunately, women's magazine portals keep reiterating a paper design attitude and do not engage with notions of interactivity through design. Therefore, I argue that user customization of the sites is just a first step in developing notions of interactivity. For new ways of communication to be developed, it is crucial that the approach to interactivity and its meaning has to change from notions of "simple" participation to evolved ideas of design strategies.

In practice-embedded design terms the inclusion of notions of interactivity repositions the design process, changing its approach from dogmatic dictation to fluid negotiation of the best communication strategy. Through the introduction of alternative design strategies that invite female users to engage with the visual and textual content, fluidity and flexibility become apparent. Female users will be in a position to define their own understanding of how static meanings need to be, adding a strong temporal element to the notions of social understanding and communication. When considering a global view of the use of the Internet, female users employing the interactive process will create design strategies that allow for their stronger presence in shaping this communication technology. Such an approach to design in terms of interactive modes of communication may lead to broader social, cultural, and political opportunities for female users' empowerment.

At this point in time a number of different disciplines are engaging in questioning, evaluating, and critiquing the Internet and its relationship to female users. Drawing attention to designers' sense of social responsibility is a matter of great importance. It is in their power and interest to search for new ways of communication, and, as producers, to question the usefulness of their products. Using well-established design processes in combination with an in-depth understanding of the gendered technological discourse and patriarchal positioning of female users, designers can create practical outcomes that prompt a shift in social meanings. Through such investigations, new possibilities for digital visual grammars will emerge, and the new discursive platform will provide a place where users, activists, designers, and producers with diverse interests can meet to achieve common goals.

Notes

1. This investigation is part of a larger research project and the subject of my doctoral study at Goldsmiths College, University of London. It engages with the issues of gender within women's publishing positioned in the context of the Internet.

2. Women's periodicals have historically instructed women in how to understand themselves and their surroundings. Shevelow (1989) describes the social role of women's magazines in the following terms:

> [I]n this eighteenth-century progressive view of women's education, a "little learning" was not a dangerous thing, for it was not only enough to suit the capacities of the softer feminine mind, but was also sufficient to serve its primary function of regulating and channeling women's intrinsic domestic genius. ... Rather than the ameliorated course of instruction in quasi-scientific subjects offered by the mid-century women's magazines, late-century magazines began to instruct their readers in the arts of femininity itself. (p. 188)

3. The taxonomy used by Aitchison and Jordan (2001) is derived from research into the imagery of women's magazines. Their research methods also include interviews with women's focus groups involved in leisure activities, the commercial sector (health and fitness clubs), or the public sector (health promotion) (Aitchison & Jordan, 2001). The following is a summary of the five categories, according to my understanding of their underlying meanings.

The category of the "homogenized" encompasses representations of women that do not allow for variation. It embodies the normative systems, imposed by society, of desired femininity. This femininity is to be sought by all women, and supports a homogenous understanding of the ideal body. Therefore, the images of women's bodies included in women's magazines do not reflect the diversity of reality but are created to represent the ideal. Through continuous reinvention of this homogenized ideal in every new issue, this understanding is cultivated and maintained.

The category of the "sexualized" addresses the objectification of women's bodies in reference to sexual context. It represents images of femininity in preparation or as invitations to a sexual encounter. The readers of women's magazines are encouraged to see the portrayed women's bodies as objects of sexual desire open to scrutiny, admiration, and imitation.

Women's magazine images that fall under the category of the "disciplined" are of controlled bodies. The portrayed bodies are seen in the context of differences and imperfections. Only discipline provides a way to overcome these differences. Therefore, the discourse of the images focuses on taking control of one's own body and its environment and turning it into the desirable norm, where control equals strength. In this case the norm seems to be unobtainable, since with each new issue, more effective ways to achieve this control are described.

The images that represent the "scrutinized" category revolve around the idea of a role model, quite often a celebrity or celebrities. Portraying women who represent a certain lifestyle—"the rich and the famous"—allows these images to be normalized as achievable realities, which can be reviewed and scrutinized by magazine readers. Once accepted as an expression of an ideal, this "reality" becomes "an object of desire." The images that represent this reality function as female icons and can be mimicked by following a regime of discipline and control.

The category of the "invisible" embodies the idea of the "other" that exists outside the norm. Most of the time the publishing industry discourse does not engage with the representation of the "other." If the "invisible" women's bodies are represented, they are most likely positioned for scrutiny, in order to be disciplined into the homogenized norm of femininity.

4. As stated by Cohen (1994), initiation is a relationship of constant tension between "selfhood (the substance of 'me' of which I am aware) and person-hood, the definition of me as a social entity which society imposes." The two forces act from opposite directions, where "the individual's developing sense of self, and the processes through which society presses that self into a matrix of its [society's] making, are often contemporaneous" (Cohen, 1994, pp. 56–57). Therefore, I suggest that one should consider women as representing single individuals with a relationship to and role in society. Ferguson sees women's social position as "one which requires separate consideration and distinctive treatment" supported by the fact of the existence of the women's magazine industry (Ferguson, 1983, p. 1).

5. As of August 31, 2001, IPC Media has taken BEME.com offline due to the downturn of the Internet economy. This decision suggests that what Internet sites offer to female users does not necessarily answer their needs. The lower financial returns point to less active engagement with the site.

References

Aitchison, C., and F. Jordan. (2001). *Beauty and the Beach: Discourses of Tourism and the Body*. Women's Studies Network 14th Annual Conference, Cheltenham and Gloucester College of Higher Education, UK.

Beetham, M. (1996). *A Magazine of Her Own?: Domesticity and Desire in the Woman's Magazine, 1800–1914*. London: Routledge.

BEME.com. (2001a). Celebrity Fashion Blunder: Emma Bunton, BEME.com. www.beme.com

BEME.com. (2001b). Get Expert Diet Advice, BEME.com. www.beme.com

BEME.com. (2001c). Turn Your Office From Sweatshop to Style Oasis With our Do and Don't Guide for Summer in theCity, BEME.com. www.beme.com

BEME.com. (2001d). Ugly or Pretty: Angelina Jolie, BEME.com. www.beme.com

Cohen, A. (1994). *Self Consciousness; An Alternative Anthropology of Identity*. London: Routledge.

Ferguson, M. (1983). *Forever Feminine: Women's Magazines and the Cult of Femininity*. London: Heinemann.

Freeland, K. (2001a). Fitness for Lazy Sods, BEME.com. www.beme.com.

Freeland, K. (2001b). Personal Trainer: When Toning Turns to Moaning, BEME.com. www.beme.com.

Hawthorne, S., & R. Klein, Eds. (1999). *CyberFeminism; Connectivity, Critique and Creativity*. Melbourne: Spinifex.

IPC Media. (2001). IPC Media Home Site, www.ipcmedia.com.

Pattanaik, B. (1999). Home and the World: The Internet as a Personal and Political Tool. In S. Hawthorne and R. Klein, eds., *CyberFeminism; Connectivity, Critique and Creativity* (pp. 19-32). Melbourne: Spinifex.

Plant, S. (1997). *Zeros + Ones; Digital Women + The New Technoculture*. London: Fourth Estate.

Pollock, S., and J. Sutton. (1999). Women Click: Feminism and the Internet. In S. Hawthorne and R. Klein, eds., *CyberFeminism; Connectivity, Critique and Creativity* (pp. 33-79). Melbourne: Spinifex.

Scott, K. (1998). "Girls Need Modems!" Cyberculture and Women's Ezines. *Women's Studies*. York, Canada: York University. Accessed at http://www.stumptuous.com/mrp.html

Shevelow, K. (1989). *Women and Print Culture: The Construction of Femininity in the Early Periodical*. London: Routledge.

Stewart Millar, M. (1998). *Cracking the Gender Code: Who Rules the Wired World?* Toronto: Second Story Press.

Tran, M. (2001). Xmas Shoppers Widen the Net, Guardian Unlimited. www.guardian.co.uk

Weale, S. (2000). Women of the World Click Here! Guardian Unlimited. www.guardian.co.uk

Websites Fork Out on Gender Appeal. (2001). *Metro*. London: Associated Newspapers.

Part Two

Addressing Women

Chapter 5

Selling the Internet to Women: The Early Years

Mia Consalvo

If you are a woman, sometimes cyberspace can get ugly.
—*The Washington Post, June 14, 1994*

It's a woman's web.
The numbers are in: women are the net's next wave.
—*MediaWeek, September 7, 1998*

Introduction

In the early 1990s, the Internet appeared as a strange new world in print media stories. It was populated by the weird and used by only a few people, mostly academics and government researchers. A very small percentage of these were women, but no one seemed to notice. Notice only came as a few more women ventured online, and suddenly the Internet was "hostile" to women, and a dangerous place if you couldn't take care of yourself. In spite of this, though, the numbers of women (and the overall population) online rose drastically, and by the late 1990s women were hailed as the "next wave" of the Internet. Although pockets of the Internet might still be dangerous, cyberspace now was a place for men, women, and children to chat, browse, and most importantly, buy. And tellingly, the Internet had become a place associated with the distribution of information and potential consumption, rather than a lawless, unexplored territory where business had no place and communication was the main attraction.

These changes occurred with lightning speed, and it is hard even to remember how the Internet "used to be." Statistics about women's use of the Internet are hard to find if they're not about the current year. And women are now overtaking men in their use of the Internet, although researchers are also starting to investigate differential uses, becoming more sophisticated than simply measuring being online or not. Yet the early world of the Internet, at least as it was portrayed in the popular media, is important to remember and study. The metaphors used in describing the Internet and the ways people were positioned in regard to their use (or non-use) of the Internet need to be scrutinized in order to better understand the Internet we have now.

This chapter takes up that challenge, examining early media attention to the Internet, especially the discourses surrounding women and metaphors in relation to cyberspace. Necessarily then, this chapter is concerned with the past. Not the distant past, but the years 1990–1998. During this period, the Internet advanced technologically and became better known popularly. This chapter is concerned with making better sense of that period—reconciling personal experiences with popular discourses.

One thing to do immediately is limit this critical analysis to print media outlets, including popular magazines. Why exclude the Internet itself? Although there are and have been many good stories coming from the Internet itself, this chapter focuses on print because during the period under examination that's where most people in America (and elsewhere) got their information about the Internet—as secondhand information. As more people went online they could compare their experiences to what they had read about, but in the beginning there were only other voices talking about some strange "electronic network."

Another limitation needed for this analysis is the choice of focus. To establish a general baseline this chapter examines one news magazine (*Newsweek*) for its general discourse about the Internet, but it also focuses on representations of women as users of the Internet, and the ways metaphors for the Internet figure into that discourse.

This chapter studies the ways women have been included in and excluded from this discourse because the presence of women online during the period changed dramatically. Women went from a small minority of users to parity, and are predicted to overtake men as a percentage of all users within a few years. Clearly, women have been interested in the Internet, and this chapter investigates what popular discourse about the Internet has said about women and their experiences (or lack of experiences) online. How closely women followed this discourse and whether women's rush online helped change this discourse are also discussed.

More personally, I'm interested in how women were talked about because my online experiences during that period accord with some accounts of the Internet but differ from others. When I first learned to use a computer, in 1989, the only information to access was the material stored on the hard drive or on a floppy disk. But upon my return to graduate school in 1993, I was assigned my first email account, and by the next year I had purchased a home computer, a 486 PC with an astounding 8 megabytes of RAM and a 14.4 modem. I quickly learned how to access our school's server, and then spent several months attempting to install various software programs on my Unix account in order to gain access to the graphical side of the World Wide Web. The Internet intrigued me, and soon I had completely changed my thesis topic and was engaged in research on a Usenet newsgroup and the fans of one television show.

During this time my experience was overwhelmingly positive, and I never thought to question whether my experience was "typical" or not. Yet, had I been more attentive to the news media and their representations of the Internet, I might have been more concerned. During this time the Internet was sometimes depicted as a place hostile to women, where few women were welcomed and indeed few women spent their time. I didn't know I was part of a minority of users, or that other media reports were encouraging women to venture online. So my interest in studying how women were addressed or represented in discourse about the Internet during 1990–1998 grows partly out of this disparity with my own experience.

Metaphors are also included in this analysis, because they've been important in helping people think about new technologies historically. For example, when the telephone was first developed, it was referred to by AT&T as "a highway of communication" passing by homes and businesses (Fischer, 1992, p. 255). The Internet has been described in similar metaphorical terms ("information superhighway") as well as with other metaphors ("electronic frontier").

Understanding a new technology by looking at it through the lens of a metaphor has "a profound impact on what will be seen" (Kent, 2001, p. 360). Metaphors magnify or encourage a certain way of looking at the world or a technology. They may make a new technology "more understandable" but only in terms of technology that has arrived previously. Metaphors "circumscribe the ways we understand how future technologies will affect our lives" (Berdayes & Berdayes, 1998, p. 111). So the metaphors that have been used to describe the Internet have both helped and hindered by presenting certain "visions" of what the Internet is or could be. Understanding the ideologies implicit in various metaphors is important in helping to determine how metaphors encourage or discourage certain ways of seeing. And if these metaphors are scrutinized to determine what they suggest about women, or gender, further understandings about this new technology should emerge.

The three components examined in this analysis are the Internet, women, and metaphor. First, the study is theoretically grounded, then a review of relevant literature concerning women, the Internet, and new communication technologies is provided, and finally the evidence and argument are presented. The four research questions driving this study are the following:

R1: How have representations of the Internet changed in traditional media from 1990 to 1998?

R2: How have women been portrayed in relation to the Internet during 1990–1998?

R3: How can metaphors help or hinder us in understanding various experiences on the Internet?

R4: How do all of these factors interrelate?

Communication and Communication Technologies

Theoretical attention to the Internet and to new communication technologies is growing daily. In addition, theories concerned with older communication technologies, and communication generally, can be drawn upon to help understand the Internet and the discourse about it. What is important for this analysis is to understand the fluid, dynamic nature of communication as well as communication technologies. To illustrate this point and draw useful parallels, this section briefly surveys selected histories of communication technologies to show how their use changed over time, in relation to both producers' and users' intentions.

In conceptualizing the Internet it helps to remind ourselves that the medium is a communications medium, first and foremost. Because the Internet transmits words, sounds, pictures, thoughts, and ideas, it has the potential to shape, alter, and produce our reality. James Carey writes that "communication is at once a structure of human action—activity, process, practice—an ensemble of expressive forms, and a structured and structuring set of social relations" (1989, p. 86). These social relations help to create understandings of the world and a sense of place within it. The Internet is becoming a vital space for this production of reality, because it is, for now, a place where there are fewer limitations on access to a means of mass communication than with television or radio.

Reports such as the United States Government's study of the digital divide ("Falling Through the Net: Toward Digital Inclusion," 2000) make the credible case that access for minorities and other disadvantaged groups is not equal, nor likely to be so in the near future. But the Internet still provides Western societies (and I use the term consciously—we are still nowhere near wiring the globe) a place where more individual voices can be heard (Bolter, 2000). These voices are largely absent from other media, due to concentration of ownership, economies of scale, and our structures of corporate capitalism (McChesney, 2000). Yet the Internet, for the moment, provides a place for more people to express ideas, concerns, and realities that may not be expressed elsewhere. Therefore, the Internet (while not perfect) actively gives shape to and is shaped by human communication in varied forms.

Examining mediated messages about the Internet also helps us to better understand the ideological underpinnings of discourse surrounding it. What was the dominant message concerning the "nature" of the Internet? How did it appear in initial coverage, and then in later years? The history of the Internet can be traced by examining the metaphors surrounding it, but built into these metaphors are differing ideologies that promote differing world-views. The frontier metaphor was one of the first metaphors used to describe the Internet, and this metaphor received a great deal of attention (Rheingold, 1993). The metaphor rests on an ideology of libertarian individualism, which promotes a narrow role for government regulation of the Internet and self-government for people in cyberspace. This metaphor perpetuates the belief that the Internet is somehow "naturally free" from regulation or control due to its very structure (Lessig, 1999). However, this early metaphor and ideology failed to adequately address the rise of commerce's role on the Internet, and the question of how commerce could be understood within an ideology of rugged individualism. So here the dominant metaphor shifts to the information superhighway, which is ideologically better suited to accommodate ideas about orderly regulation, whether by government or by commerce. Efforts to control the Internet through legislation, for example, become more prevalent, and the notion that the Internet "cannot" be regulated or monitored disappears, at least in regard to certain types of online communications.

In addition to considering how ideological constructions of the Internet have changed, the social construction of the Internet as related to gender can also be examined. At the beginning of its development, the Internet was constructed and used almost exclusively by men. However, this gendering remained invisible, as norms usually do. When women began to participate in Internet spaces, gender suddenly became an issue for online users as well as for the traditional media covering the Internet (Cherny & Weise, 1996).

Previous studies have argued that just as communication is dynamic, so too are communication technologies. How they develop, who uses them, and for what functions are variables that can and do change over time, and often in unexpected ways. This theoretical line of inquiry is examined next.

Gender, Women, and Communication Technologies

Most scholarly writing about gender and communication technologies addresses the case of women (or girls), acknowledging that women have often been excluded from or marginalized in historical and contemporary accounts of (as well as the actual processes of) the development and use of these technologies (Balsamo, 1996; Haraway, 1991; Rakow, 1992). For example, although Ada Lovelace developed the first computer-programming language, and women helped program the first computer (ENIAC), the history of women's involvement in computing has largely been erased (Plant, 1997). Women have instead largely been constructed as consumers of technologies, although their uses or appropriations of these technologies are not always what the producers intended (Wajcman, 1991).

For example, writing about the use of the telephone in women's lives, Lana Rakow (1992) makes the argument that communications technologies are not static objects that stand outside social relations or historical contexts. These technologies are historically placed processes that change and can be altered, are fluid and unstable. Communication technologies can only be understood through examining their uses, and their uses can and do change over time. Rakow argues that the history of the telephone reveals just such a change, as its use was contested by business and personal forces, which saw the telephone in different ways. While the developers of the telephone initially conceived it as a business tool for men, women in the home saw it as a personal communication device, and began using it for social rather than business activities. There were struggles between these two groups over this use—for example, telephone companies issued "etiquette" guides for proper use of the telephone by women, including warnings about poor manners and pronunciation, as users were "judged by their voices" (p. 4). Yet women and their particular uses of the medium triumphed and the telephone is now considered a "female" medium, rather than the "male business tool" that it was envisioned as when it was first developed. Rakow explains that while the telephone "changed gender," gender was also in flux at the time, as the chore of keeping in touch with family members, or organizing volunteers and social activities, via the telephone came to be understood as women's work. Thus, the telephone and gender both interacted with each other and shaped notions of each other—what the telephone was considered best used for, and what "women's work" on the telephone entailed.

"Changing the gender" of a communications technology can also be attempted by the producers of the medium in question, as was the case with radio. Early radio was considered an activity for hobbyists, who built their own radio sets and tuned them in to stations near and far (Smulyan, 1994).[1] Most of the people who built their own sets were male, including father and son teams that would work on their project as a family activity. But as commercial developers began to see a potential market for radio broadcasts (as well as a market for the sale of receivers), the audience for these broadcasts had to be expanded to include women as well. So, more "attractive" receivers were designed and marketed to women as suitable for display in a middle-class living room, and in addition to the more general evening programming (targeted mostly to men and to families generally), daytime programming targeted to appeal to women in particular was initiated through the development of programs such as "soap operas" (Smulyan, 1994). Actions such as these helped make radio more acceptable as family entertainment; but the acknowledgment that women were an important part of the radio market was critical.

The rise of commerce or the increasing importance of commerce in a medium can provide an impetus to change the gendered uses of a medium, to make the medium more "appropriate" for women, who are and have been the principal consumers in American households. This demonstrates the flexible nature of technological innovations, commercial interests, and beliefs about appropriate gendered activities. Thus, in addition to women claiming communication technologies for their own purposes, women's position as a potential audience is important enough to producers to ensure that women are included in marketing efforts related to "new" media.

The changing uses of the telephone and radio suggest that communications technologies are fluid and adaptable, and can deviate from their expected or determined use. Also, gender can interact with communications technologies, potentially changing both in the process. It is important to understand this potential for interaction and transformation because the Internet is still a new medium, and likely still far from its final form. How different users interact with the medium will shape its form to some degree, and this use will probably shape the users as well. And as the number of women online continues to grow, women become an increasingly important group to consider in this development.

Metaphors for Communication Technologies, Past and Present

Just as discourses about gender and communication technologies can interact to shape each other, metaphors applied to communications technologies can also help shape, define, or limit the ways these technologies will be perceived and used. Additionally, some of the same metaphors have been used to help the general public "understand" new media forms. Perhaps the most extensive use of a metaphor is the transportation metaphor, which has been applied to the telephone, the radio, and now the Internet (Berdayes & Berdayes, 1998, pp. 110–111). The early telephone was referred to as a "highway of the air" on which invisible signals passed through electrical lines overhead. Later, radio became associated with transportation, although now without the help of physical wires. Berdayes and Berdayes note that early debates about radio deployed the transportation metaphor to open "a space for increased government intervention in the media. In magazine articles in the 1920s, for instance, President Hoover became a "traffic cop" who's main job was to police the airwaves and to relieve the "congested lanes of ether"" (p. 111).

The transportation metaphor, in addition to legitimating a role for government intervention in media, also associated communication with a market approach. Other authors have argued that the information highway metaphor "encourages discriminatory practices" (p. 111) by giving an impression of accessibility that is not actually present.

Underlying the discourse about the Internet are new and old metaphors for understanding this technological form of communication. The earliest metaphor for the Internet ignored transportation and focused on place. Early Internet user and journalist Howard Rheingold (1993) detailed the history of the

Internet in his book, *The Virtual Community: Homesteading on the Electronic Frontier*, and is associated with the first influential metaphor to be applied to the Internet. His book focused on the unregulated atmosphere that initially prevailed, where "anything went" and users were expected to take care of themselves. The dominant metaphor, reflected in the title of his book, was of the Internet as an "electronic frontier" where there was little established "law and order" and people were seen mostly as individuals responsible for their own actions. This was deemed an unfriendly place for women from the beginning.

This metaphor is now sharing space with (or perhaps has given way to) the more capitalist-friendly metaphor of the Internet as an "information superhighway." As Berdayes and Berdayes argue, this metaphor "associates the communication infrastructure with economic growth and, therefore, provides a rationale for the federal government to commit public resources to its construction" (1998, p. 111). While this metaphor appears on the surface to be ungendered, it masks the critical function of (re)positioning women from users to consumers. This displacement has as an effect the repositioning of the Internet as more "woman-friendly," but "woman" should really be read as "consumer."

Finally, Kent makes the argument that the best metaphor to describe the Web (as against the Internet as a whole) is "managerial rhetoric" (2001). He believes this new formulation better describes the Web of commerce that has developed, which is based more on persuasion than information delivery. Kent writes that the persuasion of the Web "seeks to predict, control, and alter the behavior of the masses through the individual. In their tradeoff for (imagined) 'anonymity,' freedom of expression, and the ability to obtain 'valuable' information 24 hours-per-day, users of the Web are codified, commodified, and compartmentalized" (pp. 369–370). Kent does not suggest how this metaphor is gendered, but his description of the user of the Web as basically a consumer is similar to the information superhighway metaphor, where women become once again consumers, albeit invisibly hailed.

Whether or not the metaphor suggested by Kent will emerge in popular discourse, metaphors in general set boundaries for the ways we understand how new technologies shape or affect society as well as individuals. Metaphors are helping to shape the discourse about the Internet, and metaphors are also helping us to understand the Internet as a particularly gendered place.

The Internet, Women, and Metaphors

Early research concerning women and the Internet tried to either debunk or downplay the rhetoric of the Internet as a dangerous place for women. Volumes such as *Wired_Women: Gender and New Realities in Cyberspace* (Cherny & Weise, 1996) and *Women @ Internet: Creating New Cultures in Cyberspace* (Harcourt, 1999) explored the potential advantages available to women in cyberspace, as well as the pitfalls. More theoretical scholars, such as Sherry Turkle (1995) and Allucquère Stone (1996), explored how gender was potentially transformed when faced with new media forms, as the Internet allowed users to experiment with constructing gender in a medium where visual cues no longer applied. In contrast, scholars such as Anne Balsamo (1996) argued that cyberspace, as with other new media, often worked to reinscribe gender in predictably sexist ways, including the popular practices of Virtual Reality (VR) that objectify women's bodies and privilege male interests.

More recent research has begun to go beyond VR and text-based online communication to explore the World Wide Web and the ways in which women have been represented (if at all) in print publications about digital culture, including *Wired* magazine (Millar, 1998), and in online spaces (Cutting Edge, 2000; Green & Adam, 2001). Further, the notion of gender as a problematic identity marker has been explored and critiqued (Fuchs, 2000; Morse, 1997/2001). Perhaps most relevant for this study, Warnick (1999) has studied how print media discourse has urged women to go online. She found that popular media outlets that urged women to go online in the period 1995–1997 "valued activity, aggression, currency, technology and wealth, and they devalued their opposites—passivity, hesitancy, convention, and poverty" (p. 6). Warnick's research into print media articles that encouraged women to venture online helps us understand how appeals were made specifically to women, but the research covers a limited period, and does not address print articles about women that did not specifically urge women to go online. Thus, the present research gives a broader picture of women and their relation to the Internet during the years 1990–1998, and also explores the role of metaphors in this construction.

Method

This study takes both a broad and a deep look at the discourse about the Internet generally as well as the more specific issues of women and metaphors. It does so by using critical discourse analysis to scrutinize media texts for the themes that emerge about these topics. The themes follow from the research questions posed previously, which ask how the Internet was represented during 1990–1998, as well as how women and metaphors were represented in relation to the Internet during the same period.

This chapter relies on relevant news magazine articles. To obtain a generalized view of discourse about the Internet, a Lexis-Nexis search was performed on all issues of *Newsweek* during the period under study. Almost 400 articles (excluding brief—less than 200 words—columns or briefs from either Cyberscope or Periscope) that dealt with the Internet were identified. These articles were studied for the inclusion or omission of signifiers such as gender and class, and to determine how these terms related to the focus of the story—as explanatory, exploratory, cautionary, or celebratory. Also, the focus of coverage was examined: whether the Internet was treated as something new or integrated into daily life, as something to aid communication between friends or strangers, as an education or information source, as a tool for business, as a place to shop, or as a site for marketing. Next, a search of the *Reader's Guide to Periodical Literature* was performed for the same period, for the terms "women" and "Internet." Sixty-eight articles were identified as relevant to this research (occasionally an article dealt with the Internet, mentioned women only peripherally, and did not scrutinize the relationship of any one woman or group of women to the Internet). These articles were also studied for focus of coverage and signifiers especially as relating to women, and were also studied for tone (warning, welcome, help, neutral, etc.) as well as for placement within a particular magazine.

Metaphors were not separately searched for, but the analysis examined how metaphors were used in the articles already identified for study. Further, metaphors were examined more generally as pertaining to the periods when they were dominant, competing for dominance, or fading from view, and in relation to women and the Internet.

The Analysis: Communication/Consumption/Commodification

To analyze how print media coverage constructed women, the Internet, and relevant metaphors, some further conceptual tools are needed. In examining how this coverage progresses over the years, certain overarching themes become important, as they compete for dominance in any given period. These themes are communication, consumption, and commodification. Although these themes are not mutually exclusive, they are different enough in tone and meaning to suggest how overall coverage of the Internet (including women and the use of metaphors) shifted from period to period. A focus on communication means that the coverage of a period largely treats the Internet as a place for the exchange of ideas and information, including one-to-many, one-to-one, and many-to-one forms of communication. Individuals are considered to be "citizens" of the Internet in some unspecified way. Coverage that takes "consumption" as a central theme suggests that the Internet is a place for buying and selling, and individuals are beginning to be defined as potential consumers (although perhaps not exclusively as consumers). Finally, "commodification" is a theme of coverage that starts to aggregate individual users online, who are interested in either communication, or consumption, or both. Their grouping into identifiable interest groups or demographic categories represents a discourse about commodification. This theme is an expansion and intensification of the theme of consumption, as it suggests that individuals are not only going online to purchase things, but that their presence online is something that can be measured, studied, and sold to someone interested. All these themes can be present in one particular period, but it is important to track their progression overall.

Early Period (1990–1993): Communication

Although the Internet had been in existence since the late 1960s, the period 1990–1993 saw very few articles about the Internet. In mainstream publications no articles were found concerning women and the Internet, and in *Newsweek* only eight articles about the Internet in general appeared. Breaking the numbers for *Newsweek* down further, no articles at all were found that addressed the Internet in 1990, and only one relevant article appeared in 1991.

Articles were mostly found in the "society" section of the magazine. These pieces focused mainly on issues such as getting connected, beginning life online, and explaining this "strange new world" to outsiders. The titles of the pieces reflect how new this world was to the general public: "The Highway to the Future," "Lost on the Information Highway," and "How to Hook Into the New Global Net" are typical. However, there are interesting differences in how the articles are titled, and the content they contain.

Although many of the pieces allude to an information highway, the tone of the articles and the content itself paint a picture of an electronic frontier. For example, although articles do mention the business potential of the Internet (including the ever-promised video-on-demand), it is admitted that this is still potential—no one has yet figured out how to make money using the Internet, although this may become an important future concern. Instead, pieces focus more on nuts-and-bolts issues including how to get connected, and what you can expect to find online. Here, a focus on the wilder side of the Internet emerges. People who use the Internet for various purposes are mentioned, as are their interests: in the spleen, in financial advice, in dating people you've never met, in contributing to bondage-discussion groups, and even "weirder stuff." Although the Internet is demonstrated to be a place where relevant and important information can be found, it is also a place where privacy allows you to "sit with Cheez Whiz in your hair and chili running down your face ... and in the most un-P.C. terms you can get things out" (Kantrowitz, September 6, 1993). By focusing on the new, strange, and alternative, the discourse provides a sense of a place without social constraints or boundaries. Regulation is not discussed, and is not seen as needed. Although bondage is discussed, it is adults that are doing the talking, and no one appears offended.

According to Carolyn Marvin, in the late 1880s an article appeared that "instructed readers about how to recognize women telegraph operators out in the Wild West, the symbolic boundary of civilization, where the pressures of savagery against the social virtues represented by women were strongest" (1988, p. 26). Although she is talking about the "real" western frontier, the comparison to the Internet is apt. In the early articles, women are indeed quoted and mentioned, yet their presence is not remarked on as unusual. These women are shown as independent and strong, comfortable with using the Internet, even if some of their interests (including paganism and polyandry) are far from the norm. During this time, approximately 5% of all users were women ("GVU's first WWW user survey results," 1994/2001), but this fact is not mentioned. Women are shown as comfortable in this new and unexplored space.

During this time, gender is not an issue that is addressed. The norm for Internet use is ungendered, which usually means a default to the masculine. During this period, the Internet is mostly for the *odd*, not for the normal, citizen, and this construction of the "typical" Internet user displaces consideration of how many men and women (and percentages of each) are actually online.

One major concern of this period is hackers, and this tends to remain a dominant concern through all the periods studied. Hackers are presented as troublesome (and fearsome) individuals capable of invading and destroying computer systems with their exceptional skills. While all hackers discussed in the coverage are male, their gender is not remarked on, reflecting the masculine norms of computer and Internet use. This focus and omission continues throughout the coverage examined.

Finally, the overall theme of coverage of the Internet during the early period is one of communication. During these early years, business is discussed as a potential future activity, but most authors admit they have little idea of how Internet commerce will actually evolve. Instead, most discourse constructs the Internet as a wild place, where people congregate to share information or communicate socially. During this time, users of the Internet rely on text-based browsers or text-based programs such as Usenet and email, which have little in the way of graphical flourishes, and have more to do with writing and the exchange of ideas. This will all change in the next period to be examined.

Middle Period (1994–1995) Flux Time: Communication/Consumption

Over the next couple of years, attention to the Internet exploded. In 1994 *Newsweek* carried 30 relevant articles and in 1995 that number increased to 70 (these numbers don't include the many smaller pieces concerning the Internet that appeared in the special sections "Periscope" and "Cyberscope"). Clearly, popular attention to the Internet was beginning to increase, and news articles became more diversified in content and tone, and began to spread to various areas within *Newsweek* beyond the "Society" section—to business, the arts, and a special section titled "Focus on Technology."

During this time many of the articles focused on the Internet as a space for communication, but there was also a growing interest in consumption. The Internet was becoming a place where businesses could make money—if not through online selling to consumers, then through the development of Internet-related technologies, and the development and sale of Internet companies themselves. Articles profiled new technology companies and the Internet-related products they were developing, while other pieces explored how corporate CEOs were going to "computer camp" to learn how to use the Internet (Meyer, June 20, 1994). Technologies such as intelligent agents, the clipper chip, and Mbone (for music broadcasting) were profiled, and there was a growing amount of information pertaining to online investing as well as technology stock investing. Many of the articles were concerned with what businesses were doing online or for the online world, suggesting to readers that the Internet could be a place for commerce and consumption, even if it wasn't quite at that point yet.

While the business possibilities for the Internet were being explored, a great deal of attention was still being paid to communication online that was not business or commerce related. Articles on how to get connected or become Internet literate were common, as were educational and social opportunities online. The text-based social space LambdaMOO was profiled (Hafner,

November 7, 1994), while other articles began to consider issues of access to this new communication technology (Samuelson, February 27, 1995; Stone, July 3, 1995).

More women came online during this period. The percentage of women users of the Internet jumped to approximately 17% of all those on the Internet ("GVU's fourth WWW user survey," 1995/2001). Corresponding with this rise, articles and features addressing women and the Internet began to appear across the spectrum of print media. The magazine *Working Woman* was an early and consistent promoter of why women should go online, and detailed for women many of the perceived benefits associated with using this new technology (Fryer, March 1995; Hafner, January 1995). Likewise, more traditional women's magazines, such as *Glamour, Vogue, Harper's Bazaar,* and *Essence* all gave space to discussing the Internet and how women could use it generally (Morgan, 1995; Thomas, 1994), as well as for information about beauty and sports products (Clarke, 1995; McCune, 1995).

Articles about the dangers women faced online began to appear. *Newsweek* as well as other periodicals (such as *Ms., GQ,* and *Time*) informed women about offensive, sexist materials online, and the fact that women had been targets of Internet harassment and abuse (Herz, October 1994). For example, an article in *Newsweek* in May 1994 examined the issue of limited female participation on the Internet, and mentioned online hostility as a possible reason: "women have learned to tread their keyboards carefully in chat forums because they often have to fend off sexual advances that would make Bob Packwood blush" (Kantrowitz, May 16, 1994). There are also stories about teenage girls discussing sex with men on the Internet (Bennahum, 1995), the prevalence of porn online (Elmer-Dewitt, July 3, 1995), and the case of Jake Baker, who was arrested for distributing to a newsgroup three graphic sexual stories that used the name of a female student in one of his classes (Elmer-DeWitt, February 25, 1995).

Advice on ways to avoid or discourage harassment and arguments minimizing the extent of the "dangers" also appeared (Sherman, 1995). Other stories addressed the low percentages of women online as related to larger trends concerning women and technology, such as the small number of women in computer science, and the general lack of interest among girls in video and computer games (Kantrowitz, May 16, 1994).

Although the news concerning women was both positive and negative, it was their position as a minority group on the Internet that was their defining factor. Women were "marked" either as being targets for trouble online, or as having to constantly fight against difficulties or harassment. The effect of this positioning cast women as "other" in cyberspace, where they became notable for having a gender and bringing "gender troubles" to this new space. Prior to this period, although women were mentioned (infrequently) as participating in online life and activities, their gender was not an issue. Neither, of course, was men's gender. And during this mid-period, men were still largely perceived as un-gendered—when gender was mentioned as a part of online life or activity, it was generally with reference to women.

The result of this was a construction of the Internet as by default a "male" space. If women were the new arrivals and were the few experiencing the troubles that were reported, then the original Internet was constructed as a male space, although not specifically referred to as such. This reified another technology as masculine, and kept articulations of "general" users as men un-critiqued.

Further, the coverage of women and the problems they faced began to suggest that the Internet could be a potentially "troublesome" space, where the lawlessness of the frontier was causing problems. Laura Miller (1995) makes the argument that gender implications are constituted within the metaphor of the electronic frontier, and these implications are clearly illustrated in the media attention to the Internet. Miller believes that

> The classic Western narrative is actually far more concerned with social relationships than conflicts between man and nature. In these stories, the frontier is a lawless society of men, a milieu in which physical strength, courage, and personal charisma supplant institutional authority and violent conflict is the accepted means of settling disputes. The Western narrative connects pleasurably with the American romance of individualistic masculinity; small wonder that the predominantly male founders of the Net's culture found it so appealing. (p. 52)

Miller goes on to say that the civilization (or taming) of the frontier occurs "because women and children are victimized in conditions of freedom" (p. 52). Thus, in the early stages of development of the Internet, most "settlers" are men, and lawlessness is reinscribed as "freedom." Women who travel in this domain are expected to live by the rules of the land, which is masculine by definition. Hostile treatment and resentment of their presence is considered normal—in part because women are seen as "the coming of civilization" and thus the end of the "true" lawless frontier. But it is also because these women are in such small numbers, making them easier to single out and harass, that misogynistic behavior is given tacit approval—the classic "boys will be boys" defense.

Lawlessness is also reflected in continuing attention to the issue of hackers, who are addressed in several articles during this period. However, while all of these hackers are male, hacking is not identified as a "male" or "masculine" problem. Hackers remain individuals not marked by gender, while women experiencing problems online lose that individuality and become subsumed by their gender.

In addition to the reification of the norm of masculinity, middle-class status is also marked during this period as a baseline against which to measure other groups' access. So, for example, *Newsweek* ran an article discussing how families "can buy a good home computer and all the software you'll ever need for under $2,500" (Croal, November 1994). The article goes on to detail the books and other accessories that are necessary for a home computer, but does not make the point that many families do not have $2,500 in disposable income to spend on a computer.

However, another article from the same year reports on Internet access in schools, explaining that schools are not equally wired, those left out being "poor urban districts or rural districts with limited resources or blue-collar districts with very tight budgets" (Kantrowitz, March 21, 1994). While the US government had not yet named or studied the "digital divide," it was already becoming apparent that computers and Internet access were more prevalent in middle- and upper-class families and schools, while equipment and access was an "issue" for those with less money. Thus, again, the "nature" of the Internet as being "naturally" for the middle class (and for men) was developing during this period, and debates about universal service were absent.

The articles addressing the issues of women and the Internet also fail to address the issue of class and access, merely pointing

out the opportunities available online for those women presumably able and willing to explore the Internet. Magazines
addressing women reflect this middle- and upper-class-specific
bias as they include *Vogue, Working Woman,* and *Harper's Bazaar.*

Finally, the cultural capital needed to operate a computer and
the know-how needed to search the Internet is not addressed in
this discourse. Although there are still articles on "how to get
connected," and definitions of search terms, basic computer
knowledge is taken for granted in these pieces, and the idea that
some people might not know the "basics" is never addressed.

To sum up then, although the metaphor of the information
superhighway had appeared in the previous period, during the
period presently under discussion, this metaphor and the business
activity to support it have become dominant. The superhighway
metaphor is still in competition with the electronic frontier
metaphor, which is not heard of as much, but is still used when
describing the more "dangerous" sides of the Internet.
Consumption is becoming an issue, while communication is still
important. Individuals are not the only actors in cyberspace
anymore however—corporations are beginning to gain a presence,
even if online shopping or e-commerce has not fully developed.

Individuals have become valuable on the Internet during this
period not only for their communication potential (how they can
add to the cultural conversation) but also for their status as
potential consumers. These potential consumers are still fledg-
lings, as are businesses online. No one really knows how to
market, sell, or buy online yet, but the expectation is that all these
activities are coming. However, the Internet is still portrayed as a
somewhat dangerous place, where not all consumer groups have
yet appeared. And perhaps more importantly, they are not yet
conditioned to expect the Internet to be a place for consumption.

Late Period (1996–1998) Stabilizing Meanings:
Communication/Consumption/Commodification

By 1996 the Internet has become a routine part of the news,
and reports have become more specialized. Articles now report on
Internet investing, socializing online, and the success of dot-com
businesses. The "newness" of the Internet is gone, but excitement

over the possibilities it presents is still apparent. Internet stories that focus on communication still appear, but articles increasingly focus on consumption and commodification.

Communication online is still important, and articles about the demographics of Internet users and new uses of the Internet for education, science, and socializing still appear. However, more articles are concerned with business and the commercialization of the Internet. Articles about the "browser wars" between Netscape and Microsoft appear in this period, and the strength and power of Bill Gates and Microsoft in general are explored in depth. People now know (or think they know) how to make money from the Internet, and wild speculation about its commercial future appears. The idea of the Internet as a place for the commodification of audiences also develops during this time. Articles with titles such as "The Web: Infotopia or Marketplace" (McGrath, January 27, 1997) and "Stealth Marketing" (Kaufman, March 3, 1997) point to the growing focus on the aggregation of online audiences into consumers and consumer groups. This represents a refinement of the idea that individuals can buy products online: an acknowledgment that groups of individuals are an even more valuable product to sell to other businesses. Individuals venturing online to chat or shop are potential products themselves.

More than 50 articles appear during this period addressing women and the Internet, focusing on women going online as well as exploring how women are becoming a valuable group of online users. Although articles focusing on the dangers (cyberstalking and cyber-rape) women face online are still present, they are declining in number (Marsa, 1998; Michale, 1997). Of all these articles, only 4 out of 53 are cautionary in tone, with most of the rest taking a celebratory or informational approach.

The growing number of articles related to women and the Internet mirrors the growing number of women online. Statistics vary, but some indicate that as many as 42% of all Internet users were women in 1996, and by 1998 that percentage had risen to 48% (Gibbons, 1999). These women are being profiled in articles ("Kim Polese," 1997), their needs and interests online are explored (Bruckman, 1996; Kantrowiz, December 16, 1996), and their potential as an audience is examined (Mannix, Bernstein, & Flynn, July 1, 1996; O'Connell, August 13, 1998). During this period a much greater emphasis than before is placed on the role women can play in developing the Internet economy and culture. Articles encouraging businesswomen to use the Internet for marketing and networking become common (Parch, 1998; Sherman, 1998). Clearly, women are emerging as an important force in the online world, and the coverage reflects this.

Women during this time may be more successful in using the Internet and going online, but they are still mostly marked by their gender, while notable men are not singled out in this way. Gender in relation to the Internet, then, remains linked with the feminine, but it is being reworked as an asset for Internet use, rather than being the liability it was one or two years earlier. Men are already acknowledged to be online, but as they are not the major purchasers of household goods, they are not the goldmine to marketers that women seem to be.

For women, then, gender is still a marked category, and this category has become commodified as a desirable demographic for consumption. Women in these articles are not urged to go online to diversify newsgroups, but to engage in the business of the Internet and be sold to—both as individuals and as part of the larger group of "women online."

The electronic frontier metaphor largely disappears, and the information superhighway metaphor gains dominance. This new metaphor does not connote lawlessness, but instead order and regulation. This emphasis on regulation is demonstrated through coverage (and growing critique) of Microsoft CEO Bill Gates and his business practices with regard to the Windows operating systems, the Internet Explorer browser software, and the development of the online service provider, MSN.com. Questions are raised about the potential need for greater governmental regulation of businesses like Microsoft. This is also consistent with the superhighway metaphor in that the need for regulation is mostly centered on business, although other attempts at regulation (such as the Communications Decency Act, which is supposed to protect children from obscenity online) appear during this time.

The superhighway metaphor, however, is also gendered. While the frontier metaphor implied lawlessness and wild men who resented the arrival of women in need of "protection," the information superhighway metaphor suggests regulation and commerce. The frontier has been tamed, and business can now safely set up shop.

It is no accident that commerce has arrived in tandem with women. Women are an important demographic for marketers, and the Internet during this period has become more of a place for selling than for exploring or creating. While earlier media accounts stressed the danger the Internet posed to women, there were also dangers for business. Little regulation was present and rules for behavior (and the verification of identities) were mostly nonexistent. The subsequent "settling" or taming of the Internet to make it more appealing to women was a cover; the actual reason for the taming was to make the Internet safe for commerce. Businesses *want* women to feel safe online, because if they feel safe, they'll stay online and hopefully buy online. And this is the future of the Internet that the information superhighway suggests. The future of the Internet, from a capitalistic point of view, is not about safety for the individual's sake, but safety for commerce's sake. And with women such an important demographic for marketers, the ordering and regulation of the Internet is inevitable.

Conclusions

Although the chapter covers less than a decade, it was a time of many changes. The Internet's population exploded, and the percentage of users that were women went from a miniscule 5% to near parity. Despite the warnings and cautions, the Internet proved either too intriguing or too valuable (or both) for women to pass it up. And now, the "feminization" of the Internet appears to be occurring, as female users are increasingly courted and appealed to in online business. Yet, this feminization has its limits. While women are acknowledged to be enthusiastic users of the medium, their presence in technological jobs related to the construction and maintenance of the Internet is severely limited. Most Internet businesses are still headed by men, and the programming and technical jobs related to the Internet are still done largely by men (see Dorer, this volume). So while women are taking their place as equal partners in the use of cyberspace, their role in its production or maintenance is still quite small. Women are equal in their consumption, but consumption has traditionally been regarded as a female trait. It would have been remarkable if women had *not* eventually become the targets of online consumption and commodification. Yet, while most news accounts took celebratory approaches to the increasing power of women to shop online, it was little remarked that women had much less power to create online, or to aid in the creation of online spaces. So, although the Internet in terms of consumption might now be a feminine-coded area, production remains a masculine domain. This is also reflected in the continuing attention to hackers throughout all the periods, and the stories' lack of attention to the gender of the perpetrators. Creating technology, even "bad" technology, is the unmarked territory of men.

Metaphors helped construct the discourse of the Internet. It is likely that other metaphors would have produced alternate meanings associated with the Internet, yet the ones chosen have developed meanings, resonances, and histories that must be explored. And whether the latest metaphor, the information superhighway, becomes displaced by another term, we have yet to see.

In conclusion, the development of a history of media attention to the Internet and the role of women is important in establishing a baseline from which future attention and scrutiny can draw. Now that more women are online, and greater numbers of people overall are exploring the Internet, the stories will become more diverse. Analysis can also turn to the stories and accounts found on the Internet itself, as many more people have firsthand access to this communications technology now than did even 10 years ago. It will be important to watch for the development of new metaphors for understanding the Internet, as well as to continue looking at whether the Internet is balancing the concerns of communication, consumption, and commodification, or attempting to create other models. And how this occurs on a global scale is critically important.

Notes

1. The practices of early radio users are not greatly different from the practices of early hobbyist Internet users. Both groups enjoyed spending large periods of time configuring and tinkering with their "signal" in order to see what content was "out there" in the larger world, and how far away it was.

References

Balsamo, Anne. (1996). *Technologies of the gendered body: Reading cyborg women.* Durham, NC: Duke University Press.

Bennahum, David. (September 1995). Lolitas online. *Harper's Bazaar.*

Berdayes, Linda Cooper, & Berdayes, Vicente. (1998). The information highway in contemporary magazine narrative. *Journal of Communication, 48*(2), 109–124.

Bolter, Jay. (2000). Identity. In Thomas Swiss (Ed.), *Unspun: Key concepts for understanding the World Wide Web* (pp. 17–29). New York: New York University Press.

Bruckman, Amy. (January 1996). Finding one's own space in cyberspace. *Technology Review.*

Carey, James. (1989). *Communication as culture: Essays on media and society.* Boston: Unwin Hyman.

Cherny, Lynn, & Weise, Elizabeth. (1996). *Wired_Women: Gender and new realities in cyberspace.* Seattle: Seal Press.

Clarke, Mary. (August 1995). Beauty online. *Vogue.*

Croal, N'gai. (November 1994). Seeking shelter in books and magazines. *Newsweek, Special Issue on Computers and the Family.*

Cutting Edge. (2000). *Digital desires: Language, identity and new technologies.* London: I. B. Tauris.

Elmer-Dewitt, P. (February 25, 1995). Snuff porn on the net. *Time.*

Elmer-Dewitt, P. (July 3, 1995). On a screen near you: Cyberporn. *Time.*

"Falling through the net: Toward digital inclusion." (2000). http://www.digitaldivide.gov

Fischer, Claude. (1992). *America calling: A social history of the telephone to 1940.* Berkeley: University of California Press.

Fryer, Bronwyn. (March 1995). Job hunting the electronic way. *Working Woman.*

Fuchs, Cynthia. (2000). Gender. In Thomas Swiss (Ed.), *Unspun: Key concepts for understanding the World Wide Web* (pp. 30–38). New York: New York University Press.

Gibbons, Sheila. (Winter 1999). Media report to women: Selected statistics on women and media. *Media Report to Women* 27(1), 19.

Green, Eileen, & Adam, Alison. (Eds.). (2001). *Virtual gender: Technology, consumption and identity.* London: Routledge.

GVU's first WWW user survey results. (1994/2001). http://www.gvu. gatech.edu/user_surveys/survey-01-1994/.

GVU's fourth WWW user survey. (1995/2001). http://www.gvu. gatech.edu/user_surveys/survey-10-1995/.

Hafner, Katie. (November 7, 1994). Get in the MOOd. *Newsweek.*

Hafner, Katie. (January 1995). Adventures online. *Working Woman.*

Hall, Stuart. (1980/2001). Encoding/Decoding. In Meenakshi Gigi Durham & Douglas Kellner (Eds.), *Media and cultural studies: Keyworks* (pp. 166–176). Malden, MA: Blackwell.

Haraway, Donna. (1991). *Simians, cyborgs and women.* New York: Routledge.

Harcourt, Wendy. (Ed.). (1999). *Women@Internet: Creating new cultures in cyberspace.* New York: Zed Books.

Herz, J. C. (October 1994). Pigs in (cyber) space. *GQ.*

Hilts, Elizabeth. (November 15, 1997). How women are changing the web. *Editor & Publisher, 130*(46), 40.

Kantrowitz, Barbara. (September 6, 1993). Live wires. *Newsweek.*

Kantrowitz, Barbara. (March 21, 1994). The information gap. *Newsweek.*

Kantrowitz, Barbara. (May 16, 1994). Men, women and computers. *Newsweek.*

Kantrowitz, Barbara. (December 16, 1996). Modem moms. *Newsweek.*

Kaufman, Leslie. (March 3, 1997). Stealth marketing. *Newsweek.*

Kent, Michael. (2001). Managerial rhetoric as the metaphor for the World Wide Web. *Critical Studies in Media Communication, 18*(3), 359–375.

"Kim Polese." (July 1997). *Current Biography.*

Lessig, Lawrence. (1999). *Code and other laws of cyberspace.* New York: Basic Books.

Mannix, Margaret, Bernstein, Amy, & Flynn, Mary-Kathleen. (July 1, 1996). Welcome, women. *U.S. News & World Report.*

Marsa, Linda. (June 1998). Stalker alert. *Glamour.*

Marvin, Carolyn. (1988). *When old technologies were new: Thinking about electric communication in the late nineteenth century.* Oxford: Oxford University Press.

McChesney, Robert. (2000). So much for the magic of technology and the free market: The World Wide Web and the corporate media system. In Andrew Herman & Thomas Swiss (Eds.), *The World Wide Web and contemporary cultural theory* (pp. 5–36). New York: Routledge.

McCune, Jenny. (July/August 1995). Gone surfing. *Women's Sports and Fitness.*

McGrath, Peter. (January 27, 1997). The Web: Infotopia or marketplace? *Newsweek.*

Meyer, Michael. (June 20, 1994). The fear of flaming. *Newsweek.*

Michale, Debra. (March/April 1997). Cyber-rape: How virtual is it? *Ms.*

Millar, Melanie. (1998). *Cracking the gender code: Who rules the wired world?* Toronto: Second Story Press.

Miller, Laura. (1995). Women and children first: Gender and the settling of the electronic frontier. In James Brook & Iain Boal (Eds.), *Resisting the virtual life: The culture and politics of information* (pp. 49–58). San Francisco: City Lights Books.

Morgan, Joan. (April 1995). Adventures in cyberspace. *Essence.*

Morse, Margaret. (1997/2001). Virtually female: Body and code. In David Trend (Ed.), *Reading digital culture* (pp. 87–97). Malden, MA: Blackwell.

O'Connell, Pamela. (August 13, 1998). Web erotica aims for new female customers. *The New York Times.*

Parch, Lorie. (March 1998). Cyber schmoozing. *Working Woman.*

Plant, Sadie. (1997). *Zeros and ones: Digital women + the new technoculture.* New York: Doubleday.

Rakow, Lana. (1992). *Gender on the line: Women, the telephone, and community life.* Urbana: University of Illinois Press.

Rheingold, Howard. (1993). *The virtual community: Homesteading on the electronic frontier.* Reading, MA: Addison-Wesley.

Samuelson, Robert. (February 27, 1995). The myth of cyber inequality. *Newsweek.*

Sherman, Aliza. (July/August 1995). Claiming cyberspace: 5 myths that are keeping women offline. *Ms.*

Sherman, Aliza. (May 1998). New jobs for the next millennium. *Working Woman.*

Smulyan, Susan. (1994). *Selling radio: The commercialization of American broadcasting 1920–1934.* Washington: Smithsonian Institution Press.

Stone, Allucquère. (1996). *The war of desire and technology at the close of the mechanical age.* Cambridge: MIT Press.

Stone, Brad. (July 3, 1995). Low-tech parents aren't powerless. *Newsweek.*

Thomas, Susan. (August 1994). Women rate the online networks. *Glamour.*

Turkle, Sherry. (1995). *Life on the screen.* New York: Touchstone.

Warnick, Barbara. (1999). Masculinizing the feminine: Inviting women on line 1997. *Critical Studies in Mass Communication, 16*(1), 1–19.

Chapter 6

"There's 'O Place' Like Home": Searching for Community on Oprah.com

Leda Cooks, Mari Castañeda Paredes, and Erica Scharrer

Oprah Winfrey is one of the most successful and influential women in the world, with a personal fortune estimated at a half-billion dollars (Tannen, 1998). She is the head of a media empire that includes an ever-popular television talk show watched by some 14 million US viewers per day, a recently launched but immediately prosperous magazine, a film and television production company, and a web site kept busy by visits from faithful fans. Her impact on the book publishing industry has been dubbed the "Oprah effect" and the presentation of a book on her show virtually ensures that copies will fly off the stands into the hands of eager readers.

Yet, Oprah Winfrey is unique not only in her financial success but also in the degree of esteem in which she is held by millions of women throughout the world. She is well loved by her primarily female audience and is viewed by many as a trusted friend, a confidante, and an ally. The feeling of closeness with audience members that she inspires through her remarkable use of multiple mass media avenues overcomes any perceptions of the impersonal nature of any one medium. Winfrey interacts with audiences both present in studio audiences and tuning in through the media, allowing insights into her own life and establishing a rare sense of intimacy (Haag, 1993; Tannen, 1998). In this chapter, we analyze one of Oprah Winfrey's more recent media ventures, her web site, called "O Place" and found at Oprah.com, as a vehicle and a path through which relationships and rapport are fostered.

The Oprah.com web site is a fascinating place to observe. It is a place where women go to seek support from others, to give one another advice, to voice an opinion or describe an experience, and to come together as a community with Oprah fanhood as a common bond. In this chapter, we study the formation of relationships and community in this particular corner of cyberspace through an analysis of the written contributions of the web site users. We also assess the characteristics and qualities of the space itself, the opportunities it affords by providing a forum for women, and the constraints it imposes by virtue of its commercial nature and rather structured form. What results is specific to the "Oprah experience" but also points to universal themes regarding gender, community, identity, media, and communication.

Can We Find Community in Cyberspace?

Scholarship on communities (on- or offline) can be traced back as far as Socrates, to a concern with oral community as the foundation of democracy. The debate over the nature and consequences of what "counts" as relationship or community in computer-mediated communication generally results in predictable disjunctures: between the unitary body located in physical space and the fragmentation of identities in cyberspace; between the virtual space of information and the material space of day-to-day reality; between the authentic and the imaginary spaces of community; between spaces of anonymity, isolation, difference, and hierarchy and affiliation, relationship, and solidarity. These tensions are at the center of the scholarship on computer-mediated communication, whether it espouses modernist/critical, postmodernist, postcolonial, and/or feminist philosophy.

Acknowledging the problems as well as the virtues of naming a virtual community, Baym (1998) argues that perhaps determining the "authenticity" of particular communities should give way to a focus on, to quote Anderson (1983), "the style in which they are imagined" (p. 6). Baym (1998) provides a set of pre-existing structures that are useful for analyzing an online community's style (the scaffolding that helps provide a context for interaction): external contexts (the cultural contexts that shape people's use of and meanings they give to their online interactions); temporal structure (synchronous or asynchronous, fleeting or long term); system infrastructure (physical configurations, system adaptability, and level of user-friendliness); group purposes (whether discussing particular topics, providing advice, or participating in a community of Oprah fans); and participant characteristics (ranging from the size of the group to members' experience with and attitudes toward new technologies).

While it is beyond the scope of this chapter to fully examine all of the criteria that Baym suggests, they provide a useful framework against which we can measure the meanings given to the contexts that structure participation in Oprah.com. Our goal, then, is to elaborate not only the "style" in which the Oprah community is fashioned but to examine the ways the articulations of that style are presumed in the medium and structure of the site as well as the ways women participate on the site. These articulations are made meaningful in the movement back and forth between the symbolic representations of community and the relationships that produce them. Adams (2001) notes that

> Even in circumstances where a community can be observed as springing from a few interpersonal relationships, once a community has formed, it is no longer simply the product of those relationships. As a community it takes on functional and structural characteristics and those characteristics alternately shape the interpersonal relationships carried on in the context of that community. (p. 39)

Feminist, cultural, and communication theorists in particular are concerned about how discourses in and about online communities are produced, to whom they matter, and to what use they are put. Feminist and gender research on computer-mediated communities in particular has examined questions of substance and dominance in cyberspace, focusing specifically on the ways women are empowered or alternatively oppressed through their participation in or absence from virtual communities. Arguing that virtual communities can be affirming spaces for women, Dietrich (1997) notes that

> In this sense an electronic community of women becomes a symbolic space, an engaged social space that defines itself through a particular

textualized culture. Overriding geographical limitations, women can
gather together in ways that challenge the constraints of time and space,
allowing them to explore the potent relations among agency, authority,
and discursive community. (p. 179)

Others remain unimpressed with the power of the "information revolution" to change the material and social realities of
women's everyday lives (Addison & Hilligoss, 1999; Kramarae,
1998; Spender, 1995) or for that matter to change the nature of the
spaces that they occupy online (Blair & Takayoshi, 1999;
Bruckman, 1996; Herring, 1996; Kendall, 1996). For those of us
who are feminist and gender theorists, concerned with the
political and hegemonic nature of "community" as well as with its
role in social struggle, analyzing the places idealized and
realized/experienced as community helps us to better understand
the larger social, political, and economic consequences of such
formations. Thus, in addition to the style through which
communities articulate themselves, the goals toward which such
articulations are accomplished also matter for those concerned
with social change.

Given our concerns with the structure of Oprah.com as well as
the substance of and consequences for the interactions produced
there, the following questions are central to our analysis. How is a
space for community constructed on Oprah.com? Does women's
participation in this space constitute a community? And, if so,
what role do spaces such as these play in advancing women's
voices, issues, and struggles?

To answer these questions we have divided our analysis into
three sections. The first section offers a descriptive and structural
analysis of the Oprah.com web site, providing the scaffolding for
the community, and the categories and themes deemed relevant to
the show (and, by extension, to women). Next, to address the
question of how or whether community is experienced online, we
analyze the ways women use the site, message boards, and chat
rooms, and the underlying social, cultural, and economic premises
for their participation. In the third section we analyze the political
economy of the site, as one part of Oprah's marketing strategy of
media convergence. Our analysis of the discourse produced on the
site as well as the space created for that discourse will help us to
find out both whether this site can be considered a community
and for whom such a designation might be important.

Method of Analysis

Ethnographic methods provide useful tools for analyzing the patterns of behavior given cultural meanings by specific groups. While ethnography is often based on in-depth research in a field of real-life practices, a growing number of authors have analyzed the behaviors of virtual or online communities (Baym, 1995; Cooks, 2001; Wakeford, 1997; Watson, 1997) from an ethnographic standpoint. Ethnography adds to previous analyses of the Internet by focusing on the communicative behaviors online that (can) create a sense of "we-ness." Baym (1998) notes: "This work has shown that even the most mundane interactions require that people draw on preexisting resources endowed with social meanings that create and evoke event types, identities, relationships and norms" (p. 50).

In what follows we utilize Baym's (1998) criteria to analyze the relationship between preexisting structures, cultural resources, and everyday practices. If, as Dietrich (1997) observes, "female users [write] themselves into virtual community," they do so as subjects of culture—as consumers, mothers, daughters, professionals, activists, and so on. Thus, this "imagined" space of community is perhaps already marked or shared through the mundane practices of everyday life.

Where offline ethnographies utilize field notes, informants, and time in the field to describe and interpret cultural practices and communal systems, online ethnographies (still analyzing the behaviors of humans in social contexts) rely on time spent observing and interacting on the site, interactions with members, and analysis of ritual communicative practices and sense-making as cultural data. Our online ethnographic fieldwork is perhaps restricted by the lack of nonverbal cues and access to the offline personae of the women who participate on Oprah.com. In studying the interaction among online participants, we are limited to what they can provide: their words and textual expressions of emotion.

Procedures

Our analysis is based on eight months of observation and six months of participation on the Oprah.com site. We did not identify ourselves to the Oprah.com community as researchers, nor did we ask questions explicitly related to our project goals. While the ethics of researcher anonymity is an often-debated topic among Internet ethicists (Hamilton, 1999), our observations were not based on false pretext nor did we intervene to promote or change the topics discussed on the boards or in the chat rooms. As is the case with most "virtual" ethnographic work, the discourse posted on this site was/is considered to be public information (Wood & Smith, 2001), accessible to those who logged on to the site or signed up for the chat rooms. Our participation on the site bulletin boards and in the chat rooms was based on our own interest in the topic or its relevance to our everyday lives. Our observation of the bulletin boards or chat spaces was wide-ranging and focused on the themes or threads of discussion produced by the online participants. To analyze the discourse, we downloaded the messages from the bulletin boards and recorded (via handwritten notes) the interactions in the chat rooms. We then searched for common and unique terms for describing the space of the web site, plus common and unique terms for relating to or describing the experiences of others on the site and the actions and behaviors that occurred and were understood by members as contributing to a shared sense of community.

While the term "community" may not have been mentioned explicitly in the discourse, expressions of comfort, unity, commonality, and safety in this space were taken to be indicators of a shared sense of membership. Rather than membership, however, feminist theorists such as Haraway (1991) are concerned with the building of "coalitions" that have the power to create new signifying practices that "mark the world" through the fusion of body and technology. To answer our second research question, whether or not the space created by and through Oprah.com is a space for women, we look at the values expressed through the site, the recognition of women's struggles and actions, and the projections toward changing women's lives for the better.

In the next section, we describe the site of our research and cyber-fieldwork: the structure and space of "O Place." The duration of our fieldwork in this site was relatively brief (from January 2001, to August 2001); however, due to the structuring of communal space on the Internet, the intertextual nature of this particular community (members of the web site are also clearly fans of other Oprah-related media), and the rather fleeting expectations of and commitment to virtual communities, we feel that our description of the site presents an adequate depiction of the current activity in this cyberspace.

The Structure and Space of O Place

O Place, on Oprah.com, is the official web site linking the major components of the entertainment offerings of Oprah Winfrey. The title area of the site includes the phrase "Live Your Best Life," an overarching theme. The page features numerous opportunities for exchange and interactivity for users. One example is an area in which written contributions to *O: The Oprah Magazine* are also solicited by the use of a button that invites users to "contribute your ideas and experiences." On April 2, 2001, the topic provided was "School Shootings and Bullies." Clicking on this topic takes the user to a page on which a brief introduction is provided (e.g., "In light of the saddening incident that took place in Santee, California, recently, we at the Oprah Magazine want to know what questions you have about school shootings and bullies"). The user's age and contact information are requested and then a box is provided with "Tell Us Your Story" as the only prompt. Thus, users are asked to post descriptions of personal experiences or opinions and/or to pose questions about the topic. This interactive feature allows women to take ownership of the issues raised in the Oprah television show by applying them to their own experiences. Community can be formed, then, in this space through women's responses to each other around a common topic.

Many features of the site allow for easy feedback and expression of opinions. This interactivity is important to users' perceived relationships with Oprah because they may feel that she is "listening" to their opinions. Another important opportunity that interactivity provides is the opportunity for users to take information and concepts advanced in Oprah's show or magazine or on the web site and apply them to their own lives. Users of the Oprah site make sense of and utilize information provided by Oprah in their own diverse and unique fashions. Interactivity also allows for mutual support between and among women who post messages on the message boards and chat in the chat rooms. Community is formed virtually across space and time through conversations that take place on the Oprah web site, encouraged through such language as, "Have you completed Dr. Phil's 10-week plan? Stay on track with your weight loss goals—return to this board for continued support and motivation!" or "If you're on the road to pursuing your passion and need encouragement, visit our Finding Encouragement chat room."

The content of the web site is often gendered. The idea of discussing people in one's life who have "performed miracles" ("The Angel Network"), of nurturing one's spirit ("Your Spirit"), of asking an expert for advice about relationships ("Relationships/Dr. Phil"), of exchanging healthful and tasty recipes ("Food"), and of improving one's attitudes and approaches to life ("Lifestyle Makeovers") are all traditionally viewed as concerns of women. Similarly, the form that many of the feedback mechanisms take, such as writing in a journal or "talking it out" with others, is also widely viewed as women-oriented. The bulk of the content provided by the site that helps structure conversations is "self-help" in nature, which provides an opportunity for advertisers to proffer products and services that ostensibly assist women in this pursuit (see later section of this chapter). There is also a decidedly spiritual tone, noticeable in much of the language used on the site, as in "The Mission Calendar" ("Click on a date below for daily inspiration").

Gathering Places: Message Boards and Chat Rooms

Oprah.com's chat rooms and message boards are used fairly frequently. We tracked the amount of activity on the message boards by examining the numbers of discussions listed under each content heading over time. We began on April 2, 2001, and noted the numbers of discussions that had been posted by that date for each major topic. We then compared that to the number posted 9 days later, 18 days later, and finally 30 days later (see table 6.1 at end of chapter).

Each division of the message boards contains several folders and files for discussion. For example, "Your Spirit" section contains discussion folders such as "Remembering Your Spirit," "Gratitude," "The Best Part of Today," "Random Acts of Kindness," "Meditation," and "Favorite Quotes." The chat rooms are divided in much the same way, with rooms based on the show, on relationships, and on lifestyle makeovers, and the more general "Lobby." In the chat format, users are required to adopt a pseudonym and to remember their password in order to participate in online chatting. When a user enters a chat room, she is presented with a dialogue box that contains several lines of conversation indicating the nature and flow of the discussion. To the right appears a box which indicates the people who (using pseudonyms) are online at the moment and when they exit or which other room they enter. An open area at the bottom of the screen is used for entering a comment for discussion.

As indicated in table 6.1, analysis of the activity occurring on the message boards over approximately a month suggests that, in general, the Oprah.com web site is, indeed, a fairly active site. Women appear to use the message boards and chat options rather frequently, engaging in recurrent conversations with one another. The largest numbers of postings in the message boards in general during the period were for "Ideas Exchange" under the heading "Oprah's Angel Network," "Remembering Your Spirit" and "Favorite Quotes" under "Your Spirit," "Simplify Your Life" under "Lifestyle Makeovers," and "One Simple Change" under "Mind and Body." Each of these topics had garnered well over 1,000 discussions by our last day of observation, though we have no way of knowing how many had been posted before we began monitoring and, in some cases, the percentage increases in postings over the period examined were rather modest. The topics with the largest numbers of postings have much in common in that each invites users to discuss specific strategies and techniques used to maintain physical and psychological well-being. Each involves self-help, through attention to spirituality ("Remembering Your Spirit"), ways to relieve stress and maintain order in life ("Simplify Your Life"), and healthful diets, non-smoking strategies, and exercise efforts to maintain physical health ("One Simple Change"). The popularity of "Favorite Quotes" suggests users are also fond of sending advice via statements made by others, in addition to reporting personal experiences.

The remaining topic that stands out as being particularly popular, with well over 1,000 discussions in one file and several hundred in a series of additional files, is "Oprah's Book Club." Conversations around the book *Icy Sparks*, for instance, generated the highest percentage increases in postings in the month of our analysis, attesting to the phenomenal influence of Oprah's Book Club on reading and purchasing. Other topics that inspired frequent activity in the month we monitored the site, as seen in percentage increases of postings, included "In Need of Prayer" (in "Oprah's Angel Network"), "Remembering Your Spirit," and "Meditation" (both in "Your Spirit").

Cultural Premises for and
Social-Cultural Effects of Participation

We now conduct a textual analysis of the Oprah web site, message boards, and chat rooms. We base our interpretation of the participation and activity on the message boards on several criteria: the usefulness of the activity for identifying and solidifying a sense of *we*-ness, the depth of feeling the activity provides or provokes, and the number of responses/amount of interest the activity generates.

Participation is at the center of our analysis of the ways in which a virtual community is created and maintained around the media image of Oprah. In what follows we analyze the ways people—primarily women[1]—coordinate their actions to create and uphold meaningful membership in the Oprah community as a valid cultural form. We identify several rituals of activity based on repetition and the frequency with which they occur as well as their salience for the members of the community. Women use the message boards and chat rooms to attempt to both affirm and transform themselves and others, using Oprah's image and story as their guide.

Taking Responsibility for Ourselves

In line with Oprah's philosophy of transforming communities through self-transformation, a major method of participating on the message boards and in the chat rooms was through claiming responsibility for one's own actions. As the majority of the messages indicate, "claiming" and "naming," but not "blaming" are key rules for participating, either for telling one's own story or for offering advice to others hoping to change their relationships, their weight, their lifestyle, and so on. Members chastise each other for not "owning your own stuff" and not "tak[ing] responsibility" for weight gain, relationship problems, and (most importantly) reporting back to the community about their progress. Much of the discourse around taking responsibility can be directly linked to the underlying theme of Oprah's show, magazine, and web site, taking charge and changing your life.

Asking/Giving Support or Advice

A typical activity for many of the participants on the sites that also affirmed the community and the connection among members was asking for and receiving advice and support. This activity occurred frequently and was replicated on all the discussion groups, whether on spirit, on relationships, or in the general talk around the show. While many discussion threads could be cited to demonstrate the frequency of this form of participation, one from the "Relationships" board exemplifies the importance of both asking for and receiving advice and support. After one woman posted a message asking for relationship help, she received many responses that both affirmed her struggle to distance herself from a bad relationship and provided advice and support for "going on" without it. Other threads illustrate the ways women on the site communicated an empathetic understanding of relational difficulties while urging the woman with the problem to acknowledge her own "addiction" and seek help from a higher power. While the responses from other members of the community often indicated their support, the underlying message was that it was up to the suffering woman to "recover" from her addiction.

The activity of asking for and receiving advice or support on the message boards paralleled the structure of the Oprah show, and of other talk shows where a guest or audience member would present a problem (often a very personal problem) and the host, along with the ever-present guest expert and audience members, would offer an answer or register an opinion. This form of participation, disclosing a personal problem and receiving advice or support was well understood by all the members of the community and was coordinated in a very sophisticated fashion among members who acknowledged both the individual and the communal feeling about the topic.

The rhetoric of addiction and recovery was present in all the message areas, whether the subject was weight, relationships, or simplifying one's life. The movement from doing it on your own (as in the discourse of Dr. Phil's contributions on the show and in the magazine) to giving up control and giving yourself over to a higher power is consistent with the contradictory cultural messages that pervade contemporary media and self-help literature (Cooks & Descutner, 1993).

Another tension present in this mix is the tension between individualism or self-sufficiency as a dominant cultural value, and community and relationships as a cultural value for groups with a minority representation in the society. The ways women in particular utilize self-help literature and participate in self-help communities have been documented elsewhere (see, for example, Cooks & Descutner, 1993; DeFrancisco & O'Connor, 1995; Grodin, 1995); however, for our purposes, it is useful to note that the cultural premises for self-help talk ("addiction" and "recovery" through a higher power) were understood and shared among the participants on most of the message boards.

Affirming Community

Women participated frequently on the message boards to affirm others who were "struggling along the path" and to ask for affirmation from other members of the community. Often the women would discuss the ways that their relationships in physical space had let them down, and would look to this space for cyberfriends, or offer validation that members of this community would not let them down. As faithstep[2] put it, "I truly enjoy reading about peoples little victories. A whole bunch of those add up to a big result. I thank you all for sharing your hearts. And if you are struggling I want to hear that too. The world is too full of fair weather friends. I do not think there is any such thing as over praising or being too nice."

While faithstep (and others) cited a higher power or some other source of strength, they also thanked women on the message boards or Oprah herself for helping them get through the really hard times. "We're here for you" was the frequent refrain from the community after a story of tragedy and personal struggle.

On the official messages boards for spirit and for simplifying one's life, many of the women told stories of hardship: of poverty, abuse, hard work, and difficult emotional times. They connected their stories with others on the site, people on the show, and Oprah herself. On these boards in particular, Oprah was often represented as the center or as representing the core values of a community marked by self-empowerment, self-transformation, good will, and friendship. Although the rules for participation in this supportive setting were rarely violated, when they were, the reaction was often one of pain, anger, and frustration among members, and subsequently a reinstatement of the format for participation in the community. As junebug observed: "I am much more comfortable reading some of the most personal stories I see on these boards than with conflict over what was meant by what we said. Why do we need to fight with one another? This is a place for support."

Marking, Regulating, and Tracking Virtual Community

Messages indicating movement through the virtual spaces of the community allow others to track their movement/progress through a weight loss program, for example, as well as keep tabs on the members. This message board actually framed participation in terms of where a member was in her progress toward the goal. Thus, a member might post at week 5, if that indicated her progress in the plan. Other members might regulate the postings on this board by asking errant members to limit their posts to the particular week they were working on at that time. In week 10, for instance, several members became upset when a few posts indicated that women were at an earlier stage in their diets.

Often, when the discussion in the chat rooms or on the message boards went into areas not recognized as the official format of the web site or as appropriate topics for the community, the members would pull the discussion back to a safer theme, either through directing the member back to the lists of rules for participation, through discussion of what topics were valued by the community, or through the use of humor. One humorous redirect occurred in the "Lifestyle Makeover" chat room after several members had been engaging in some (fairly tame) cybersex: "When they said that this was the lifestyle makeover room, I didn't think they were talking about this kind of lifestyle." Subsequent entries responded to this use of humor (indicated by the repeated use of LoL for Laugh out Loud or RoFL for Roll on the Floor Laughing) and then the discussion shifted back to the previous topics: bizarre diets, gas remedies, and eating disorders.

While each of these ways of participating, taking re-sponsibility for oneself, asking/giving support or advice, affirming community, marking/regulating and maintaining community is mirrored or reflected in women's participation in other forms of community life, it is important to note that cyberspace communities differ in terms of the continuity of conversations and in the fluidity of and commitment to participation. Members of virtual communities enter and leave the community with very little personal risk (that is, risk to their social presentation of self). Cyberspace preserves physical anonymity, and to some extent online personae are protected by the different pseudonyms and identities users can adopt.

Additionally, the formats of chat rooms are often marked by discontinuity and fragmentation in conversation, which reduces expectations for commitment to sustaining threads of conversation for long periods of time. The format of the chat room itself is set up so that members are free (and to some extent encouraged) to leave at any time to pursue subjects in different rooms. This leads to a third difference in virtual communities: commitment to the conversation/topic and to other members participating in that conversation. While the conditions of anonymity, discontinuity, and flexibility in time and space may lead to decreased responsibility to others in the community, these same conditions can also be said to actually increase participation in and commitment to the community. As we have seen in the previous section, members felt free to disclose very personal information that they might have been less comfortable explaining in the physical presence of others. Moreover, some members noted that they actually expected and relied more on the support of their friends in cyberspace than on the support of their "fair weather" friends and relatives in physical space.

The consequences and effects of participation in the "O Place" community cannot be isolated from the commercial space in which the community is located. In the next section, we consider how participation is also structured by economic interests and how the idea of communities in conversation becomes a sophisticated marketing strategy for Oprah, her affiliates, and the advertisers.

Community and Participation in a Commercial Space

Oprah Winfrey's appeal is not limited to the women who watch her TV show, read her magazine, or participate online. Her appeal is also evident in the world of women's marketing. According to industry reports, Oprah is a magnet for women, and media products associated with her reputation often become hits with consumers and advertisers months before they hit the retail stores. Her one-year-old monthly, *O: The Oprah Magazine*, had the highest grossing debut to date, and her daily talk show currently draws 22 million viewers, mostly women, in 119 countries per week (Rose, 2000). Harpo Entertainment Group, Winfrey's media company, views the Internet's e-commerce as an essential means of extending the commercial success of the "Oprah Brand" in the twenty-first century.

Our analysis of women's participation on Oprah.com must be examined within the larger context of commodification and the ways in which new media technologies are utilized to reach niche markets. How is the Internet being transformed into a "tool of the trade"? How is the transformation from resource to commercial space altering the participation of online users? How are Oprah.com and similar media firms imposing commercial practices on web sites? What are the implications of the commodification of women's voices in new media? It is difficult to address these questions thoroughly in the context of this chapter, but we will introduce some political-economic issues into the discussion of women's virtual space, especially as they relate to

Oprah.com.

Two important issues for marketing and advertising executives are consumer loyalty and expenditure tracking. The $100
billion women's market is chock full of merchandisers competing
for women's purse strings, particularly those of women in higher-
income households. Attracting and maintaining a loyal relationship with consumers is important for long-term commercial
success, and tracking consumption behavior is often noted as the
best method for assessing changes in the market. Internet
technologies are helping these practices along, and in women's
virtual space, Oprah.com is leading the way. According to a
Procter and Gamble executive, television content is intended to
drive consumers "to the print ad and then to the Web site, which
is supporting your direct-to-consumer and [retail traffic] ... so
there's a synergy there" (Neff, 2001). Advertisers are lured to
Oprah-related media products because they have a captive and
loyal audience and this allows Harpo Entertainment Group to
push its various outlets as primary sites for marketing to women.
In a similar vein, Unilever Bestfoods utilized its demographic and
geographic data to create the web site Slim-Fast Online for dieters
wanting additional support during their endeavor to lose weight
(Thompson, 2001).

The creation of *O: The Oprah Magazine* is another excellent
example of consumer loyalty and the magnitude of the "Oprah
brand." While the periodical was still in the preproduction stage,
its publisher, Hearst Corp., effortlessly cleared $20 million worth
of advertising for the first three issues. The publisher actually
turned advertisers away after an issue reached 166 pages of
advertising. Hearst executives were assured that the new Oprah
magazine would become an instant hit, and the company agreed
to publish the monthly although it owned various media products
that directly competed with Harpo holdings. Hearst's cable
television network, Lifetime, would soon rival Oprah's new cable
investment, Oxygen, and the publisher's online site Women.com
and the magazine *Redbook* would challenge Oprah.com and *O*
magazine. According to the president of Hearst's magazine unit,
the competitive world of marketing to women makes it almost
necessary for competitors to become synergistic partners in the
sphere of commercial media (Thompson, 2001). Companies are
developing alliances with other firms that have better name

recognition because it is difficult to maintain long-term consumer interest in specific categories as well as brands (Taylor, 2001).

Schiller (1999) notes that companies are enthusiastic about making links between traditional media content and so-called new media services for several reasons. First, it cuts reproduction costs. Much of the content on Oprah.com is a reproduction of content in the magazine and the talk show. Second, the convergence and synchronicity between the various Harpo products create a multimedia platform in which audience relationships with entertainment programs and marketing power can be sustained and extended in the digital era. While Oprah.com encourages community building for its online users, it does so within the topical confines of the talk show and the magazine. Lastly, the development of Oprah.com can be viewed as an attempt to extend the Oprah franchise into new media outlets such as the World Wide Web, in order to create an Internet hub that is customized for loyal female fans and integrated into the assorted media offerings.

By creating a reliable gathering space for women, marketers and advertisers can hone their targeting efforts in the virtual sphere. In the case of Oprah.com, the website is segmented into different topics which track specific consumers with banner, push-and-click, and pop-up advertisements such as 1-800-Flowers. Information about women's interests is considered the "strategic weapon" for successfully competing in the new economy. E-commerce is becoming a surefire way of creating virtual warehouses of information, which allow marketers to improve the focus of commercial messages (Martin, 2001).

Oprah Winfrey's investment in Oxygen Media, a new media network aimed at "empowering women" through the convergence of cable television and digital media, attests to the importance of commercial practices that link new communications technology with women's marketing. The cross-media marketing between Oprah.com and the Oxygen network aims to target the female audience across online and offline environments for advertising and research purposes. The biggest advertisements on Oprah.com are Oxygen Media products such as Ka-Ching.com (a finance web site for women), MomsOnline.com (a web site for mothers), and *Oprah Goes Online* (an Oxygen cable network show). In a crowded Internet marketplace, advertisers want to co-brand with the multimedia platforms that have the greatest potential for global recognition, mass consumer loyalty, and convergence flexibility, and the "Oprah brand" promises all three.

According to Oxygen CEO Geraldine Laybourne, the cable network's programming and its connected web sites, such as Oprah.com, rely a great deal on the information obtained from the chat rooms (Jones, 2000). The hope is to engender the following type of synergy: A television viewer may watch a program, for instance the *Oprah Winfrey Show*, and connect with the day's topic, "Taking Responsibility." At the end of the show, the TV viewer then turns to her computer and visits the Oprah.com web site, a Harpo Entertainment resource on how to "live your best life." After the viewer posts her thoughts in the "You Have to Name It to Claim It" chat room, the TV now-turned cyber fan clicks on the Ka-Ching.com link (hosted on Oxygen.com's web portal) for more information on money management and a list of financial institutions that are selling money management products and services online. Oprah television viewers can now become interactive producers via chat room postings as well as e-commerce consumers via marketing web links. Since the "Oprah brand" is one that loyal fans believe they can trust, consumer product advertisers are hoping that their association with the web site will stimulate the same kind of trust.

Turow (1997) notes that the development of new high technology, such as the Internet, direct satellite broadcasting, and digital cable, not only transformed media into instruments for tailored marketing, but also, in some ways, fractured the cultural fabric of American society. Although the rupture of "American" culture is up for debate, Turow's observations about the role of new media in multi-platform marketing strategies and the divisions this may cause ring true in the case of Oprah.com. While the participants in the Oprah.com chat rooms may indeed be creating a community, we cannot lose sight of the fact that these women are participating under the aegis of a multimedia empire that is attempting to construct a commercial cyber-version of society as a critical part of its struggle for position in the global communications economy.

Ultimately, what are the implications of commercially sponsored space for women's recovery/support? As Schiller (1999) asks, "what does advertiser sponsorship do to the media that become dependent on it? There is plenty of evidence that advertising seizes and reorients the social purpose of any media it can make dependent on it, substantially affecting their organization, content, and relationships with audiences" (p. 124), and in the case of online interactive media, it changes the relationship with users. Yet, if the belief is that "when advertisers foot an appreciable proportion of overall media costs, they come to dominate that medium's workaday self-consciousness, one effect of which is also to place determining pressures and limits on its relationship with audiences" (p. 124), how does women's participation transform those pressures and limits? Does the interactivity of cyberspace allow women to resist the limits imposed by commercial media? How does this resistance take place, and how is it coopted? These questions require further study and we hope that future scholarship will grapple with them more thoroughly.

Conclusions

Returning to Baym's (1998) sources and structures of influence on virtual communities—system infrastructure, temporal structure, group purposes, participant characteristics, and external contexts—we can perhaps answer the questions central to this chapter about how spaces for community are constructed on Oprah.com, and how women's participation online plays a role in that construction.

We find that participation on the Oprah web site is at least partially informed by the way the site visually and symbolically connects with Oprah as a transformative, powerful, and healing presence. The system infrastructure, as Baym calls it, allows for intertextual references to topics presented on Oprah's daily talk show, articles in her *O* magazine, and ongoing categories related to themes important to the women who are fans. The system also permits the dissemination of visual and aural stimuli on the site (in addition to text); however, the interaction between participants on the site occurs in a text-based form.

The temporal structure of the site permits both synchronous and asynchronous communication. The chat rooms permit immediate feedback and response in real time. Although the comments inevitably interrupt and overlap each other, the immediacy of the chat room permits a more communal feeling, and thus (presumably) an increased commitment to and responsibility for connecting with others present in the room. Message board interaction, while easier to follow and respond to, is not conducted in real time. Messages are displayed according to their posted subject, date, and time. Members can respond at their leisure and to those topics that interest them.

Commitment to the virtual community is also to some extent determined by temporality. If members can enter and exit at will and with some degree of anonymity, commitment to connecting with the other members and responsibility for responding to requests, queries, and emotional needs are based on self-interest and an individual sense of accountability.

Participant or group characteristics can be determined in part by the fact that the community is online. The women who post messages and chat must have some familiarity with and access to the Internet. The messages occasionally reveal the context in which they are written (e.g., at home, after the kids are in bed, at work, etc.), but we can presume that the members of this group are among the minority of the population who have access to the Internet either at home or through their worksite. Other characteristics that are important to this group include the commonality they share as fans of Oprah and (presumably) as readers of her magazine and viewers of her show. The assumption that the vast majority of those who visit the site are women is based on the demographics of Oprah's viewing audience and the names, pseudonyms, or referents the participants use, and their relationships, interests, and activities, revealed through the message boards and chat rooms in which they interact.

The purposes around which the group comes together can be described as primarily social. Even those posts which are more or less task oriented (seeking more information on health or spiritual topics discussed on the show or products advertised on the show, seeking advice on relationships, etc.) occur within a social or recreational as opposed to an organizational or task-defined format. More specifically, as we have noted throughout this chapter, women participate on Oprah.com primarily in roles that are extensions of their roles in everyday life. They may participate as fans, as mothers, as daughters, as survivors, as addicts, as friends, and so on. Identification based on other "marked" categories such as race, class, sexuality, and ability is less explicit and often read in between the lines of the text. The categories of "woman" and "fan" perhaps form the primary basis for online identification of membership. The women who post messages and chat online do so to tell their stories, share their struggles, and seek/give advice and support. These purposes for an online community do not deviate much from those for offline women's communities (Ashcraft, 2001) yet, as computer-mediated communication (CMC) theorists have argued, the two types of communities are different in fundamental ways. For many gender and feminist scholars, the paramount question is not is this *really* a community, but does this forum for interaction advance women's issues, promote equality, and give voice to those who have previously been invisible and inaudible.

The role of external contexts in structuring participation on Oprah.com includes the cultural, social, and (for our purposes) economic factors that give shape to this particular space. Throughout this chapter we have looked at the ways the tensions among individuals and communities, audiences and marketers are enacted online, and the ways their deployment (as part of predefined communities organized into gendered topics such as health, beauty, fashion, etc.) allow users the opportunity to create community while extending (often uncritically) the meaning given to activities and interests.

Joanne very appropriately illustrates these tensions in the following post:

> I am surprised in how the atmosphere on the community connection can change from hot to cold and back to hot again. Why does it distress me, it's because everyone has their opinion whether you agree with it or not. I think we can all agree that everyone of us has been thru the good and bad, the poor of things of the not so poor of things ... It distresses me that HarpoBoard has to come in and tell you that there is a person on the other side of the computer. Because I feel that if women can't get along behind a computer screen who is going to show the men in this world how to get along? (Mind you that is my dry sense of humour coming out) Thank you for listening, Joanne.

Joanne points to the complexities of the mediation of meaning in a virtual community. Well aware of the intervention by the "powers that be" (HarpoBoard) to structure the interactions and prevent conflict, she indicates that it is in the best interest of this virtual community of women to maintain their connections to each other through their shared experiences and their responsibility to show men how to "get along."

This tension precisely reflects the ambiguity and contradiction that Dietrich (1997), Haraway (1991), Blair and Takayoshi (1999), and Morse (1997) acknowledge is necessary for women to refashion a textual space for social change. The virtuality of this space allows the possibility for new coalitions, and for imagining new modes of solidarity. Nonetheless, as we have seen in our analysis of the conversations on the Oprah site, moments of imagination, of creating new possibilities for reshaping or rethinking everyday practices and relationships, are rare. More likely, the virtual community of Oprah.com exists in a constellation of relationships in which women struggle to define for themselves what their relationship should be to each other, to the significant others in their lives, to those people and situations that control them, and to those over which they can exercise some control.

Finally, is the space of Oprah.com a place *for* women? As our use of communication technologies evolves and women gain access and become proficient users, the possibilities for asserting those connections amidst a sea of commercial dominance and inequities of power evolve along with it. Oprah.com is both a commercial venture and a meeting place through which women have made connections to each other and to those issues that are important in their lives. The consequences of these connections are just beginning to be noticed, both on the individual and on the relational level. Where these conversations intersect the personal goals of individual women and the political goals of a movement on behalf of women will be difficult to determine. Perhaps the better question at this moment is not what women's communities should consist of, but rather *when* and *how* online spaces open up new possibilities for re-visioning our lives, both on- and offline. New criteria for public spaces mean that the spaces that make a difference in our lives and the meaning that those spaces hold are themselves changing.

Notes

1. Although we have no way of tracking the gender or sex of the people who participate, the pseudonyms or "nicks," pronouns, and references to identity

(mother, lesbian, daughter, wife, etc.), activities (giving birth), or relationships (boyfriend, husband, etc.) seemed to indicate that the vast majority of the members are women.

2. The pseudonyms used throughout this analysis are those used on the message boards and in the chat rooms. The women participating in these venues were asked to choose a name and encouraged not to use their real name.

References

Adams, C. H. (2001). Prosocial bias in theories of interpersonal communication competence: Must good communication be nice? In G. J. Shepherd & E. W. Rothenbuhler (Eds.), *Communication and community* (pp. 37–52). Mahwah, NJ: Lawrence Erlbaum Associates.

Addison, J., & Hilligoss, S. (1999). Technological fronts: Lesbian lives "on the line." In K. Blair & P. Takayoshi (Eds.), *Feminist cyberspaces: Mapping gendered academic spaces* (pp. 21–40). Stamford, CT: Ablex.

Anderson, B. (1983). *Imagined communities: Reflections on the origins and spread of nationalism.* London: Verso.

Ashcraft, K. L. (2001). Feminist organizing and the construction of alternative community. In G. J. Shepherd & E. W. Rothenbuhler (Eds.), *Communication and community* (pp. 79–109). Mahwah, NJ: Lawrence Erlbaum Associates.

Baym, N. K. (1995). From practice to culture on Usenet. In S. L. Star (Ed.), *The cultures of computing* (pp. 29–52). Oxford: Basil Blackwell.

Baym, N.K. (1998). The emergence of community in CMC. In S. Jones (Ed.), *Cybersociety 2.0: Revisiting computer-mediated communication and community* (pp. 35–67). Thousand Oaks, CA: Sage.

Blair, K., & Takayoshi, P. (1999). Introduction: Mapping the terrain of feminist cyberspaces. In K. Blair & P. Takayoshi (Eds.), *Feminist cyberspaces: Mapping gendered academic spaces* (pp. 1–20). Stamford, CT: Ablex.

Bruckman, A. (1996). Finding one's own space in cyberspace. *Technology Review, 99*(1), 48–55.

Cooks, L. M. (2001). Negotiating national identity and social movement in cyberspace: Natives and invaders on the Panama-L listserv. In B. Ebo (Ed.), *Cyberimperialism? Global relations in the new electronic frontier* (pp. 233–252). Westport, CT: Praeger.

Cooks, L. M., & Descutner, D. (1993). Different paths from powerlessness to empowerment: A dramatistic analysis of two eating disorder therapies. *Western Journal of Communication, 57,* 494–514.

DeFrancisco, V.L., & O'Connor, P. (1995). A feminist critique of self-help books on heterosexual romance: Read 'em and weep. *Women's Studies in Communication, 18*(2), 217–277.

Dietrich, D. (1997). Re-fashioning the techno-erotic woman: Gender and textuality in the cybercultural matrix. In S. Jones (Ed.), *Virtual culture: Identity & communication in cybersociety* (pp. 169–185). London: Sage.

Grodin, D. (1995). Women reading self-help: Themes of separation and connection. *Women's Studies in Communication, 18*(2), 123–134.

Haag, L. L. (1993). Oprah Winfrey: The construction of intimacy in the talk show setting. *Journal of Popular Culture, 26* (4), 115–122.

Hamilton, J. C. (December 3, 1999). The ethics of conducting social science research on the Internet. *The Chronicle of Higher Education,* pp. B6–7.

Haraway, D. (1985). A cyborg manifesto: Science, technology and socialist feminism in the late twentieth century. In *Simians, cyborgs and women* (pp. 127–148). New York: Routledge.

Haraway, D. (1991). *Simians, cyborgs, and women: The reinvention of nature.* London: Free Association Books.

Herring, S. (1996). Posting in a different voice. Gender and ethics in CMC. In C. Hess (Ed.), *Philosophical perspectives on computer-mediated communication.* Albany: State University of New York Press.

Jones, L. (January 30, 2000). "The mightiest names in American television are launching a channel for women." *The Independent.*

Kendall, L. (1996). MUDder? I hardly know'er! Adventures of a feminist MUDder. In L. Cherny & E. R. Weise (Eds.), *Wired women: Gender and new realities in cyberspace* (pp. 207–223). Seattle: Seal Press.

Kramarae, C. (1998). Feminist fictions of future technology. In S. Jones (Ed.), *Cybersociety 2.0: Revisiting computer-mediated communication and community* (pp. 100–128). Thousand Oaks, CA: Sage.

Martin, C. (March 5, 2001). "Relationship revolution: Internetworking, not Net, is key." *Advertising Age,* p. 22.

Morse, M. (1997). Virtually female: Body and code. In J. Terry & M. Calvert (Eds.), *Processed lives: Gender and technology in everyday life* (pp. 37–65). London: Routledge.

Neff, J. (February 12, 2001). "IVillage may not be big enough for both of them." *Advertising Age,* p. 24.

Rose, M. (2000, April 3). "In Oprah's empire, rivals are partners." *Wall Street Journal.*

Schiller, D. (1999). *Digital capitalism.* Cambridge: MIT Press.

Spender, D. (1995). *Nattering on the net: Women, power and cyberspace.* Melbourne: Spinifex.

Tannen, D. (June 8, 1998). Oprah Winfrey. *Time, 151*(22), 196–199.

Taylor, C. P. (2001, May 21). "E-Business falls back to earth." *Advertising Age,* pp. 32–34.

Thompson, S. (April 3, 2001). "Slim-Fast sets out to beef up web club." *Advertising Age,* p. 26.

Turow, J. (1997). *Breaking up America : Advertisers and the new media world.* Chicago: University of Chicago Press.

Wakeford, N. (1997). Networking women and grrrls with information/communication technology: Surfing tales of the World Wide Web. In J. Terry & M. Calvert (Eds.), *Processed lives: Gender and technology in everyday life* (pp. 52–65). London: Routledge.

Watson, N. (1997). Why we argue about virtual community: A case study of the Phish.net fan community. In S. Jones (Ed.), *Virtual culture: Identity and community in cybersociety* (pp. 102–132). London: Sage.

Wood, A. F., & Smith, M. J. (2001). *Online communication: Linking technology, identity & culture.* Mahwah, NJ: Laurence Erlbaum Associates.

Table 6.1 Charting Activity on Oprah.com's Message Boards

Topic	April 2	April 11	April 20	May 2
			Date, 2001	
		Number of messages and percentage increase		
The Oprah Show				
April	5	10 (100%)	20 (100%)	–
May	–	–	–	4
Information From Past				
Shows Here!	918	941 (2.5%)	967 (2.8%)	1,001 (3.5%)
Oprah Magazine				
April	7	7	7	7
May	–	–	1	1
Looking for				
Information?	758	759 (0.1%)	765 (0.8%)	–
Oprah's Cut	–	–	–	7
Oprah's Book Club				
Icy Sparks	143	212 (48.3%)	254 (19.8%)	327 (28.7%)
What Authors Have				
Inspired You?	364	362 (-0.5%)	377 (4.1%)	416 (10.3%)
Recommended Kids'				
Books	879	889 (1.1%)	905 (1.8%)	919 (1.5%)
Book Suggestions	1,456	1,480 (1.6%)	1,505 (1.7%)	1,576 (4.7%)
Build Your Own				
Book Club	617	629 (1.9%)	635 (1.0%)	645 (1.6%)
Non-Book Club Books				
Seen on Oprah	239	239	245 (2.5%)	254 (3.7%)
Oprah's Angel Network				
Inspired by the Use				
Your Life Award	75	94 (25.3%)	98 (4.3%)	102 (4.1%)
Use Your Life				
Award	170	173 (1.8%)	174 (0.6%)	175 (0.6%)
Kindness Chain	237	253 (6.8%)	257 (1.6%)	271 (5.4%)
In Need of Prayer	221	258 (16.7%)	300 (16.3%)	326 (8.7%)
Making a Difference	373	390 (4.6%)	399 (2.3%)	412 (3.3%)
Ideas Exchange	959	1,000 (4.3%)	1,011 (1.1%)	1,029 (1.8%)

Continued on next page

Table 6.1—Continued

Your Spirit				
Remembering Your Spirit	1,385	1,564 (12.9%)	1,726 (10.4%)	1,906 (10.4%)
Gratitude	664	775 (16.7%)	848 (9.4%)	904 (6.6%)
The Best Part of Today	301	319 (6.3%)	326 (2.2%)	333 (21%)
Random Acts of Kindness	133	152 (14.3%)	162 (6.6%)	176 (8.6%)
Meditation	93	113 (21.5%)	127 (12.4%)	134 (5.5)
Favorite Quotes	802	849 (5.9%)	882 (3.9%)	1,071 (21.4%)
Relationships—Dr. Phil McGraw				
Getting Straight with Your Weight	9	11 (22.2%)	11	11
Getting Real with Your Relationship	2	2	2	2
Relationship Rescue	7	7	7	7
Family	8	8	8	8
Relationships	9	9	9	9
Food				
Oprah.com Recipe Review	5	7 (40.0%)	8 (14.3%)	10 (25%)
Recipe Exchange	4	4	4	4
Healthy Eating	4	4	4	4
We Want to Hear From You	70	71 (1.4%)	74 (4.2%)	86 (16.2%)
Cooking Questions?	193	200 (3.6%)	208 (4.0%)	219 (5.3%)
Art's Recipe Box	25	25	29 (16.0%)	28 (3.4%)
Recipe Review: Spa Breakfast	–	–	–	5
Lifestyle Makeovers				
Weekly Challenge	11	12 (9.1%)	14 (16.7%)	15 (7.1%)
Lifestyle Makeover	17	17	17	17
Pursuing Yr Passion	1	1	1	1
Simplify Your Life	1,078	1,105 (2.5%)	1,125 (1.8%)	1,149 (21%)

Continued on next page

Table 6.1—Continued

Oprah Winfrey Presents				
The Movie: *Amy*				
and Isabelle	116	117 (0.9%)	118 (0.9%)	121 (3.5%)
The Book: *Amy*				
and Isabelle	16	16	16	16
Mind and Body				
Your Mind	9	9	9	9
Your Body	13	13	13	14
Spa Girls	3	3	3	3
One Simple Change	1,642	1,689 (2.9%)	1,735 (2.7%)	1,800 (3.7%)
In the News				
Science and Health				
News	58	63 (8.6%)	65 (3.2%)	–
Sports News	9	9	9	9
Election 2000	365	366 (0.3%)	367 (0.3%)	–
Headline News	134	145 (8.2%)	150 (3.4%)	–
Good News!	48	51 (6.3%)	54 (5.9%)	–
Hometown News	30	30	30	–
Political News	176	181 (2.8%)	186 (2.8%)	–
Business News	17	17	18 (5.9%)	–
Journal Message Boards				
Community Gratitude				
Journal	–	–	–	25
Daily Journal	–	–	–	157
Gratitude	–	–	–	50

*Omissions in the table indicate that the topic in question did not appear on the message boards on that day. Omissions in the percentage increases indicate that the number of messages posted remained the same between the dates indicated, therefore there was a zero percentage change.

Chapter 7

Join Now, Membership Is Free: Women's Web Sites and the Coding of Community

Karen E. Gustafson

Introduction

This chapter will explore the factors that control and monitor behavior on three well-known women's sites, iVillage (www. iVillage.com), Women.com (www.women.com), and Oxygen, (www.oxygen.com). Users of these sites are controlled in a variety of ways, through community rules and norms and the sites' architecture, or code. Drawing upon Lawrence Lessig's recent work, *Code and Other Laws of Cyberspace*, I will examine how use of these three sites is organized along these axes of control. In doing so, I also explore the rhetoric of community surrounding popular women's sites, both investigating the ways in which community is designed on these sites and looking at the feminization of community online. According to a survey released by Media Metrix and Jupiter Communications in August of 2000, women now outnumber men online (Flynn, 2000). While this is significant in that it reverses the "gender gap" of 1990s Internet use, it also introduces the questions of what women are doing online, and how Internet sites are designing themselves to appeal to women users. After examining the mainstream and marketing press coverage surrounding these three women's sites and looking at the sites themselves, I argue that while women are a growing Internet population, they are being discursively constructed on the Internet as community-seekers and as consumers, traditionally feminine roles. Furthermore, I find it significant that these women's sites, which advertise themselves with rhetoric of community, are actually commercially controlled structures. While this may seem immediately obvious—of course iVillage.com is private and commercial—it is the juxtaposition of community and commercialism that intrigues me.

While the Internet has frequently been invoked as a potential site of community idealism, "community" has now become a buzzword for commercial portals such as America Online (AOL), or the more niche-oriented women's sites I examine here. What does it mean that online community is now frequently something deliberately designed, especially to attract a particular (albeit broad) demographic group, such as women Internet users? How is community constructed and controlled through these sites' rules and coding? The Internet has been popularly promoted as a tool of freedom and liberation, but Lessig suggests that "left to itself, cyberspace will become a perfect tool of control" (1999, p. 6). Coding decides to what degree users have privacy, access, and the ability to engage in free speech with other users. The Internet was first hailed in the early 1990s as a potentially powerful democratic community space, and this rhetoric of community continues to exist on a large scale within the sites examined here. This chapter will interrogate how these three sites are using tropes of community, and how community is being framed on these sites through rhetoric as well as through site design and Lessig's concept of code. These particular sites were chosen because of their status as women's portals—comprehensive web sites oriented specifically toward women. As a portal, each site attempts to offer a variety of services related to women-specific interests, and in each case, women are hailed with the promise of online feminine community. Women.com and iVillage established themselves as leaders in the women's online market in the late 1990s; according to Media Metrix, these two sites had among the highest concentrations of women users in late 1999 (Flynn, 2000). The Oxygen site appeared during the peak of the older sites' popularity, aiming to take advantage of the newly visible market of wired women. Because Oxygen, iVillage, and Women.com are such large sites, I will focus on a few common elements, including each web site's home page, community page, membership form, and terms of service agreement.[1]

Oxygen Media

The Oxygen web site accompanies the recently launched Oxygen Media cable network, which targets a variety of women viewers. Although Oxygen Media is popularly associated with talk show celebrity and actor Oprah Winfrey, Oxygen is actually headed by Geraldine Laybourne, who is known for her success with the Nickelodeon network in the last decade. Oxygen is supported by its partners America Online, Winfrey's Harpo Entertainment Group, Paul Allen's Vulcan Ventures investment firm, and the CWM television production company. The web site, which appeared in the summer of 1999, synergistically accompanies the cable network, with a considerable crossover of content. In mainstream commentary on women's web sites, Oxygen has also been noted for having a feminist and political edge (Piller, 2000).

Of the three sites I examine here, Oxygen.com is probably the most inclusive, with no reference to membership forms or benefits. The Oxygen home page is subtitled "A Woman's View of the World," and offers a few features, including articles on sex toys, genetically modified foods, and holiday recipes. The sidebar lists several more categories of interest, including entertainment, family, health, issues and action, shopping, and of course, Oxygen TV. The top menu is more general, with the headings of Topics, Sites, Schedule (for the cable network), Interact, Newsletters, Tools, Search, and Shop. The site represents itself as offering a wide variety of content choices and activities, while not directly requesting any investment by the user. At the same time, the home page display discursively constructs the user as a family-oriented consumer of cultural and material goods. The ideal user might be a mother who is concerned about her family's health and pays attention to the national political scene, while still finding time to be sexy for her spouse. This sort of user is hailed by the site's featured content, while her activities on the site are constructed in code.

The Interact page itself offers various forms of online interaction, including chat, message boards, and games. Chats and boards occur around a variety of preselected topics, such as Oxygen television shows and gift guides for the holidays, and several, including MomsOnline and ThriveOnline, a "sexuality salon," require users to be members of America Online. Other Oxygen chats and message boards can be joined by providing minimal information, including email address, user name, and password—in terms of information collection, this site appears to be the least invasive of the three I examine here. The registration form includes optional information, such as sex and personal home page URL, but is relatively brief. Although the topics are already articulated, often in support of the cable network television shows, one link is offered for "open chat." Except for this link, all avenues of conversation are directed toward preselected topics, subtly guiding the user while providing the impression of open contact and social opportunity. Finally, the site registration form refers the user to the terms and conditions agreement, which I will discuss next.

The terms and conditions, like other commercial sites' terms of service, are lengthy and highly detailed. Briefly, this page lists the terms under which the Oxygen site may be used, discussing issues of intellectual property, editorial policy, and legal disclaimers. Although many of the terms listed may be seen as fairly standard for a commercial web site, it is revealing to interrogate them in the context of community spaces. Those rules most salient to community rhetoric include intellectual ownership and the editing of material in chat rooms and on message boards. While all content produced by the Oxygen site is protected by copyright law, Oxygen also gains perpetual publication rights to all submitted material:

> By posting on the Oxygen Sites, you grant (or warrant that the owner of such rights has expressly granted) Oxygen and/or relevant affiliated companies the worldwide, perpetual, nonexclusive right to use your questions, comments, and postings, in their original or edited form, in television programs, books, articles, commentaries, or in any other medium now known or later developed. (Oxygen terms and conditions, November 22, 2000)

Despite the rhetoric of community on this site, it is clearly not a relationship of equals between the corporate and individual producers. By contributing to the discussions that make Oxygen a community site, users waive publication rights to their own content, in exchange for Oxygen's provision of technical structures which encourage forms of online community, such as chat rooms and message boards. This is one instance in which the rules governing site usage reveal commercial rifts in the egalitarian rhetoric of community.

Another example of this is seen in the web site's editorial policy, which is similar to that of many paper-based publications. Oxygen reserves the right, at its sole discretion, to delete or modify material and messages that are found to be "infringing, offensive, abusive, defamatory, obscene, stale, or otherwise unacceptable." Furthermore, the site may edit material "for any other reason" (Oxygen terms and conditions, November 22, 2000). While it may be hard to argue with certain standards on the site, such as the prohibition of abusive or obscene material, it is important to recognize two elements in this policy: First, the editors at Oxygen have sole discretion over what is *defined* as defamatory, infringing, and so on. Second, while these standards may be acceptable or even desirable to many users, the rules of use are not created by the "community" of Oxygen users. People accessing the site's boards, chat rooms, and other material must agree to the terms and conditions, but this is a situation of prefabricated community standards existing prior to any actual users' interaction. Through this contract, Oxygen maintains control over the issues discussed in its online community, and helps to ensure that online interaction is channeled in commercially appropriate ways. For instance, could a user harshly criticize an Oxygen-backed product, or would this be construed as defamatory? Using the power of definition, the editors of the site can exert a fluid and invisible control over users' interaction, while not actually forbidding any topics outright.

Oxygen's privacy policy also demonstrates the commercial nature of this community site, both through "opt-in" product promotions and through the use of aggregate market data. With users' individual permission, Oxygen may use personal information for marketing and promotional purposes. Although users may choose to opt out of these product and service promotions, Oxygen notes that they "may not be eligible for certain benefits for which a name, e-mail address, telephone number or other personal identification information is needed" (Oxygen privacy policy, November 22, 2000). In this case, although the user is allowed to protect her personal information, this may be to her detriment. In addition, Oxygen may release personal information about its users under court order, subpoena, or search warrant. This is especially significant in light of data storage capabilities. Not only can the user's private information be released; her actual online conversations can be retrieved and made available. Finally, in the form of aggregate information, Oxygen collects data on the user's browser and computer type, as well as the user's movement within the Oxygen site and beyond, to extra-site links. Although this information may be shared with third parties, the privacy policy stresses the impersonal nature of this data collection, justifying surveillance in the name of better service. This data collection mechanism is coded into the site through cookies—a technology that enables the site's server to request pieces of information about the user, such as name or interests, to be stored on her computer. Cookie files can be repeatedly accessed by the server and, as in the case of personal information, opt out may mean the user misses out on potential participation benefits. Although Oxygen admits the possibility of refusing cookies, it asks users to "please note that some parts of the Oxygen Sites, such as message boards, chats, shopping, contests and game areas, may not function properly" (Oxygen privacy policy, November 22, 2000). If the user chooses not to contribute to Oxygen's aggregate information collection, she is prevented from effectively using many of the site's interactive features. As Lessig points out, this sort of coding is frequently naturalized in discourse but is the product of deliberate, conscious choice. Cookies are constructed as a necessary characteristic, and as part of the site's quest to better serve users. While the user has the choice of rejecting cookies, this means remaining a community outsider. According to the rules on the terms page, users must agree and adhere to Oxygen's requirements to use the site, and according to the code built into the site, users must allow data collection to occur in order to access many of the site's features, especially the interactive tools that enable the communal nature of the site. Although these editorial and information-gathering requirements are not uncommon on commercial web sites, I argue that these rules are strange bedfellows with the community rhetoric that occupies the bulk of the site. Still, Oxygen is less aggressive than some sites—other community sites such as Women.com are more strident in their demands for personal information and member registration.

Women.com

Of the three sites discussed here, Women.com is most closely tied to the traditional women's magazine. Backed by a number of Hearst names such as *Cosmopolitan, Country Living,* and *Marie Claire,* Women.com was originally begun under the name of Women's Wire in 1992 (Garcia, October 13, 1999). Functioning as a community space as well as a link to online versions of paper-based publications, Women.com is perhaps more baldly predicated on the concept of women as consumers than is Oxygen. In a January 2000 *Time* article, Women.com CEO Marlene McDaniel articulated this, stating, "Women are coming online in droves, and they're going shopping," commenting on the statistical increase of women e-commerce customers (Krantz, January 31, 2000). Like Oxygen, Women.com attempts to efficiently arrange a variety of information for a wide range of mainly female users, and for Women.com, this strategy is tied directly to the prospect of women as a powerful commercial market.[2] In a feature in trade magazine *Brandweek,* Women.com is noted for its use of the "advertorial" model of content provision, blending sponsorship and marketing with writing (Mara, May 22, 2000).

This sponsorship is immediately apparent on Women.com's home page, which offers a sidebar listing special sponsor sections, including a "Women in Motion" feature backed by General Motors. The main links from this home page include stories of motherhood, cooking advice for Thanksgiving, information on aphrodisiac foods, and tips on business travel. Other sidebar offerings include links to a variety of traditional magazine sites, as well as a shopping feature, and other links to current department store sales. The daily poll asks, "Are your periods regular?" and the "Community" section of the home page asks users to explain when they begin their holiday decorating. Other message boards linked to the main page include parenting, diets, and fashion, chats with celebrities and experts, and clubs, which list investments as a potential interest. A minimal amount of business information is offered by this page, but the majority of Women.com's home page discourse revolves around very traditional, and in many cases biological, definitions of femininity, with a focus on decorating, cooking, reproduction, and sex. The main menu bar at the top of the page organizes these interests, listing Channels, drawing on a television metaphor, as well as links to Magazines and Sites, Shopping, Community, and an offer to "Join Women.com, Free!"

The "Community" page of Women.com features more links to magazine sites as well as a generic listing of chats, boards, bingo, and clubs. The top of the page asks, "First visit? Join FREE" and requests members to log in. Whereas the membership discourse on Oxygen is understated and mainly appears on chat and message board links, Women.com more aggressively cajoles users to register with the site. Users are encouraged to "Join others who share your interests and concerns. We welcome your participation and ideas. Visit us often" (Women.com, community standards, November 23, 2000). Featured community links from this page include holiday cooking disasters, office politics, single motherhood, and a "bragging area" for new mothers—again, the emphasis is on women as homemakers and parents. Reinforcing the pressure to join this community, there is a list of "members-only offers," which include a holiday quiz, free newsletters, and a retirement guidebook. Whereas Oxygen discursively plays down the issue of community membership as an exclusive privilege, Women.com consistently emphasizes the importance of joining, and not just surfing, the site. Steve Jones, in *CyberSociety 2.0*, discusses the significance of identity authentication on community sites, noting the fluid nature of cyberspace personae. On commercial sites based on advertising and sponsorships, unidentified users are not as valuable as identified users, and thus the fluidity referred to by Jones is being coded out (Jones, 1998, p. 28). Users must reveal information about themselves to receive the full benefits of these community sites, and often, if a user's information is found to be false or even "inappropriate," she is cut off from the community. This insistence on identification on Women.com relates to Lessig's concept of *traceability*, both in terms of membership files and through on-the-fly data collection, where the web site can trace users' interactions and movements constantly. The aspects of traceability and *trackability* are especially relevant to the status of Women.com and other commercial community sites as commercial services, which not only enable a user to interact with other users but also allow her to purchase goods online. Women.com and the other sites discussed in this chapter collect aggregate data on users' purchasing habits and tastes, in order to more efficiently serve users as consumers. Coding choices, such as the necessity of cookies and user identification, demonstrate the link between online community sites, implicit social controls, and the drive for online commercial enterprise.

Women.com's membership form lists a variety of reasons for users to join, such as promotions, sweepstakes, personalized tools, and members-only discounts, as well as interactive access to the community of Women.com through message boards and chat rooms. Users are required to give first and last names, gender, birthday, email addresses, and geographical location by zip code. In addition, Women.com suggests that users allow the site to get to "know you a bit better," by providing optional information, including home address, education level, marital status, and household income. After establishing a member name and pass-word, users may volunteer to be contacted about promotions from Women.com and "partners" of Women.com, and are auto-matically signed up to receive the site's newsletter. To finalize membership in Women.com's community, users must accept the membership agreement, which appears in a small scrolling box on the registration screen. Stating that "we've created these rules and guidelines to protect you and to ensure that becoming a member and participating in our community is fun and safe for everyone," the agreement contains several points concerning liability, content provision, privacy, and intellectual property (Women.com terms and conditions, November 23, 2000). Like Oxygen, Women.com has perpetual and sub-licensable rights to all content posted on its sites. Also like Oxygen, Women.com gives itself considerable latitude in editing content posted by users, ostensibly to address dangers of libel or spamming (the electronic equivalent of junk mail), but also in other cases. The third point of Women.com's membership agreement warns, "we may choose to remove some or all of your content at any time," and also reserves the right to terminate membership "if we are unable to verify or authenticate any information you provide to us" (Women.com terms and conditions, November 23, 2000). This insistence on identity authentication echoes Jones's observation—the principle of marketing requires that commercial community sites know who their users are, and this erodes the fluidity of identity that can exist in noncommercial milieus. Women.com is more concerned with this authentication than is Oxygen, but both reserve the right to edit the postings to these online communities, undercutting any possibility of an entirely free exchange of ideas. Both of these sites actively structure the possibilities of member's interaction, through rules, editing, and discursive agenda-setting—especially on Women.com, the traditional feminine roles of mother and homemaker are emphasized and highlighted as desirable topics of discussion for community members. Although users may choose which chat room to enter or which message board to access, the topics of interaction are already selected. Although Oxygen's scope seems wider than that of Women.com, there is considerable emphasis on media consumption, whereas Women.com frames its community along the lines of shopping and raising children.

Women.com further regulates users' behavior through a list of community standards, which are linked to the registration page. Some of the rules listed here are concerned with legal issues, such as appropriation of other sites' content or threats of violence to other users. Other rules, however, extend the policing power of the site over its community members beyond public law. Although the justification for these standards is stated in very inclusive terms, these rules are not established by community members; they are established by the site itself. The introduction to the "Community Standards" section suggests, "like any community, our community has certain rules of behavior that we all must adhere to as part of the community" (Women.com community standards, November 23, 2000). Those registering with the site are urged to select user names in good taste, lest Women.com should decide a name is "inappropriate," "vulgar," or misrepresents a user's true identity. The standards also prohibit a variety of content, from that which is racist, obscene, or defamatory, to that which is "disruptive," spamming, or disparaging of a company's goods or services. Like the standards set by Oxygen, some of these rules are hard to argue with, but others, including those prohibiting disparaging material, drive home the status of Women.com as a *commercial* community site, devoted to encouraging consumption. Also, the subjective nature of these rules makes the site the judge of all violations, and members must acknowledge the right of the site to cut them off at any time for any perceived transgression. Members of this community are subject to a wide variety of rules, and these limit the potential of open discourse and deliberation. This sanitizing, of course, is all in the interest of making the community safe, fun, and useful, according to the site's rationale.

Beyond providing a pleasant experience, however, Women.com, like many other commercial sites, is concerned with data collection. Although the registration form and the prohibition against providing unverifiable information support this mission, other mechanisms of information gathering are coded into the site via cookies and the tracking of Internet Protocol (IP) addresses. In its privacy policy, Women.com explains the use of data collection technologies in terms of enhancing the users' experience, as well as helping the site sell advertising. As on the Oxygen site, a user may disable cookies on her browser, but this will inhibit certain functions of the site, again presenting a trade-off of information for the benefits of community and site tools. Whereas much of the information collection is aggregated, the site also collects personal information, but stresses that this is on a voluntary basis, explaining that this information is necessary for membership registration or promotions. This repeats the trade-off situation of the cookies—users may withhold their personal information, but by doing so, they lose access to community benefits. Also, Women.com warns that users' personal information may be used in the investigation of complaints made by other users or third parties. The policy states that

> [I]n the unlikely event we need to investigate or resolve possible problems or inquiries, we can (and you authorize us to do so) disclose any information about you to private entities, law enforcement or other government officials as we, in our sole discretion, believe necessary or appropriate. (Women.com terms and conditions, November 23, 2000)

User information may be used to market the user to sponsors, to market directly to the user, or to investigate the user for a perceived infraction. This produces a combination of rules and code similar to that discussed in Lessig. Identity authentication and the sharing of personal information are phrased in terms of providing safety and convenience, but are enforced through a combination of explicit rules and implicit coding decisions. For a last example of this interweaving of rules, code, and community rhetoric, I will now turn to the iVillage.com site.

iVillage.com

Ivillage.com originated as a parenting site in 1996, appearing on America Online and on the Web. Candice Carpenter, former chief executive officer, and cofounder Nancy Evans started iVillage as "a baby-boomer site focused on parenting, health, and work," not intentionally targeting a female audience (Krantz, January 31, 2000). Carpenter and Evans began ParentSoup, which they referred to as a "channel," on AOL and iVillage in 1996; this attracted notice for its blend of editorial content, advertising, and commerce (Wylie, February 6, 1996). By fall 1998, iVillage had more than half a million members, most of them women, and in April 1999, iVillage experienced a very successful initial public offering, although its stock prices plummeted shortly afterward (Hickman, Levin, Rupley, & Willmott, October 20, 1998). In retrospect, the content provision company was criticized for expanding into e-commerce uncritically, without forethought (Evans, June 5, 2000). Despite the stock setback, iVillage was rated the most popular site for women over 18 in spring 2000, and nearly 4 million women have logged on to iVillage or Women.com per month, according to a Media Metrix study from the first half of 2000 (Sparta, June 5, 2000). America Online and NBC are major iVillage shareholders.

Media coverage of iVillage has emphasized it as a women's community site. In a *Forbes* article from May 2000, Carpenter comments on the importance of the Internet for female users, and the significance of iVillage for its target users, women aged 25 to 54. "We seek to get women all the way from a problem to the solution. That's why the Internet is so powerful for women. It allows each woman to find her own best life, and to have fun" (Lee, May 29, 2000). An article on Carpenter in the *New York Times* emphasizes the central place of community on this site. Referring to an earlier job as an outdoor instructor, Carpenter states,

A lot of my passion for community came from seeing these strangers come together, help transform one another, then part. I carried this idea forward to iVillage.com. It's the real issues that make it happen. Thousands of things in a person's life go right to the bone: your child has an illness, you hate your job, you have breast cancer. (Carpenter & Lawlor, November 3, 1999)

In these ways, iVillage has been framed as an empowering space that will facilitate women coming together. Rhetorically, this is similar to the discourse surrounding Oxygen and Women.com. Next I will examine the coding and discursive framing of community on the actual iVillage site.

Of the three web sites I examine in this chapter, iVillage is perhaps the most insistent about membership, and this is expressed through both coding and discourse. Like Women.com and Oxygen.com, iVillage urges users to join the site community: "When you join, you become a member of the entire iVillage network and receive great member benefits." A sidebar lists these benefits, which include a free email account, a web site, and access to a variety of "tools" and sweepstakes. These tools mentioned by iVillage range from a gift reminder service to a financial health evaluation to a pregnancy and first year of life calendar. The three-page membership form begins with basic questions, similar to those of Women.com, regarding member name and password, gender, first and last names, email address, birthday, country, and zip code. This information alone is enough to create a detailed profile. In addition, the user is asked to agree to abide by the site's terms of service. Significantly, all these forms must be filled out before the user can progress to the next page of the membership application. This coding forces a potential member to identify herself and agree to the iVillage terms of service before even viewing most of the membership application.

The second page of the form invites the new user to subscribe to a number of newsletters produced by iVillage, including parenting, jokes, dieting, beauty, astrology, and travel. Although these newsletters are billed as a benefit of membership, this form is another way of gathering information on user profiles and interests. The third page contains an "optional survey," which includes questions on whether or not the user is pregnant, whether or not the user already has children, and whether or not she shops online, and on potential interests. The user is requested to check the appropriate boxes if she is planning on losing weight, starting a family, buying a home, or having a wedding, among other things. This final survey is promoted as a service to the user. "Why are we asking these questions? The better we know you, the more we can tailor iVillage to meet your needs" (iVillage membership, November 23, 2000). At the same time, the site reassures the user about the harmlessness of this information-gathering, urging the user to consult the site's privacy policy: "Getting to know who you are and what interests you is core to our business, but we do NOT sell your personal information to third parties. That's not part of our business" (iVillage membership, November 23, 2000). Although the site repeatedly states that this information-gathering is for the convenience of its individual members, it also ensures the traceability and trackability of the user. To access many of the iVillage site features, the user must sign up with the site, providing her legal identity as well as detailed demographic information. Moreover, there is no option allowing the user to examine the membership form before applying; all spaces on each page must be filled out before the user may progress to the next part of the form. This characteristic may increase the user's initial investment in the site's community, encouraging adherence to pre-specified community standards and expectations.

In this way, the site can regulate members' behavior without overt shows of force, promoting members' self-surveillance instead. An iVillage community member, knowing that she has given up a range of personal information, will be more likely to observe the rules of the community, which are established not by other members but by the corporation that oversees the network. This Foucauldian confession of identity and habits can bind the user to the site's community, while promoting the appearance of entirely voluntary acceptance of and participation in community norms. By surrendering personal information, the user becomes part of the site's prefabricated community, but this decision to join is encouraged by the site's rhetoric and coding.

The terms of service begin with a broad justification that explains the need for a contract, while also urging members to report other users who are not properly observing these rules. The first paragraph of the contract states:

> By joining iVillage.com: The Women's Network, you're agreeing to abide by the Terms of Service below. We've created these rules and

guidelines to protect you and to ensure that iVillage is safe and fun for everybody. This way, should someone use bad language, make a harassing statement or otherwise make a pain of herself, we are able to do something about it. If you encounter another member who isn't abiding by these rules, please write to us. By agreeing to these terms, you're taking responsibility for your own actions. (iVillage terms and conditions, November 23, 2000)

The 16-point contract outlines a variety of restrictions and waivers. As on Women.com and Oxygen, community members waive intellectual property rights to any material posted. In addition, iVillage reserves the right to offer various third-party products and services according to the user's personal profile, and to suspend all services to the user if her registration information is found to be inaccurate. This further enforces the identification requirement while assisting iVillage in "better knowing" its user base. If the user posts content that iVillage determines is "inappropriate" for the community, iVillage may delete her content, terminate her membership, and report her to the legal authorities, as well as taking any other action that iVillage "deems to be appropriate." This ambiguous language, prohibiting "inappropriate" member names and content, leaves all discretion to iVillage. In another section, iVillage lists types of prohibited content, including "material that is unlawful, harassing, libelous, defamatory, abusive, threatening, harmful, vulgar, obscene, profane, sexually oriented, threatening, racially offensive, inaccurate, or otherwise objectionable material of any kind or nature" (iVillage terms and conditions, November 23, 2000). Again, while it is difficult to argue with some of these rules prohibiting racist or defamatory material, it is important to remember that the guidelines are imposed from above the "community," rather than from within it. Furthermore, the list of prohibited content is impressively broad, including anything having to do with sexuality, anything harmful, and finally, anything otherwise objectionable. This gives iVillage a great deal of latitude in governing content, and any infractions by users can lead to membership termination.

The trackability of iVillage users is detailed in the privacy section of the site, which notes that iVillage currently archives information it collects on its members and visitors. Information is collected via cookies, as well as by server log files and IP addresses, and is used to "make your visit to iVillage as relevant and as valuable to you as possible" (iVillage privacy, November 23,

2000). This information is also used to create aggregated portraits of the iVillage community, and although the user has the option of disabling the cookies, this makes many of the site's tools inaccessible. In addition, the user's personal profile is updated with survey answers and other information, so that personally identifiable information accumulates while the user interacts with the community. This individual information can be shared among the iVillage network, its affiliates, and its subsidiaries, all of which are interested in both the user's identity and her web surfing patterns on the site. Of these three sites, iVillage is perhaps the most overt in its intention to promote tailored marketing and encourage organized, traditionally feminine modes of consumption. Surveys and discussion groups may bond community members to one another, while serving the broader purpose of providing detailed marketing information.

Conclusions

In some ways, the sites discussed above could be viewed as merely transactional; users exchange personal information for access to particular web services. In the case of Oxygen, Women.com, and iVillage, those visiting the sites give up a certain amount of privacy in order to gain access to the chat and bulletin board infrastructure of the online community, as well as to contests, quizzes, and newsletters. These three sites, however, are making significant discursive moves. First, each firmly frames women in the traditionally feminine role of consumer and seeks to attract women users with the promise of community. Second, these sites are redefining the idea of online community. Whereas earlier works such as those of Howard Rheingold (1993) or Sherry Turkle (1995) discuss virtual community in terms of self-directed, consensus-driven social structures, these contemporary online communities are decidedly hierarchical, with a divide between those who run the communities and those who are members of the communities. These women's sites create a simulation of community—users are told that their interests matter, and are even polled about their opinions, but this is for the sake of marketing, not governance. The actual rules and penalties of the community are already decided, and any user on the site has automatically agreed to them. Is this the new form of online community? While Rheingold's and Turkle's analyses address the dynamics of specialized, often consensus-driven communities, these more recent women's portals demonstrate the naturalization of online community as marketing maneuver. In *CyberSociety 2.0*, Steve Jones reviews past interpretations of online community and emphasizes the malleability he sees in community and computer-mediated communication, arguing that "CMC allows us to customize our social contacts from fragmented communities and to plan, organize, and make efficient our social contacts" (Jones, 1998, p. 11). Although these sites do allow all these advantages, it is in exchange for member information and for the termination of users' access for perceived violations. The power of both coding and discourse on these sites makes online community less innocent than it originally appeared in the early 1990s. Will new formations of online community be sponsored and firmly controlled? How significant is it that women, a powerful marketing category, are the targets of these emerging mega-communities?

Although women may be marketing targets of these women-tailored portals, this angle of marketing has not continued to prove successful, at least in terms of the three sites examined. While iVillage debuted with an impressive initial public offering in the late 1990s, the company's stock value was dropping by 2000, following the downward trend of many online enterprises. Early in 2001, iVillage agreed to acquire the Women.com site for about $47 million in stock and cash (*Dow Jones News*, May 15, 2001). Although iVillage was in danger of being delisted on the Nasdaq Stock Market due to its drop in share price, the companies merged the following summer, causing substantial layoffs in both companies ("Net iVillage Workforce Cut in Half," June 23, 2001). Meanwhile Oxygen Media, parent of the Oxygen site, was described as "troubled" in the *New York Times*, due to both financial and regulatory problems (Schwartz, December 28, 2000). Oxygen has continued to support its web site with the help of funding from Paul Allen's Vulcan Ventures investment firm (Seward, December 5, 2000). Despite the fanfare surrounding the emerging online women's market in the late 1990s, revenue growth has been much slower than expected. Online advertisers have removed their support from many commercial community sites, and the relationship between online community and consumption is becoming questionable. While some women may be alienated by the sites' discourses of traditional femininity, other users may gladly join the sites' community networks without taking the next step of spending money on sponsors' products. So far, desire for community does not seem to produce willingness to consume. While users are still commercially useful to the portals as sources of marketing information, this may not be enough to hold the interest of the web sites' advertisers.

The ability of these communities to bring groups together cannot be entirely discounted. In his article, "Public Space, Urban Space, and Electronic Space," Mike Crang (2000) notes the way in which the Internet increasingly creates "perfectly simulated capitalism" through e-commerce and "dataveillance," and acknowledges the issue of closure of public space. At the same time, however, Crang points out that many of the classic spaces of public interaction were also commercial. Criticizing the invocation of an authentic, noncommercial public space, Crang suggests that commercial "public" areas still offer benefits. The users of Oxygen.com and the newly merged iVillage/Women.com sites may take advantage of these prefabricated community spaces, forming meaningful relationships with one another, while ignoring the call for site-supported consumption. At the same time, the users must reveal a certain amount of personal information and accept mechanisms of data storage like cookies in order to use these sites.

Many of these issues still come down to code. As long as these sites are discursively and literally coded for information gathering and monitored social contact, the sites will be shadows of community. Although it can be argued that the users of these online communities can access these sites with their eyes open, aware of privacy issues, other coded aspects of the sites make consciously made decisions appear natural and inevitable. An example of this is the cookie issue that is mentioned on each site—users are free to disable cookies, but this bars them from significant areas of the online community. The sites want to optimize information gathering, so cookie acceptance is strongly encouraged. This is more than a technical issue, it is a conscious decision. The discourse of community is likewise deliberate; by using rhetoric of empowerment and self-direction, these sites can attract women and encourage them to form predefined affinity groups, neatly packaged for marketers. As Lessig argues in *Code*, it is important to consider the deliberation that underlies coding decisions, in this case to discover alternatives to the current norm of popular online communities. Can a more democratic application of community coexist with commercial purposes, or can the bandwidth and design benefits to be had on large commercial sites come only with the trade-off of privacy and freedom of expression? Finally, do the recent challenges presented to these sites signal users' rejection of commercial, consumer-defined community?

Notes

1. Each of these sites was analyzed during the week of November 20, 2000. Although the three sites maintain a basic general structure of "channels" or categories of interests, specific content, such as featured health concerns or film reviews, changes frequently.

2. Although it is very likely that Oxygen.com's management also keeps women's strength as a market foremost in their thoughts, popular coverage of Women.com refers to this commercial aspect much more frequently.

References

Carpenter, C., & Lawlor, J. (November 3, 1999). A passion for community. *New York Times*. Retrieved April 18, 2000, from Lexis-Nexis Academic Universe database at: http://web.lexis-nexis/universe/.

Crang, M. (February 2000). Public space, urban space and electronic space: Would the real city please stand up? *Urban Studies, 37,* 2.

Dow Jones News. (May 15, 2001). IVillage, Women.com merger in trouble. *Newsday*. Retrieved August 30, 2001, from Lexis-Nexis Academic Universe database at: http://web.lexis-nexis/universe/.

Evans, B. (June 5, 2000). E-commerce: Reality bites. *InformationWeek*. Retrieved August 22, 2000, from Expanded Academic ASAP database at: http://web6.infotrac.galegroup.com.

Flynn, L. J. (August 14, 2000). Internet is more than just fun for women. *New York Times*. Retrieved August 22, 2000, from Lexis-Nexis Academic Universe database at: http://web.lexis-nexis/universe/.

Garcia, E. (October 13, 1999). Women online for a Wall Street debut. *New York Daily News*. Retrieved April 18, 2000, from Lexis-Nexis Academic Universe database at: http://web.lexis-nexis/universe/.

Hickman, A., Levin, C., Rupley, S. & Willmott, D. (October 20, 1998). Keyword: Women. *PC Magazine, 17,* 18. Retrieved August 18, 2000, from Expanded Academic ASAP database at: http://web6.infotrac.galegroup.com.

iVillage. (November 22, 2000). iVillage membership. Retrieved November 22, 2000 from http://www.ivillage.com.

iVillage. (November 22, 2000). iVillage privacy. Retrieved November 22, 2000 from http://www.ivillage.com.

iVillage. (November 22, 2000). iVillage terms and conditions. Retrieved November 22, 2000 from http://www.ivillage.com.

Jones, S. (1998). *CyberSociety 2.0 : Revisiting computer-mediated communication and community*. Thousand Oaks, CA: Sage.

Krantz, M. (January 31, 2000). What do wired women want? The great online makeover. *Time*, 155:4. Retrieved April 18, 2000, from Expanded Academic ASAP database at: http://web6.infotrac.galegroup.com.

Lee, S. (May 29, 2000). What do women want? *Forbes*. Retrieved August 22, 2000, from Expanded Academic ASAP database at: http://web6.infotrac.galegroup.com.

Lessig, L. (1999). *Code and other laws of cyberspace*. New York: Basic Books.

Mara, J. (May 22, 2000). The halo effect. *Brandweek*, 41:21. Retrieved August 22, 2000, from Expanded Academic ASAP database at: http://web6.infotrac.galegroup.com

Oxygen. (November 22, 2000). Oxygen privacy policy. Retrieved from http://www.oxygen.com.

Oxygen. (November 22, 2000). Oxygen terms and conditions. Retrieved from http://www.oxygen.com.

Piller, C. (May 30, 2000). Sites struggle as they connect women to Web. *Los Angeles Times*. Retrieved August 22, 2000, from Lexis-Nexis Academic Universe database at: http://web.lexis-nexis.universe/.

Rheingold, H. (1993). *The virtual community: Homesteading on the electronic frontier*. Reading, MA: Addison-Wesley.

Schwartz, J. (December 28, 2000). Oxygen.com to make changes. *New York Times*. Retrieved August 30, 2001, from Lexis-Nexis Academic Universe database at: http://web.lexis-nexis.universe/.

Seward, C. (December 5, 2000). Oxygen Media gets $100 million. *The Atlanta Constitution*. Retrieved August 30, 2001, from Lexis-Nexis Academic Universe database at: http://web.lexis-nexis.universe/.

Sparta, C. (June 5, 2000). Click time. *MediaWeek*, 10:23. Retrieved August 22, 2000, from Expanded Academic ASAP database at: http://web6.infotrac.galegroup.com

The ticker: Net iVillage workforce cut in half. (June 23, 2001). *New York Daily News*. Retrieved August 30, 2001, from Lexis-Nexis Academic Universe database at: http://web.lexis-nexis.universe/.

Turkle, S. (1995). *Life on the screen: Identity in the age of the Internet*. New York: Simon & Schuster.

Women.com. (November 23, 2000). community standards. Retrieved at http://www.women.com

Women.com. (November 23, 2000). Women.com terms and conditions. Retrieved at http://www.women.com

Wylie, M. (February 6, 1996). A fly in the parent soup? Upstart iVillage blends editorial, advertising, and shopping in a bold, risky recipe. *Digital Media*, 5, 9.

Part Three

Everyday Uses

"So I Got It Into My Head That I Should Set Up My Own Stable ... " Creating Virtual Stables on the Internet as Girls' Own Computer Culture

Virpi Oksman

> I believe that this virtual stables culture has brought girls to the Net and taught them skills in how to make home pages. Cause there's hundreds of them made by Finns alone, it's really amazing how many.
> —Girl, 16

Virtual stables are a fantasy game constructed by 10- to 15-year-old girls on the Internet. They make it possible for girls to ride, race, sell, buy, and take care of make-believe horses. It seems that the creation and maintenance of virtual stables and other personal content production has in a short space of time become a part of girls' own computer culture in Finland. Through studying the experiences girls have with virtual stables it is possible to broaden our perception of women's attitudes toward technology. In this chapter I will consider the opportunities for bringing out the voices of girls and young women in matters related to technology[1] and for supporting their positive engagement with new technologies through the case of virtual stables. The observations are mostly based on thematic interviews and surveys conducted as part of various projects looking into the interaction between people and new communication technologies.[2]

Contextualizing Gender in the Computer World

> I don't like computers. They control people's lives too much. The
> thought of being FORCED to learn the use of computers in the
> university makes my skin crawl. ... You're nothing these days if you
> don't know how to use the Internet and other cosmic programs. People
> value computers far too much. At times, they have raised them to the
> level of gods.

This quotation is an extract from a text written by a 19-year-
old female university student on the subject "Information Technology and Me." The student's technology aversion may be
exceptional in her age group, but the passage is also illustrative of
a phenomenon: Several empirical studies have shown that women
(perhaps also people in general) have a somewhat ambivalent
attitude to computers in their everyday lives. Computer aversion
(see for example Brosnan & Davidson, 1994), for instance, is a
phenomenon that has surfaced in a number of interviews, though
it has usually been mentioned in passing and the issue has not
necessarily become a central theme in the discussion. What is
surprising, however, is that fears of technology continue to
emerge in research at a time when the notion that young people
are all skilled and enthusiastic users of technological devices has
become prevalent in society. One should remember, however, that
girls and women by no means constitute a homogeneous group as
users of computers and the Internet.

It has been theorized that the Internet would be the
information technology application to narrow the gender gap in
use of technology. Several recent surveys indicate that Internet use
by men and women in Finland and in other Nordic countries is
almost equal in quantity (Aula, 1998; IBM, 1999; Nurmela, 2000).
Social and creative features of the Internet, such as using chat
rooms, emailing friends, and designing web pages, seem to appeal
to girls and women in particular. Interview studies also support
the idea that it is the interactive features of the Internet and
computers that are of particular interest to women and girls (see
Håpnes & Rasmussen, 2000).

While conducting interview-based research on the relationship
between people and new information technologies for various
projects, I have observed that a wide range of attitudes toward
technology are possible within a single generation. One interview

in particular was a turning point which opened my eyes to considering how young people experience technology in their daily lives. In the interview, two girls from Rovaniemi in the north of Finland related that they suffered from computerphobia and went to great lengths to avoid the use of computers. The computer anxiety experienced by these two girls, who at the time were attending upper secondary school, was surprising to me, as both surveys and the Finnish media tend to present a picture of young people with highly advanced computer skills and a positive attitude toward technology in general. I began to wonder whether there really could be young people who go through comprehensive school without acquiring basic skills in computer use. The interview also struck a familiar chord: it is not uncommon to hear women expressing similar views on how difficult and inconvenient computers are to use.

The creation of virtual stables can be seen as an opposite case for another minority of girls, who are averse to computers. What is relevant is girls' own fascination with the virtual world: interesting enough content can make technology seem manageable. In the case of virtual stables, it is particularly interesting to observe the phenomenon as part of girls' own computer culture and to study the culture as experienced by girls themselves: Does it constitute a new way of acquiring knowledge and skills, one that draws on girls' actual needs and experiences? Vehviläinen (2000) stresses the importance of women's starting points and women's knowledge in the process of analyzing gender as social and cultural relations (p. 23). It is important to look at young people's relationships to technology from the point of view of the consequences for the individual: If at the age of making occupational decisions (generally in her late teens) a girl is afflicted by computer anxiety, this may limit the options she considers for herself. Do girls who create virtual stables view their abilities and opportunities more broadly than girls have traditionally done? Or will they too continue to see technology as a "nerdy," odd and uninteresting world? As research accumulates, the picture of how women experience information technology in their lives becomes more complete. The general picture offered by survey data may be enhanced by empirical interviews and personal narratives. Qualitative research may provide a more detailed understanding of areas such as the quality of the experience and the characteristics of different computer cultures.

Games and Children's Relationship to Technology

Virtual stables as a computer-related interest of girls are exceptional in the sense that computers as recreation are very largely used by boys and men: many researchers have concluded that for both genders they constitute "boys' toys" (Cassell & Jenkins, 1999, p. 13) and "worlds without women" (Vehviläinen, 1997, p. 3). A major way to become familiar with computers is through computer games, the most popular of which frequently fall into categories such as action, adventure, or car racing. They have been produced with the interests of boys more than those of girls in mind, and, as such, invite masculine identification. Playing computer games is a convenient way to learn basic skills in the use of a computer: the use of a mouse, basic commands, hand-eye coordination, and basic problem-solving. Like toys, computer games played in early childhood are significant for the individual on another level: Through games and playing, children pick up skills that steer girls and boys toward their later roles in society. Furthermore, toys act as social mediators between the imaginary world of a child and the reality of adult life (Bloch & Lemish, 1999, p. 284). For the playing experience to be immersive, the player should become absorbed in the action and the narration of the game but in most cases also be able to identify with the characters of the game. In games, fantasy and identification enable children to feel stronger, more powerful, and more courageous than they could ever be in real life, and through games, children reach for higher levels of development:

> In play a child is always beyond his average stage, above his daily behavior, in play it is as though he were a head taller than himself. (Vygotsky, 1978, p. 102)

Numerous studies have revealed that the combination of violence and masculinity and the narrow and stereotypical ways in which women are represented in computer games position girls as spectators, which, according to Alloway and Gilbert, results in girls becoming nonplayers (1998, pp. 95–96). In computer games, women are usually represented as maidens in need of rescue or as passive brides for superheroes. Games targeted to girls are more difficult to find, and they tend to provide little in the way of challenges with the consequence that girls grow tired of them quickly (Cassell & Jenkins, 1999, pp. 8–9; Kangas, 2000, pp. 48–49; Sjöberg, 1999, pp. 19–20; Thomas & Walkerdine, 2000). Studies that have investigated children's playing of computer games through methods such as video-recording their playing have shown that girls were less enthusiastic about the games, they played for shorter periods of time, and their playing was less intensive (Thomas & Walkerdine, 2000). Results like these may raise the question: Are the games currently on the market really the most convenient way for girls to become acquainted with computers? Overall, there are fewer fun things to do with computers that girls feel suit their personalities than there are for boys. For example, the action narrative manages to hold the interest of boys and inspire their playing, whereas girls frequently find it boring.

Interviewer: What's a good computer game like?

Informant: Pretty gruesome.

Interviewer: (laughs) How do you mean gruesome?

Informant: Well, not terribly gruesome but pretty gruesome, you know.

Interviewer: So it has to have violence in it?

Informant: Yea.

Interviewer: Why does it have to have violence?

Informant: It's more fun that way. (Boy, 10)

Interviewer: What's great in a good game, is it colors or?

Informant: Colors and kicks and guns and things like that. (Boy, 8)

Interviewer: You don't care too much for games with shooting in them, do you?

Informant: It's always the same thing, you start to shoot them, you shoot them once, and then they die. (Girl, 9)

Interviewer: What type of games do you like then?

Informant: Well, I like games with horses and also other animals where you don't kill them, you just bounce on top of them and they disappear. (Girl, 12)

Parents are more likely to interfere with girls' playing than boys', and girls are often encouraged to engage in other activities and give priority to social interaction. An Australian study revealed the parents' fear that as a result of a too intensive involvement with computers girls might become alienated and put on weight (Thomas & Walkerdine, 2000). According to a Norwegian study, many 14- to 16-year-old girls avoid computer games, because they do not want to be identified as game-playing "asocial computer nerds" (Håpnes & Rasmussen, 2000, pp. 2, 18). Immersion in the world of the computer is not necessarily considered a form of social interaction suitable for girls. Girls themselves may worry that extensive playing may reduce their social networks. A Swedish study (Sjöberg, 1999, p. 80) reflected the notion that girls' norms about what is considered proper social behavior are stricter than or at least different from boys'. Girls prefer to spend time with friends rather than "waste" it on computers, and they believe that friends are more likely to lose their interest in someone who is constantly staring at a computer screen.

Girls and women usually learn technologies at school or at work or they are taught by others (Nurmela, 1997, p. 31). A study of young people's media culture concluded that boys as young as 10 to 15 years of age have faith in themselves as users of information technology, whereas girls do not (Saanilahti, 1999, p. 73). In the inquiry I carried out, gender differences were clearly visible in the acquisition of computer skills. The boys had usually started to use computers at an early age, generally under the age of 10, by playing computer games. Through the games, the boys had mastered basic computer skills, and by programming games themselves, they later picked up the basics of computer programming. In school-aged children, the boys' computer skills were far superior to girls'. The girls started to use computers at a later age than the boys, often somewhere between 13 and 18. The girls used computers mainly for things they considered "work": writing essays, doing homework, using email and doing information searches, whereas the boys used computers for both recreation and work. Through programming and playing computer games, some of the boys had familiarized themselves with the world of information technology at a young age:

> Well, basically, my first contact with a computer was when I was 6 years old. At the time I would just play the games but … I think at the age of 12 or 13 I started to use a computer more deeply in a way, and after that I never played anymore, I've just done programming and things like that ever since. (Mikko, 16)

In his answers Mikko created the impression of being an expert in his field: He has worked as an information technology professional since the age of 14. Mikko's case reflects the reality that through playing computer games many boys learn the use of computers and acquire basic skills in programming, thus achieving a general confidence in computer use. For the boys and young men interviewed, games and other computer-related activities did not necessarily constitute work. The following is a description by a 24-year-old male student of his relationship with computers:

> I use computers for playing, studying, and "work." As a user I'm a very conventional male interested in computers: I know all the keyboard shortcuts for the functions that I use, I fix the appearance of my personal desktop to suit me, and sit in front of the screen for too much of my life.

It should, however, be noted that a person's relationship to technology does not necessarily signify a static, unchanging attitude toward computers: The relationship may comprise several layers and it may be subject to change in different life stages. Johanna Uotinen has gathered stories informants have written on their experiences with computers (Uotinen, 2001b). In her study she describes the multilayered nature of people's relationships with computers and the changes that may occur in these relationships in the lifespan of a young person (Uotinen, 2001a). On the one hand, a person with a reluctant attitude toward anything to do with computers may evolve into a home page wizard or a computer game virtuoso, and on the other hand, a person once skilled in the coding of computer programs may temporarily lose interest in computers only to find out after a while that his or her skills are no longer valid.

A number of studies indicate that females use information technology mainly as a tool for work, whereas males use computers both for work and for entertainment. Girls find it more difficult to perceive the computer as something they could see themselves absorbed in learning about or as a device they would enjoy spending their time using.

> I have sometimes tried ... I try to copy something, for instance, and the computer always starts going on and on about the same thing. Then I lose patience completely, I get this "I don't need this anymore," I just want to throw the thing out the window. I always get a "bad command or file name" or whatever, and I think not again! In the end it's just a machine and it's stupid! (laughing). (Girl, 16)

A rapid technologization of everyday life has taken place in Finland in the latter half of the 1990s, resulting in a number of equally rapid generational changes. Children are growing up in a technological environment that is markedly different from that of earlier generations. The new technologies have existed for as long as today's children and teenagers can remember, and thus do not constitute new media for them, as stated by Kirsten Drotner (2000, p. 167), who has conducted research on Danish teenagers. Yet, many girls still have an ambivalent attitude to computers and their own skills in using them. Interviewed in 2000, a 17-year-old girl attending upper secondary school said she had used the Internet since the age of 15, mostly to look for information on her hobby, live role playing. Despite her daily use she expressed a somewhat negative attitude to the Internet:

> I personally am not that interested in using the Internet. I just use it when I have to. ... I have this certain type of technophobia. There was a

chapter in our English book about it. The way it fit me was really interesting. I'm not ... it's just not interesting to me at all. If I need it for something, the computer, I will learn to use it just enough to get the benefit and that's all. But I have no inclination to create any stuff of my own in there.

Regardless of many years of use experience, some girls may continue to have reservations about computers, especially if they have no particular field of interest that would motivate them to use computers. Though new technology has for some years been part of the everyday life of teenagers, this has not always been unproblematic. One wonders if the generation of girls now between the ages of 10 and 15 will become the first with an unprejudiced enough attitude to technology for them to begin to independently learn the use of various technologies and to develop their own innovations.

Virtual Stables, Virtual Fun

Figure 8.1 A virtual stable. Used with permission of the creator.

In February 2000 my email friends told me about virtual stables. I spent a lot of time in other people's stables and took care of other people's horses to see if I was up to it. That went well so I bought a couple of horses. That seemed easy enough, so for some reason I got it into my head that I should set up my own stable. (Girl, 13)

Girls' computer activities, ranging from virtual horse stables or kennels to diaries, may be considered a new type of skill or knowledge that originates from girls' own interests. Numerous virtual stables set up by girls have sprung up on the Internet. Virtual stables reflect a spectrum of girls' computer culture: In addition to stables in active use, the Internet houses many stables that have been destroyed or that have ended their operations for other reasons, announcing their current status in a laconic tone: "The stud-farm is closed down. All the horses are up for sale."

Virtual stables are a good example of how, once they find an inspiring enough option, girls adopt an experimental and unprejudiced attitude to information technology and learn to use the newest applications by trial and error, having accepted the impossibility of instant perfection. Virtual stables and kennels can be seen to function as role-playing games of a sort, as people use them to simulate, produce, and practice reality. Virtual role-playing games offer experiences of freedom and fantasy but, like other games, they can also serve as places of learning—of acquiring new knowledge and skills and getting prepared for future roles in society. Rosa, aged 13, keeps a virtual stable and has the following to say about her hobby:

I made my first pages on Sunpoint [a Finnish Internet portal] and they were published on Valentine's Day February 14, 2000. To be perfectly honest, they were absolutely LOUSY. Then I discovered GeoCities, which I learned to use all by myself. And my ventures have proved fruitful: When you try all sorts of stuff, you find all sorts of stuff!

According to a Norwegian study, the Internet as an information technology is well suited to the maintenance of girls' culture generally and to girls' individual identity work. The girls in the study were fascinated by the fact that technology could be used for communication via the Internet. Through the Internet, technology enabled them to interact with people living in different places and communicating in different languages (Håpnes & Rasmussen, 2000). For girls, interaction, creativity, and the making of new acquaintances seem to be the most powerful sources of inspiration for the use of new technology: This is evident in the case of virtual stables.

> In real life, I only know three people who are into this virtual horse thing. You make friends easily here. I've met one of my best friends through the Internet: She takes care of one of my horses. ... We've met each other as well, even though we live on two opposite sides of the country!

Virtual horses have become a hobby in which girls immerse themselves. It can even be said that "virtual worlds offer experiences that are hard to come by in real life" (Turkle, 1995, p. 192). Girls become deeply involved in the simulated worlds of the game, as if they were dealing with real animals, looking after them and riding them. In the virtual worlds of girls, the competition revolves around nurturing, though bullying and mischief are just as much a part of the girls' world as they are of the boys' world. Girls' bullying may, for instance, take the form of publicizing the names of bad caretakers.

> I usually spend about two to four hours a day on my stables. I don't update it just every day, but I do it at least two or three times a week. Sometimes we gather to ride, take care of the horses, or just to talk in chat rooms. That takes a little longer. But anyway, I have this most adorable virtual Finnish gelding that I take care of on Mondays, Wednesdays, and weekends. His owner says I'm the best person she's had to look after him ever.

Studies suggest that girls are often more interested in finding out what they can accomplish with information technology and whom they can contact with it, whereas boys may find the devices and technologies fascinating in themselves. The visual side and the appearance of the software and the computer itself are often more important for girls than they are for boys.

The girls who keep virtual stables and their active stable hands break with the tradition that women learn to use information technology through others, as is the case in school and in various courses (Nurmela, 1997, p. 31). The girls often learn to make home pages together and share their knowledge over the Internet.

> About the text at the beginning of the stables. ... You had typed "Index" at the end of the "In the Stable" section. You don't need it, you don't

> need to type anything there, that's if you've saved your front page as Index. You don't even need to put in .html. If you don't get it, sorry I can't explain it any better ... =((message in the guestbook of a virtual stable)

Virtual stables reinforce the idea that women are generally interested in producing personal content: Girls use the Internet to publish their own poems, short stories, recipes, drawings, diaries, friends' statements under the heading "My Friends' Opinion of Me," photos of pets, themselves, and their friends, and introductions to their own pop and rock bands. In this sense, the Internet seems to be a democratic and interactive medium, through which one can gain publicity for one's own products of the mind more effectively than in mainstream media. The 14-year-old Emma has constructed a home site that has gradually evolved from its original two pages into an increasingly complicated structure. Emma has a busy virtual life: She has dozens of friends whom she meets in chats. The acquaintances often proceed gradually from chatting to visiting each other's home pages to exchanging mobile phone numbers and active text messaging; Sometimes they even meet in person. The creativity and interaction involved in building a home on the Web inspire Emma to go on building her home site:

> I keep adding new stuff in there. I just made some fun questions, it's nice to read all the different answers you get. You get answers from complete strangers. I ask something like, "What do people use fluffy toys for?" and they answer with their own imagination.

One of the most popular ways of using the Internet for producing personal content among women is virtual diaries, where people publish their experiences and ideas about life for public readership. A 25-year-old student of literature has kept a diary on the Internet since 1995 and does not seem to find programming problematic:

> That's my way of spending my free time. Others knit sweaters, I code html: two plain, two purl.[3]

> A diary on the Internet is an intersection of my private and public life. I write what I want to remember of myself, not everything, not always

being truthful. Agrippa is real like dreams and memories are real: It is selected, edited, molded. (from Agrippa, a virtual diary)

Somehow the fact that one is dealing with a technological medium of communication is pushed to the background here, with the more interesting things stealing the spotlight. Technology ceases to be the first priority, though its presence is still felt: "Coding" and "learning by oneself" remain activities worth mentioning.

Reality Strikes Back

Though the virtual world affords possibilities for fantasy, trying out different roles and experimenting with identity, the young horse enthusiasts were soon to discover that the rules and regulations of the "real world" were also present in the virtual universe. One central question of theirs concerned the lifespan of virtual horses: How do they live and age and how soon does a newborn foal develop into a horse people can ride? The girls were not willing to go along with real-life limitations that do not allow for riding until the horse is three years old. Thus they felt it necessary to agree on a set of rules. This was the beginning of the Virtual Stables Union, the Virtual Horse Riders Union, and the Virtual Breeders Union. The solution was that all horses and all stables were to be registered. Making up horses yourself was no longer allowed: Horses were to be born in stud-farms operating under supervision. The unions agreed on rules according to which all foals would age one year in one month. Within these rules and the time they have available, girls can participate in raising virtual foals and training them as riding horses. In Rosa's opinion, however, rules like these place too many limitations on virtual fantasies:

I no longer want to be a part of the Virtual Stables Union. I really don't see why you shouldn't make up horses in the virtual world?! Sounds crazy to me. I'm sure this way virtual horses would soon become extinct!

Another set of regulations that prompted some discussion among the girls concerned copyright. A 16-year-old Icelandic horse enthusiast named Anna maintains horse pages, where she publishes her own articles and translations. For a small fee, she also makes home pages for an Icelandic horse stable. When Anna's family purchased a computer, Anna's father, who "knows virtually everything there is to know about computers," taught her how to use it. Later Anna, too, was able to advise her father, in areas that she was better acquainted with. Anna had long been saving money to rent a real horse with a friend. She is also interested in photography and publishes on her web pages photos she has taken of the real-life stables where she goes riding regularly. Anna was shocked to find that a girl a few years younger than her had copied a picture and invented character traits for the horse:

> It's not all that nice to see a picture of your horse as some virtual hack with a text underneath saying it's vicious. You get a little emotional with stuff like that, but when you think of it it's also taught me a lot about copyright.

Anna began a campaign to get back her pictures and now publishes copyright rules on her page. In addition, photos taken by Anna usually carry her signature. In this way, many younger girls have become acquainted with the basics of copyright.

The girls were hit by a third aspect of reality when it appeared that the virtual world was no more sunny or benevolent than the real world. Hacking is as common in the girls' virtual world as it is in areas dominated by men: Girls sometimes sabotage each others' virtual stables.

> It's a cruel world and the same goes for the virtual one. There are some really nasty people out there who guess stables' passwords and destroy pages. That's really obnoxious!

Anonymity in the Internet also allows bullying of many other kinds, as in the case of virtual violence. It is difficult to punish the anonymous offender in any way and it is nearly impossible to keep any Internet community entirely closed from outsiders (Zickmund, 1997, p. 204). Rosa has had a particularly unpleasant encounter with virtual harassment:

Once I thought I had got a devoted caretaker for a pony of mine. The first care history was perfectly alright. The second one was an utter shock. ... Though the pony was all muddy, the person had just saddled him, bridled him, and taken him out! The caretaker had then galloped up a steep hill tormenting the pony within an inch of his life. In the end the pony had collapsed. The person had then got a gun and shot the pony in the forehead, and the pony had died instantly. The message ended with laughter: HAHAHAHAHAHAHAH. ... People like that just shouldn't exist!

One may, of course, consider whether there is anything peculiar in girls looking after virtual animals and becoming attached to them. Are they unable to determine the difference between the virtual world and the real world and its creatures? My view is that the girls are indeed still able to differentiate between reality and the virtual world, but emotionally, an attack on one's own "creation" feels almost the same as violence against a real pet. Above all, girls playing make-believe in the virtual world are in a sense prolonging their childhood, a period of life which in contemporary society has been cut short.

Innovative Games?

Girls in their teens are occupied with make up, boys, horses etc. We do not consider these interests as potential building blocks for an innovative and emancipatory computer game for girls. (Bratteteig & Verne, 2000, p. 48)

According to some critics, games designed for girls have suffered from an undue emphasis on "girlhood" in the narrow sense of the word. Games directed to girls have thus for one reason or another failed to attract their target group. Yet virtual stables originate from girls' own initiative and through interests particular to them—they are not produced by the computer gaming industry or established media institutions. Virtual stables can thus, in the words of Fornäs, be called mesomedia, which he defines as "niched products circulated locally or within alternative public spheres, with a less sharp separation of producers and consumers" (1998, pp. 27–38). Virtual horses along with other virtual pets such as tamagotchis (Bloch & Lemish, p. 1999), being created as part of computerized games, afford privilege to traditionally male technological skills. However, their content world is about nurturing, raising, and prolonging life rather than killing (p. 296). It seems undeniable that girls' virtual stables constitute innovative computer games of a kind, as they have been constructed with creativity, invention, and imagination. They are also emancipatory in that they have persuaded girls to disregard their traditional limitations, to invent new forms of interaction, to learn, try out, and do new things, to find solutions, to teach each other, to get excited and frustrated, and often to forget that they are dealing with technology. It is through interesting activities that people lose their reservations about technology.

> Interviewer: Any chance of you choosing a technological field of study when the time comes?
>
> Anna: I've thought about that too. I've not eliminated any possibilities, I have opportunities for anything, really. I'm not going to close any doors at this stage.

With young people, the question "Why shouldn't the use of computers simply be fun if it is the easiest way to learn the skills and to 'seize control of technology'?" appears central. Bearing this question in mind, it seems difficult to maintain that girls do not need games or other "useless" computer time, as boys do, because girls use computers primarily for rational, pedagogical purposes (Bratteteig & Verne, 2000, p. 47). Approaching the subject with a predetermined definition of what kinds of use and interests are or are not innovative or emancipatory, with little knowledge or understanding of the actual everyday life and experiences of young people, also seems unhelpful.

Future research will determine the significance of virtual stables and other personal content production in computer culture. Will these independent activities change girls' attitudes to technology in the long run? Will independent content production, of which the virtual stables are one example, become a permanent part of girls' own computer culture? As computer culture continues to develop, those applications that allow for self-expression originating from teens' own interests, and thus provide the best possible means for learning computer literacies, will hold a key position.

Notes

1. In this chapter, I use the word "technology" to refer to computers, the Internet, and other comparable information technologies.

2. The interviews are from the following projects: (1) Second Generation Mobile Media and Newspapers: An Audience Study, 1998. Fifty thematic interviews were conducted during the research period. (2) Mobile Communication Culture of Finnish Children and Teenagers, 1997 to 2001. A total of 850 interviews were conducted by the research group in both urban and rural areas. The children and teens interviewed were between the ages of 5 and 18. The family backgrounds of the informants were socioeconomically heterogeneous. Aside from the interviews, various types of qualitative material were collected: observation of youth events, photographs, media diaries, picture collages by teens, text message material, and children's drawings of their dream mobiles. (3) The Media Culture Research Programme of the Academy of Finland, 1999 to 2000. In my project 20 thematic interviews were conducted and an inquiry involving 30 students aged 19 to 25 was carried out. In 1999, 129 written experience stories on information and communication technologies were collected by Johanna Uotinen.

3. An interview in *Helsingin Sanomat*, April 23, 2001.

References

Books, articles, etc.

Alloway, Nola, & Gilbert, Pam. (1998). Video Game Culture: Playing With Masculinity, Violence and Pleasure. In Howard, Sue (ed.), *Wired Up: Young People and the Electronic Media* (pp. 95–114). Bloomington: Indiana University Press.

Aula, Pekka. (1998). *Universities and the Internet. An inquiry into the use of the Internet in nine universities* (in Finnish). www.helsinki.fi/lehdet/yolehti/verkkotutkimus/html.

Bloch, Linda-Renée, & Lemish, Dafna. (1999). Disposable Love. The Rise and Fall of a Virtual Pet. *New Media & Society, 1*(3), 283–303.

Bratteteig, Tone & Verne, Guri. (2000). Feminist, or Merely Critical? In Search of Gender Perspectives in Informatics. In Mörtberg, Christina (ed.), *Where Do We Go From Here? Feminist Challenges of Information Technology* (pp. 39–56). Luleå, Sweden: Luleå University Printing Office.

Brosnan, Mark J., & Davidson, Marilyn J. (1994). Computerphobia—Is it a Particularly Female Phenomenon? *The Psychologist, 2*(7), 73–78.

Cassell, Justine, & Jenkins, Henry. (1999). Chess for Girls? Feminism and Computer Games. In Cassell & Jenkins (eds.), *From Barbie to Mortal Kombat. Gender and Computer Games* (pp. 2–45). Cambridge: MIT Press.

Drotner, Kirsten. (2000). Difference and Diversity: Trends in Young Danes' Media Uses, *Media, Culture & Society, 22*, 149–166.

Fornäs, Johan. (1998). Digital Borderlands: Identity and Interactivity in Culture, Media and Communications. *Nordicom Review, 19*(1), 27–38.

Håpnes, Tove, & Rasmussen, Bente. (2000). Young Girls on the Internet. In Balka, E. & Smith, R. (eds.) *Women, Work and Computerization. Charting a Course to the Future* (pp. 233–240). Boston: Kluwer.

IBM. (1999). The Digital Class Difference—Does It Exist? PC and Internet Habits in the Age Group 16–24 Years in Scandinavia. Norsk Gallup Institutt.

Kangas, Sonja. (2000). *Girls as the Focus Group of Electronic Games: The Science of Design Method in the Production of Computer Games for Girls* (in Finnish). Master's Thesis, Faculty of Arts, University of Lapland.

Nurmela, Juha. (1997). *The Finns and Modern Information Technology.* Report no. 1 of the project entitled "The Finns and the Future Information Society." Helsinki: Statistics Finland.

Saanilahti, Marja. (1999). *The Changing Media Culture of Children and Teenagers* (in Finnish). Tampere, Finland: Tampere University Press, Department of Journalism and Mass Communication, Series B 42/1999.

Sjöberg, Ulrika. (1999). *In the World of Computer Games. A Study on How Children Use and Experience Computer Games* (in Swedish). Lund: Lund University, Media and Communication Studies, Working Paper no. 3.

Thomas, Angela, & Walkerdine, Valerie. (2000). *Girls and Computer Games.* Paper presented at Fourth European Feminist Conference in Bologna, Italy.

Turkle, Sherry. (1995). *Life on the Screen.* New York: Simon & Schuster.

Uotinen, Johanna. (2001a). The Cybercafé at the Community Resources Center in Joensuu. Participation in the Information Society (in Finnish). In Uotinen, Johanna, Tuuva, Sari, Vehviläinen, Marja, & Knuuttila, Seppo (eds.), *Experiencing networks. Constructing a Local Information Society* (pp. 109–144). Saarijärvi, Finland: Gummerus.

Uotinen, Johanna. (2001b). They Delivered It to Our Bedroom Table on Finnish Language Day. Experience stories on ICTs. (in Finnish) Paper presented at the seminar on Societal and Cultural Research on Technology, Tampere, Finland, 2001.

Vehviläinen, Marja. (1997). *Gender, Expertise and Information Technology.* Tampere, Finland: University of Tampere, Department of Computer Science.

Vehviläinen, Marja. (2000). Understandings of Gender and Information Technology. In Mörtberg, Christina (ed.), *Where Do We Go From Here? Feminist Challenges of Information Technology* (pp. 17–37). Luleå, Sweden: Luleå University Printing

Vygotsky, L. S. (1978). *Mind in Society: The Development of Higher Psychological Processes.* Cambridge: Harvard University Press.

Zickmund, Susan. (1997). Approaching the Radical Other: The Discursive Culture of Cyberhate. In Jones, Steven, G. (ed.), *Virtual Culture. Identity & Commun-ication in Cybersociety* (pp. 185–205). London: Sage.

Other materials

Agrippa, a virtual diary. http://www.uta.fi/~ke54877/index

Panu Räty: Private Affairs for Millions to Read (2001). (in Finnish) *Helsingin Sanomat* (newspaper). April 22.

Virtual stables

A virtual pony stable: http://www.vrl.itsme.fi/miniature/

A destroyed virtual stable: http://www.geocities.com/tulihevosentalli/

A stud-farm that has closed down: http://www.comlumbus.fi/rocky.mountain/

A list of links with dozens of virtual stables: http://www.ultimate topsites.com/coolsites/jenni/links

Chapter 9

Women Veterans and the Net: Using Internet Technology to Network and Reconnect

Jennifer M. Tiernan

On the evening of September 15, 2000, five women gathered in a motel room in Kokomo, Indiana. The opening ceremonies of the Howard County Vietnam Veterans Reunion were scheduled for the following morning. The reunion, held each year in September, attracts thousands of veterans to a campground in a cornfield outside of town. Ann, Pat, Emily, Joan, and Marilyn had gathered to reconnect and to view each other's Vietnam slides. They took turns showing and describing their slides. One slide, an image of a woman in Army Special Services serving refreshments to soldiers, caught Emily's eye. "Go back two slides. You're serving Kool-Aid off of the Agent Orange barrel."[1] The women in the room, several of whom suspect their bouts with cancer are linked to exposure to the defoliant, broke into nervous laughter. Many such moments of shared remembrance are experienced over the course of the weekend together. Although it's a rare occurrence for these women to be together in person, they know each other well from shared Vietnam experiences facilitated by their participation in a listserv, InCountry Women (ICW). Online and in person, these women provide each other with a strong and supportive community.

The following morning in the cornfield, surrounded by thousands of male Vietnam veterans, these same women, who acted as a close-knit support group for each other the previous night, revert to their Vietnam roles from decades earlier. Emily, dressed in a Donut Dolly t-shirt, becomes a symbolic representative of the role she played during the war. Male veterans approach her for hugs and to thank her, not as *their* Donut Dolly, but as *a* Donut Dolly. These men just want to thank someone for the support they received, even if they can't ever thank the particular individual who brought them comfort.

The interactions in the motel room the night before were highly personal and supportive, and focused on the women's own experiences, represented by the photographs and the process of remembering. In contrast, the interactions between the women and the male veterans at the reunion are much more impersonal and casual. In the motel room and on their listserv, the women are part of a highly supportive interpretive community. In the cornfield, these same women revert to roles they played decades ago in Vietnam. Among other women, whether in person or online, they are women veterans with a set of shared experiences and common worldviews that link them together in an interpretive community. In the larger, male Vietnam veteran community, they are auxiliaries, anonymous symbols of the roles women played in Vietnam.

An estimated 10,000 American women served in the Vietnam War, yet their experiences and stories are neither well known nor adequately documented.[2] Women served in Vietnam in a variety of capacities and not all are officially considered veterans by the United States Government. As veterans Joan Arrington Craigwell and Ellen Hoffman Young note (1998), it is only recently that veteran organizations have decided to "permit women full membership, thus adding further invalidation and stigma for being a woman and serving in a combat zone" (p. 42). Women served in official military positions (as nurses, translators, administrative assistants, stenographers, typists, first sergeants, WAC commanders, and in intelligence); in Army Special Services in administrative positions, for example, librarians and recreation center/service club facilitators; as journalists and war correspondents; as civilian nurses and humanitarian workers; with the Red Cross; as entertainers and with the USO (United Service

Organization); as weather girls for AFVN television; in Operation Baby Lift; and with USAID (US Agency for International Development). The Vietnam Veterans Memorial in Washington, DC, lists the names of 6 women soldiers killed in the war. An estimated 70 military and civilian women were killed.[3] None of the civilian women receive official recognition or veterans' benefits from the United States Government.

Women veterans received a different type of recognition from the American public than male veterans. Male veterans were recognized as legitimate participants in the Vietnam War, and although some of that recognition was negative, they were not ignored. Many Americans had no idea that women participated, or they failed to discuss or understand women's experiences. Many women veterans faced double standards when they returned; people expected women to interject themselves right back into the lives they led before Vietnam without counseling, or understanding, or even recognition of how they had grown and changed during the war. There were few veteran services available for these women and many did not feel comfortable in the larger male Vietnam veteran community because of the lack of support and understanding.

For those unrecognized women veterans of Vietnam who have been isolated and marginalized for decades, the Internet provides a means for the creation of a supportive community, separate from the recognized male veteran community and focused specifically on the needs of women. "Women served alongside men in that sink-pit of war," Joan Arrington Craigwell and Ellen Hoffman Young (1998) wrote. "For the country to heal, these women need to reveal the full depth of their experiences, first to themselves and then to the rest of us. It's time for women's experiences and contributions to be recognized and acknowledged as an important part of the history of the Vietnam conflict" (p. 43). The present chapter suggests that the Internet provides the unrecognized women veterans of Vietnam with a means to build and maintain their own virtual interpretive community. In this safe space, mostly freed from their auxiliary roles in the larger veteran community, women are free to remember, support, befriend, and come to terms with Vietnam. This case study has implications for other studies of how other marginalized groups use the Internet and computer mediated communication (CMC) to create and maintain virtual interpretive communities. There is great potential for the Internet to provide "safe" spaces where those who may be marginalized in a society can communicate and connect without the burdens or restrictions imposed in their physical community.

Virtual Community and Computer Mediated Communication

A necessary starting point for any discussion of computer mediated communication and online communities is Howard Rheingold's (1993) definition of virtual communities, as "social aggregations that emerge from the Net when enough people carry on those public discussions long enough, with sufficient human feeling, to form webs of personal relationships in cyberspace" (p. 5). Some argue that virtual communities are not truly communities. Virtual communities have neither geographical boundaries nor complex social and environmental structures. They are not, by traditional definitions, "places" occupied by "people." How then, do we begin to think about "communities" on the Internet? What are the important questions to ask? Does something change in the definition when the online group is severely marginalized?

The notion of "community" brings up a variety of definitions, from the classical idea of a geographic "community" to Benedict Anderson's (1991, p. 25) "imagined community" of a nation-state united in a single national consciousness by media, to the idea of communities of meaning, or interpretive communities (Zelizer, 1997). Several scholars who study virtual communities acknowledge the dilemma of defining a non-geographically bounded group as a community (Baym, 1998; Foster, 1997; Jones, 1998; Rheingold, 1993; Stoll, 1995; Wellman & Gulia, 1999). They suggest that a good way to address this issue is to examine and analyze how members of virtual communities create and maintain relationships, build bonds that transform traditional community definitions, and define communities in terms of social networks rather than physical spaces (Wellman & Gulia, 1999).

In addition, ideas concerning gender and the Internet are important to this discussion. A small but growing literature addresses women and the Internet. While some texts serve as how-to guides, others concentrate on issues of access, feminism, uses, and implications for women and emerging technology. Internet communities can be important spaces where women feel supported and effect change. Sadie Plant (1996) argues that "Complex systems and virtual worlds are not only important because they open spaces for existing women within an already existing culture, but also because of the extent to which they undermine both the world-view and the material reality of two thousand years of patriarchal control" (p. 170). There are powerful implications for virtual communities of women and other marginalized groups. Often, members of these types of virtual communities might not have otherwise come into contact with each other, so there exists great potential for beneficial interaction or progress. With the Internet comes the possibility of bringing together people from different geographical backgrounds and cultures who might not have otherwise been able to communicate with each other. The Internet provides women with a space to express themselves, to share knowledge, and to claim a voice.

Gillian Youngs (1999) raises issues about the significance of online communication, Internet "space," and women, which are important to this discussion. Many women who participate in online communities are involved in consciousness-raising efforts and it is crucial for these efforts that they are able to communicate with other women in a safe space. The Internet provides a communication medium that allows some women, who might otherwise be silenced by structures of patriarchy and society, or disconnected by geography, to contact each other and communicate in a "safe" space. Youngs believes "the notion of 'safe' environments in which women can meet and communicate has been fundamental to the transition of feminist theory into practice through, for example, consciousness-raising" (p. 63). Women who participate in online communication with other women use the Internet as a "safe" space in which to build supportive virtual communities.

A Virtual and Interpretive Community

The technology defines the community of women veterans as "virtual," but a more useful way to describe and analyze this group is in terms of an interpretive community. An interpretive community, again, is not geographically bounded, but its members are bound together in other important ways. Women Vietnam veterans are bound in an interpretive community because they share a common use of the past, a common application and understanding of the present, and, moving beyond the literature of interpretive community, an assumption of a shared future (Zelizer, 1997). Their common belief in the importance and meaning-making power of their discourse of an event or part of a common history binds them together in an interpretive community.

The notion of interpretive community has been applied, for example, to journalism by Barbie Zelizer (1997) as an alternative to the use of theories of professionalism to characterize newswork. Interpretive communities have been described by scholars of anthropology, folklore, and literary studies. Various definitions of interpretive community emphasize shared understandings of reality, the production and interpretation of "texts" by members of a group, and the establishment of "communities of memory" (Zelizer, 1997, p. 405).

Here we might consider women Vietnam veterans who interact together online as an interpretive community sharing the experience of the Vietnam War, being women in Vietnam, and the lingering after-effects of their war experience. The Vietnam War is the primary "text" that unites women veterans as an interpretive community. And through their discourse, they collaborate in the creation of boundaries around their shared understandings and meanings of the war. In their interpretive community, they share the war as a common use, or "text," of the past. The ICW discussion group and the Women in Vietnam web site are important elements of this "text."

Women Vietnam veterans share common applications and understandings of the present because their past was shaped by Vietnam. Many women altered their political views after returning from Vietnam. For instance, some claim that although they were very supportive of the war and the political administration at the time, they no longer feel the United States should have been involved in Vietnam, and certainly not to the extent to which it was involved.

Changing political views are just one way veterans are

attempting to fit the Vietnam experience into their present lives. Ann Kelsey, an Army Special Services librarian in Vietnam, literally incorporates Vietnam into her present. She has made four trips back to Vietnam in the last 10 years, most recently in June 2001. She maintains a connection with her Vietnam experience by helping administer the ICW discussion group and by conducting her own Vietnam-related research. Emily Strange, a Red Cross "Donut Dolly" in Vietnam, maintains Vietnam in her present by writing poetry and songs about her experiences. She shares these artistic products with the "community" by posting poems, lyrics, and Vietnam snapshots on the Web.

Online, women are able to carve out isolated and safe "spaces" for their discussions and experiences, thus creating and maintaining their interpretive community. Their virtual spaces include chat rooms, email discussion groups, resources related to the Vietnam War, virtual guestbooks, and spaces for veterans looking for buddies and long-lost friends. Veterans share their "texts" and artifacts online. Web pages include photographs, poetry, fiction, opinion, music, and memories. And all these "texts" contribute to a collective identity with which women veterans can share and relate to.

Finally, women Vietnam veterans have an assumption of a shared future that is evident in their lives and reflected in their online community. They understand themselves as a Vietnam veteran community, and they are protective of and determined to ensure that their experiences will be preserved and remembered. This sense of legacy also drives the durational discourse of the online community. The experience of participating in a war, participating as women, creating memories, gathering souvenirs and artifacts, and contextualizing the Vietnam War into their everyday lives create a collective assumption of the future for the interpretive community of women Vietnam veterans. It is their "texts" that bind women veterans together through experience of a shared past, present, and future that is rooted in war experience, artifacts, and memories.

Why Do Women Veterans Use the Internet?

Women Vietnam veterans use the Internet and its technology

for three primary reasons. First, the Internet serves as a "safe place" for them to come together in an online community. This community is formed primarily through online discussion groups and email listservs, although many women who got to know each other online have since met in person. In addition, women veterans use the Internet to create web sites that serve as resources and "spaces" for consciousness-raising and for providing information about the Vietnam War and the experiences of other veterans, as artistic and creative outlets for dealing with the war, and as a vehicle for connecting and reconnecting with other women (and men) veterans. Women veterans also use the Internet to heal the physical and emotional scars incurred in Vietnam. Discussion lists and individual and group-related Vietnam web sites open dialogues that help veterans express feelings related to their experiences so they can begin to deal with these experiences and move forward with their lives. For many of the women who participate on the ICW list, this is their first opportunity to remember and discuss their Vietnam experiences with other women, or anyone at all.

A Safe Community in Virtual Space

Marilyn Knapp Litt, a native of Gas City, Indiana, started the Women in Vietnam web site and the ICW email discussion group in response to the difficulties she had finding online "spaces" and information for women Vietnam veterans. Although not a veteran herself, Litt grew up during the Vietnam era and became aware of and interested in women veterans after attending a play in Chicago in January 1993. The play was based on Laura Palmer's book of letters left at the Vietnam Veterans Memorial Wall in Washington, DC, *Shrapnel in the Heart*. Litt (1998) recalls, "My afternoon at the theater made me want to make amends for not noticing, not listening, and I suppose most of all for not caring anymore after the war about the people we sent and their families" (p. 2). She was also struck by the poetry of a nurse, "Dusty," that was presented in the production.

Litt joined a Prodigy online discussion about Vietnam, but found that only male veterans participated. Litt had joined the discussion specifically to hear women veterans' experiences, but found only men talking about their experiences. It was not until a year and a half after seeing the play that she met her first woman veteran online; this woman was Dusty. This friendship inspired Litt to create a poetry web site for Dusty, which in turn, brought her in to contact with more women veterans. These women signed the site's guestbook and Litt kept a list of their email addresses, notifying them whenever the site was updated. She wanted to keep the discussion going, but discovered it was not as easy as she had initially thought:

> One of my misapprehensions about cyberspace was that it would be easy for these women to find each other online. However, the same factors that conspire to keep them isolated, the small number who served and their general unwillingness to discuss their service with casual acquaintances, also worked online to keep them apart. There was no easy way for them to find each other. (1998)

Litt's creation and updating of the original poetry site was instrumental in bringing together the core group of women veterans who would found the email discussion group InCountry Women.

InCountry Women was started by Litt in December 1996 with just 12 members. It remains one of only a handful of lists of its kind. Ann Kelsey of Whippany, New Jersey, a veteran who served in Vietnam as an administrative librarian with Army Special Services from August 1969 to August 1970, and Dusty, veteran nurse and poet, help Marilyn run the list. Litt's purpose in starting the list was to bring women veterans together in conversation with each other. Her intent was "to provide a comfortable environment for women to discuss their service with each other and anyone who was interested" (1998). In March 2001 there were approximately 110 list subscribers, but according to Litt, only about 80 of these were active. Approximately 20 to 25 subscribers no longer participated but did not know how to unsubscribe. There were also members who did not talk on the list, preferring to listen. The largest percentage of members were women veterans, and there were fewer than 10 males, some civilians, and a few academics who monitored the list. Approximately 80% of the members were women who were in Vietnam.

Unlike many email discussion groups and listservs, ICW is not advertised anywhere online, although one can sign up for the list on Litt's Women in Vietnam web site. A link that will take site visitors to a page with instructions for signing up is located toward the bottom of the home page. This link is accompanied by a quotation from list member and Army Special Services veteran Patricia Brimeyer:

> We went to a foreign country in service of our country ... we gave aid and encouragement to a whole segment of our brothers/sisters ... we survived a war ... we are noble ... we are brave ... we are adventurous ... we are an active part of world history ... we are interesting ... we have lived such exciting lives ... we have gone far beyond the boundaries allowed to most of our sisters ... we did it together ... and we still have each other.

Brimeyer clearly identifies several elements that bind women Vietnam veterans together as a community, jumping from the past to the present and emphasizing the group's shared experiences. She also notes the "boundaries," gender and societal, that women went beyond in Vietnam. Historically, few women in "official" military or service positions have been found in war zones, yet there were many women in Vietnam. Membership in the community is limited, for the most part, to those with Vietnam experience and invited guests. Litt did not want "just anyone" signing up for the list so most people find out about it through other list members or through the recommendation of someone who knows about the list. Litt does not want to exclude people, but she does have concerns about maintaining the safe and comfortable atmosphere that the original members created. "It's not that I don't want people to join, I like as many people that are interested to find out, and also that way you don't get trouble-makers, you know, that maybe just sign on the list to cause trouble."[4]

The list has seen its share of troublemakers. One notable individual signed on to the list claiming to be a woman veteran of the marines. She posted to the list a funny story from her past. She said her name was Pat and that she had accidentally received a draft letter but later signed up for service in Vietnam. Another list member immediately responded that she had heard that story before and several members began asking Pat questions about her time in service. There were approximately 18 women marines in Vietnam. Several list members knew their names and immediately became suspicious. Pat soon left the list and has not been heard from since. Some members made postings that were hurtful to other members and were subsequently removed from the list. Litt has also removed a few members after discovering they were not who they said they were.

The list has rules and guidelines and these are emailed to each new subscriber. Litt recalls that from the list's beginning she called for civility. There are etiquette guidelines, such as courtesy toward members and respect for privacy. List members are asked to keep their postings brief and to post only a few times a day to reduce unnecessary volume. There are also privacy guidelines that are very important for maintaining the comfortable "space" in which women veterans and other list members feel safe expressing their experiences and feelings. What is posted on the list is not to be passed on unless the author grants permission for a posting to be used elsewhere. The list community assumes that members of one's household are "de facto" members of the list and may read what is posted, but access should not be granted to anyone outside the household of a member.

In general, cross-postings or forwards are not allowed. The only exceptions are research requests, questions from students (who are not members of the list), and announcements of veteran and Vietnam-related events. Postings should pertain to what women did in Vietnam, but anything related to the main theme of the list is usually welcome. The list is not moderated, so anything posted goes directly to the list, unless a post is unusually long, in which case it may bounce back to the author for editing.

New members are required to introduce themselves to the rest of the list community. This is accomplished by the member sending both the list and the webmaster a short paragraph about who s/he is and why s/he is interested in the list. While there is a core of members who are a pretty tight group because of their service in Vietnam, the introductions are meant to make everyone feel welcome and aware of who is on the list, maintaining the "safe space" of the community. The guidelines state:

> You may feel at first as if everyone knows each other, but that only makes a new voice even more welcome, so please don't be shy. Listen a bit, then speak right up and introduce yourself and say a few words about what your interest is in Vietnam and why you have joined the list. Even if you do not intend to post to the list, you need to do this. (InCountry Women list guidelines)

List members are quick to welcome new members by replying to their introductions. These introductions serve another important purpose, in that they alert members to possible false identities and thus help to maintain a "safe" environment.

List members discuss a wide variety of topics that center around Vietnam and women in Vietnam-related issues. The following list includes common topics that have been discussed: memories of Vietnam, Post Traumatic Stress Disorder (PTSD), dealing with veteran centers and VA hospitals, support for depression and mood swings, therapy sessions, reunions and other veteran's ceremonies (the Moving Wall, Memorial Day, directions, schedules), congratulations on awards and honors received, notification of birthdays, marriages, divorces, and illnesses, recaps of reunions and get-togethers, research inquiries, Vietnam-related questions, trivia, questions veterans ask of other veterans (definition of terms associated with the war or service, identifying uniforms in photos, people in photos), and announcements and discussions of TV documentaries dealing with Vietnam.

The gendered context in which the listserv exists and functions is obvious in nearly every subject discussed. From Post Traumatic Stress Disorder to remembering a typical day in service in Vietnam, the need for a place to discuss issues *as* women pervades the list. While not all the topics are specific to women's experiences in Vietnam, the fact that many of these women have not had an opportunity to discuss their experiences before joining the list makes all Vietnam-related topics important to them. For example, ICW members frequently discuss topics relating to PTSD, including depression and mood swings, treatment for depression, and the difficulties women veterans encounter in seeking treatment. Sometimes, messages about PTSD are more subtle. For example, shortly after New Year's Day 2001, the list was unusually quiet. Instead of 10 to 30 posts per day, which is the average, there were sometimes none or only a few. Pat Brimeyer posted the following message to the list in response to a posting noting the silence of the list asking, "Where is everyone anyway?"

> RE: wow, it's quiet. I'm here, too, but really in a funk. Can't even figure out why ... just keep bursting into tears for no reason ... and full of anger, but don't know at what ... not like me. But the guys at rap seem to be the same way, so maybe it's winter. What are you all doing to keep your spirits up?

Several members who responded commented that they were having similar experiences. Brimeyer mentions that the male veterans at a "rap" (discussion) group she attended were acting in a similar fashion, but it was the women on ICW she turned to for consolation and advice. In the safe space of ICW, Brimeyer felt comfortable discussing her emotions with other women veterans and asking them for advice. This thread helped to increase the volume of postings and get the list back to its usual activity level.

Discussion threads about PTSD sometimes include its effect on the relationships women veterans have with other people and the difficulties that can arise. Participants in these discussions often comment on romantic relationships, the problems they have, and the fears they have about maintaining relationships. In a posting on July 27, 2001, a list member explains,

> I have been in an isolative mode—too much thinking, I guess—have been attempting to figure out where I am in my relationship—what I want and what I deserve—what is possible and feasible—finally figured out that I am attracted to people who are emotionally unavailable because in many ways I am emotionally unavailable ... well DUH—something about the PTSD.

This member received several supportive replies in which list members commiserated, offered advice, and recalled their own similar experiences and feelings. On ICW, the women do not have to be silent about their feelings or worry about discussing personal topics. In mixed company, online and in person, they may not talk about their experiences at all, but because ICW is a space where women veterans feel comfortable discussing personal issues and know that there are many members who share their experiences, they can discuss these topics.

In addition, many more clearly gender-specific topics are discussed. A discussion thread that started in April 2001 in response to an oral historian's question asked offline dealt with pregnancy in Vietnam. This thread solicited several responses, some informative and others sarcastic, about the reactions to and repercussions of pregnancy among women serving in Vietnam. The initial posting was sent by Kelsey:

> It's my recollection that if someone got pregnant in Vietnam their contract was terminated, I'm talking about civilians now, and they were sent home. I sort of recall that that was even stipulated in the agreement

> I signed. I believe that military women who got pregnant at that time, no matter where they were assigned, were discharged whether they wanted to be or not. ... I wondered if my memory about the civilians was correct. Does anyone recall what the repercussions of pregnancy were?

This post received many responses ranging from serious answers to humorous remarks. Most women who replied recalled that women were usually sent home immediately if they became pregnant, amid anger from their commanding officers, and, depending on the relationship of the woman to the father, shame or disgrace. One list member recalled a woman who had planned to get pregnant so she could get out of Vietnam. A list member who worked with the Red Cross in Vietnam recalled that the organization "treated it like it treated everything else that could have threatened its girls (like PTSD, Agent Orange, etc.) which was that it didn't exist. The main threat we girls faced, per the Red Cross, was MARRIED MEN, which, as it turned out, was a very real threat." Several of the gender-specific issues raised by this posting are often discussed on the list, including recognized and expected gender roles imposed on women even though they were in the unusual and very male space of a war zone. Women were expected to operate according to the same social and gender norms they encountered in American society, even though these norms sometimes placed them in uncomfortable or dangerous situations.

There were many dangers women faced in Vietnam simply because they were women, and frequently, men were the source of these dangers. In addition to pregnancy, ICW members discuss how they were treated (well or badly) on a daily basis by American men in Vietnam, how they felt about the men, and the troubles they faced. Litt recalls, "I know recently they were talking about how the guys were so young. That comes up pretty often ... the way they [the women] were treated. Usually it's about how they were treated well. Sometimes they talk about being in danger from the GIs. There's a number of women on there that have been raped. I mean, I was really surprised."[5] Again, these are topics that women might not feel safe or comfortable discussing with male veterans, friends, or the general public. The "safe" space of ICW and the less intimidating, nonphysical virtual community of the Internet encourages these conversations.

Men are not barred from joining the list, but their participation is specifically mentioned in the discussion list guidelines. The section begins, "IF YOU ARE A GUY" and includes a quotation from a list member that Litt felt best expressed the overall sentiment of women veterans toward the participation of men:

> We females have had so little opportunity to discuss our own agenda that some of us are just a little bit possessive of finally having our own list. But we love to share our thoughts and stories, with you guys as well as each other, and we especially welcome questions that keep the topical conversation going. You'll find there's a lot of "substance" on this list—probably because, unlike you guys, we've seldom dealt with anything having to do with Vietnam up to this point ... so it's all new to us. Anyway, with that treatise over, glad to see you here. Just make yourself at home. (name withheld, InCountry Women list guidelines)

As this member states, one of the reasons the list is so important to women veterans is that many of them have not "dealt" with their Vietnam experiences and it is crucial that the atmosphere of the list remain comfortable for the women participating. And while the women do not want to completely exclude male veterans, as the men were an integral part of women's Vietnam experiences, they want to make it clear to the men that the list is first and foremost for the women. The men on the list post on a regular basis, asking questions, responding to the posts of others, bringing up topics for discussion, and having their queries answered.

Brimeyer agrees that men are welcome, but women need a space of their own:

> The purpose of the list is to focus on the female experience in Vietnam. You will hear me say this over and over, and I (and others) have fought to keep this list on that focus. Men have consistently joined and tried to change the focus to themselves. I've alienated quite a few men by being blunt about their intrusion, but the guys we do have on the list understand and are very supportive.[6]

Brimeyer had unpleasant experiences on other Vietnam veteran lists that focused on just the male experience in Vietnam. Women on these lists were often uncomfortable discussing anything personal, had their discussion topics taken over by men on the lists, and were unable to find adequate support and understanding from the men. Brimeyer was excited to discover the ICW list because it focuses on women and she joined immediately. This sentiment is shared by many of the list members and is an integral part of their virtual community.

Conclusions

The Internet is a valuable resource for marginalized groups, such as women Vietnam veterans, in the building and maintaining of a safe community "space" in which individuals can discuss and remember experiences, educate, practice consciousness-raising, and effect change. The opportunities for women veterans to get together in person to discuss their experiences as the five women did in Kokomo, Indiana, are rare and have limited potential and participation because of time constraints and geographical, monetary, and other problems. The Internet can provide a space in which marginalized groups are free to address their own needs with other supportive individuals.

Because members of ICW share a common past, a common understanding of the present, and a shared assumption of the future, their interactions online help establish their interpretive community. These women recall past events, discuss present implications and effects of their experiences, and plan to stick together in the future, whether online or in person. The community often expands beyond its virtual boundaries when members meet in person or talk on the phone. The list fosters lifelong and supportive friendships and has helped many women deal with the emotional and physical ailments that have lingered since their service in Vietnam. For many women veterans, ICW is the first opportunity they've had to talk about their Vietnam experiences with anyone who understands. Women veterans will carry the experience and discourse of Vietnam with them for the rest of their lives, and the community bonds and safe "space" created through InCountry Women and Women in Vietnam facilitate and help maintain their connections.

The Internet won't be truly effective as a tool for marginalized groups and people until more have the means and opportunity to gain access. The successful virtual communities now in existence represent the potential of the Internet for marginalized groups worldwide. Many of the women on ICW call the list a lifeline, and in many instances that is exactly what lists are and what the Internet has the potential to become.

Notes

1. Emily Strange, Kokomo, Indiana, September 15, 2000.

2. There are several oral histories of women veterans that primarily focus on nurses: Kathryn Marshall. *In the Combat Zone: An Oral History of American Women in Vietnam, 1966–1975* (Boston: Little, Brown & Company, 1987); Elizabeth M. Norman. *Women at War: The Story of Fifty Military Nurses Who Served in Vietnam* (Philadelphia: University of Pennsylvania Press, 1990); Keith Walker. *A Piece of My Heart: The Stories of 26 American Women Who Served in Vietnam* (Novato, CA: Presidio Press, 1985). These oral histories offer little analysis or opportunity for feedback and reflection. In addition, there are a few documentaries based on oral histories.

3. http://www.illyria.com/women/vnwlist.html.

4. Marilyn Knapp Litt, telephone interview by author, tape recording, March 7, 2001.

5. Ibid.

6. Patricia Brimeyer, email interview by author, April 4, 2001.

228 Tiernan

References

Books and Articles

Anderson, Benedict. (1991). *Imagined Communities: Reflections on the Origin and Spread of Nationalism.* London: Verso.

Baym, Nancy K. (1998). The Emergence of On-Line Community. In Steven Jones (Ed.), *Cybersociety 2.0: Revisiting Computer-Mediated Communication and Community* (pp. 35–68). Thousand Oaks, CA: Sage.

Craigwell, Joan Arrington and Ellen Hoffman Young. (January 1998). "The War was Pain and Fear." *NamNews, 2*(1), 40–43.

Foster, Derek. (1997). Community and Identity in the Electronic Village. In David Porter (Ed.), *Internet Culture* (pp. 23–37). London: Routledge.

Jones, Steven. (1998). Information, Internet, and Community: Notes Toward an Understanding of Community in the Information Age. In Steven Jones (Ed.), *Cybersociety 2.0: Revisiting Computer-Mediated Communication and Community* (pp. 1–34). Thousand Oaks, CA: Sage.

Litt, Marilyn Knapp. (April 1998). Women in Vietnam: Not Only Nurses Served. Paper presented at the annual meeting of the Popular Culture Association and American Culture Association, Orlando, FL.

Marshall, Kathryn. (1987). *In the Combat Zone: An Oral History of American Women in Vietnam, 1966–1975.* Boston: Little, Brown & Company.

Norman, Elizabeth M. (1990). *Women at War: The Story of Fifty Military Nurses Who Served in Vietnam.* Philadelphia: University of Pennsylvania Press.

Plant, Sadie. (1996). On the Matrix: Cyberfeminist Simulations. In Rob Shields (Ed.), *Cultures of Internet: Virtual Spaces, Real Histories, Living Bodies* (pp. 170–183). Thousand Oaks, CA: Sage.

Rheingold, Howard. (1993). *The Virtual Community: Homesteading on the Electronic Frontier.* New York: HarperPerennial.

Stoll, Clifford. (1995). *Silicon Snake Oil: Second Thoughts on the Information Highway.* New York: Doubleday.

Walker, Keith (1985). *A Piece of My Heart: The Stories of 26 American Women Who Served in Vietnam.* Novato, CA: Presidio Press.

Wellman, Barry and Milena Gulia (1999). Virtual Communities as Communities:

Net Surfers Don't Ride Alone. In Marc Smith & Peter Kollock (Eds.), *Communities in Cyberspace* (pp. 167–194). London: Routledge.

Youngs, Gillian. (1999). Virtual Voices: Real Lives. In Wendy Harcourt (Ed.), *Women @ Internet: Creating New Cultures in Cyberspace* (pp. 55–68). London: Zed Books.

Zelizer, Barbie. (1997). Journalists as Interpretive Communities. In Dan Berkowitz (Ed.), *Social Meanings of News: A Text Reader* (pp. 401–419). Thousand Oaks, CA: Sage.

Interviews

Brimeyer, Patricia. Email interview by author, April 4, 2001.

Kelsey, Ann. Email interview by author, March 30, 2001.

Litt, Marilyn Knapp. Telephone interview by author, tape recording, March 7, 2001.

Chapter 10

Trouble, Pleasure, and Tactics: Anonymity and Identity in a Lesbian Chat Room

Jamie M. Poster

As I think about women using the Internet, I find myself bombarded by questions about the consequences of anonymity for identity. How can we know how women use the Internet when all aspects of it are mediated and therefore anonymous? Semiotically, we can determine how web texts might hail women, what they offer, what they set up as women's Internet concerns. Or we can look for feminist politics and organizations to see how women's advocacy groups might be using the Internet. Yet none of these possibilities solve the problem that the Internet context presents. Any site may be created and/or used by any combination of users. In other words, investigating women's everyday uses of the Internet will prove to be a very difficult and slippery undertaking.

With this question in mind, I recently turned my humanities-style ethnographic gaze to the everyday uses of a lesbian chat room (#LesChat). Why not add the complication of sexuality to the already vexing question of online gender? My research produced multiple insights into the very problem of computer-mediated identity. In #LesChat, the users experience a range of responses to the challenges that (assumedly) "fixed" identities face on the Internet. In this chapter, I will introduce my research, briefly review relevant theories of virtual subjectivity and lesbian identity, and then "read" the chat room for its multiple responses to anonymity. I will demonstrate that regular users struggle against the anonymity of the Web (to stabilize identity), experience pleasure in not knowing who people really are, and, finally, utilize the indeterminacy for playful political tactics.

Technological Context

The chat room functions in a communicational mode called Internet Relay Chat (IRC). In this context, each room resides on a server connected to immense networks of other chat rooms, any of which can be accessed internationally. The technological prerequisites for chat participation are a personal computer and an Internet connection. Implicit in these requirements are financial resources, a certain level of technological knowledge, and a reasonable command of the English language. With the necessary technology and knowledge, one accesses a chat room by connecting to an IRC network and selecting a room from among 10,000 interest-based options. Communication is synchronous; all the participants communicate with one another in real time, as if they are engaging in telephone conversations using written text instead of voice. Several users contribute to one or more conversations in the public space of the chat room.

E-thnography

The ethnographic portion of my research consisted of two segments, starting with a broad focus and subsequently narrowing. The two stages consisted of (a) interviewing self-identified lesbian computer users who were regular members of the community, and (b) observing chat room interactions. I began the interview process in mid 1997 and by the end of 1999 I had interviewed 76 individuals; all of these interviews were conducted in private IRC (real-time and text-only) conversations. The structural invisibility of the interviews allowed for total anonymity, and as per the request of the interviewees, all names have been changed including that of the chat room.

I asked a room originator if I could respectfully observe room interactions. After consulting with members, she stated that my presence would be acceptable (and welcome) as long as ethical codes of privacy and anonymity were honored. In addition, she requested that I position myself as a nonparticipant observer (taking a name indicating my purpose, "researchr") and relegate my activity to observation. Nonparticipant observation involves recording and interpreting activities without taking part in them. I conducted all my observations under overt conditions; all members and visitors of the chat room were informed of my presence and asked if it was acceptable. On a few occasions I was asked to leave; several participants were interested in being interviewed but chose not to be observed. In total I collected about 200 hours of data, presently archived on disk.

I have no way of determining if the interview data represents the "real" experiences and feelings of the respondents, nor do I believe that the data is representative of "truth." The concept of "empirical truth" is a construction located in a historical moment and a particular ideological project. In the subsequent analysis, I will read the narratives with the understanding that language speaks them. However, my study is an attempt to unpack the manner in which the interviewees combine and augment familiar dialogues for the unfamiliar terrain of cyberspace. The testimonials represent the stories, ideas, and opinions of self-identified lesbian computer users as they move through the multiple and various discourses that mediate experience.

Virtual Subjectivity

Many scholarly conversations about cyberspace celebrate what has come to be called "identity play." As noted above, Internet communication is entirely mediated by technology; users have no way of authenticating or verifying the identity of their interlocutors. With the words "authentication" and "verification," I refer to the process by which individuals identify and read each other as subjects; the body plays a critical role in the process of identification. Reliance upon corporeal cues (touch, sound, sight) to read a body into an identity is suspect and problematic, to say the least. The relationship between assumed behaviors and beliefs, identity markers, and the body is socially, culturally, and historically constructed. Despite this critique, in popular exchange, the process of "reading" one another often relies on bodies as the chief identity signifiers. The mediated condition of cyberspace sets it substantially apart from "real world" circumstances. By comparing Internet contexts and "real" spaces, my intention is not to set up an easy and problematic opposition of real versus virtual. Recognizing the heightened mediation of cyberspace does not diminish the significance of the discursive mediation of what we call "reality." Nonetheless, the (troublesome) inclination to associate corporeal signs with identity essences creates an impasse in text-based electronic environments.

An advertisement for America Online depicts a woman sitting in a bay window; underneath the image the text reads, "On AOL, I can be a cowboy or an astronaut." The ad remarks that the structural anonymity of cyberspace offers individuals the option to assume different identities. The woman in the window can write herself as a cowboy or an astronaut. (She is, by sexist default, not following either occupation already, implying that such a career must remain in the realm of play and imagination.) Does the plasticity of identity referenced in the ad encourage individuals to wonder about the fixity and unity of "real" identity?

Some of the most significant scholarly work on this topic comes from the writing of Sherry Turkle, Elizabeth Reid, and Allucquère Rosanne Stone. Turkle's (1995) conception of virtual identity provides a fruitful means of thinking about multiple subjectivities in cyberspace. "What they [web sites] have in common is that they all suggest the value of approaching one's 'story' in several ways and with fluid access to one's different aspects. We are encouraged to think of ourselves as fluid, emergent, decentralized, multiplicitous, flexible, and ever in process" (Turkle, 1995, pp. 263–264). When individuals engage in different identity performances they become aware of the multiple positions people can and do maintain in "real life." Turkle also demonstrates that people are interpellated differently by the various Internet functions that they inhabit. For example, web surfing through hypertexts is a self-constructive process; various chat rooms and multiuser domains (MUDs) hail users in possibly more structured ways.

However, Turkle's use of notions such as hailing and interpellation is very distinct from Louis Althusser's use of the same terms. He (1986) suggests that identity most commonly comes from above or outside the self, from the state or ideology. The Repressive State Apparatus (RSA) is that which endeavors to govern identity and behavior by force of law or explicit rules. Aspects of personhood are overtly determined by the state; people are hailed as lawful and lawless subjects. The Ideological State Apparatus (ISA) is more vague; aspects of the self are interpellated by ideological constructs, such as the family, religion, and so forth. For both ISAs and RSAs, institutions encourage (or mandate) codes of personhood. For Turkle, and I borrow from her on this point, subject interpellation is more diffuse, lateral or even stemming from beneath. Ideology (small and large "i") is not as explicitly at work in various computer contexts (although it is most likely present in the ether). People may be encouraged to form certain types of self in different interest-based MUDs, but the act of forming oneself is, as implied, a function of agency that highlights the constructedness and multiplicity of identity.

Elizabeth Reid's (1991) research on IRC examines how users actively construct identities for themselves and others. Users must autobiographically construct their own life narrative and description. Concurrently, one must treat the screen as a palimpsest, reading the identities of one's interlocutors through layered conversations. Reid suggests that users may gain a sense of the constructedness of identity by participating in this constant process of writing the self and reading others. The subtle difference between Turkle and Reid resides in the latter's assertion that an experiential identity critique emerges from reading/ composing others, not only from writing the self.

In *The War of Desire and Technology at the Close of the Mechanical Age*, Stone (1996) presents the notion of "warranting":

Technologies that enable near-instantaneous communication among social groups pose old problems in new guises (similar to the unexpected ways in which the invention of the automobile affected postadolescent courting behavior in some industrial nations), but also pose new problems; not simply problems of accountability (i.e., who did it), but of warrantability (i.e., did a body/subject unit do it). The issue of warrantability—that is, is there a physical human body involved in this interaction anywhere?—is one such. (Stone, 1996, p. 87)

This notion of warranting, as you will see subsequently, is key for the identity negotiations in #LesChat. Users are preoccupied by the mystery of the particular body producing any given online text. While Stone is interested in the ways in which disembodied, online communication opens up possibilities for new identity (particularly multiple identity) formations, she is equally concerned with the irritations and difficulties. She presents a fascinating analysis of an extended online drag performance in which a male doctor (Sanford Lewin) enters a chat room as a disabled woman and creates important relationships with other users. After a considerable amount of time, the persona (Julie Graham) begins to fall apart, and her friends become obsessed with warranting, determining the identity of the person who speaks through her. Ultimately, Lewin is found out and the aftermath (in large part) is an environment of hurt, sore, and jaded users. The users of #LesChat fear confronting the same surprise and therefore employ complicated systems by which language and ideas are relied upon to warrant personae.

With important and distinct nuances, all the writers discussed above agree that technological mediation offers formidable challenges for modern notions of personhood.[1] Entering the conversation, #LesChat offers an example of some specific, everyday challenges that the Internet creates for people who are (partially) committed to "fixed" identities.

Identity: Lesbian and Queer[2]

There are those who regard lesbianism to be a settled, stable source of identification and a base for political action against male domination and compulsory heterosexuality. They see "lesbians" as roughly analogous to an ethnic group, who share a collective one true "self," a bounded group with a common history that is distinct from the dominant patriarchal, heterosexual society. Others, however, who understand sexuality as inherently unsettled and ambiguous, see efforts to form a collective sexual identity as fraught with potential contradictions. Rather than embrace marginalized identities such as "lesbian," they contend that the true radical act is to refuse such an identity; that the dichotomous categories homosexual/heterosexual are inherently limiting; and that the relationship among sexuality, identity, and politics is necessarily inconsistent, transient, and shifting. (Stein, 1997, pp. 2–3)

This passage from Arlene Stein's *Sex and Sensibility* (1997) succinctly articulates and summarizes a complex debate about identity. Through interviews with self-identified lesbians, Stein's book traces the impact, or movement, of lesbian-feminist ideas among different generations. Similarly, part of my examination charts the different versions of "lesbian" identity referenced by the members of #LesChat. These often-conflicting treatments will be read in the dichotomy set up by the above quote.

The first "side" that Stein mentions holds the conception that lesbianism is "a settled, stable source of identification and a base for political action against male domination and compulsory heterosexuality" (Stein, 1997, pp. 2–3). Described here is the lesbian-feminist position regarding identity and political work. Within this framework, lesbians consider themselves as a politically and socially marginalized group that should use its identity in oppositional politics to critique the center. For the purposes of this political program it is necessary to articulate and limit lesbian identity.

The lesbian feminist conception of identity has faced many forms of critique. For the purposes of this study, I'm going to focus on only one form of objection, the "other side" in Stein's quote, and the one most relevant to identity concerns in #LesChat. Postmodern and queer critiques of lesbian identity politics emerged in the 1980s. Regarded as "regulatory regimes," lesbian identity politics were/are rejected for the following reasons: destructively reifying power imbalances through the reassertion of differences, closing off identity as unified and ignoring the multiplicity of subject positions that compose identities, and overlooking pleasure and erotic experience. These criticisms, concurrent with changes in feminism and postmodern theories, contributed to the formation of a queer deconstruction of identity.

Queer acknowledges, studies, and offers a political critique of anything that falls into normative and deviant categories, particularly sexual activities and identities (Jagose, 1996). Queer theories insist that all sexual behaviors, all concepts linking sexual behaviors to sexual identities, and all categories of normative and deviant sexualities are constructs that create certain types of social meaning. This model follows feminist theory and lesbian and gay

studies in rejecting the idea that sexuality is an essentialist category, determined by biology or judged by eternal standards of
morality and truth. In queer conceptions, sexuality is a complex
array of codes and forces, forms of individual activity and
institutional power, which interact to shape the ideas of what is
normative and what is deviant at any particular moment, and
which then operate under the rubric of what is "natural,"
"essential," or "biological."

Queer visions of identity have been heavily influenced by the
work of Judith Butler (1989); her theory of performance argues
that gender is structurally imitative. She traces heteronormative
gender differences to an indefinitely deferred referent. Gender,
without the anchor and precedence of biologically determined
codes, becomes an imitation of no original. Gender coheres, in a
sense, around the repeated performance of itself, its socially and
historically generated codes. As individuals reiterate gender
categories they constantly remind themselves, and others, of the
strictly imitative condition of gender. Possibilities for the subversion of gender binaries can be found in the gaps of this gender
performance; with every reiteration, gender is at once both reified
and opened up for misiteration (semiotic resistance).

While this brief (and admittedly reductive) review of lesbian
feminism and queer theory may seem chronological, both of these
sentiments are evident concurrently in the conflicting treatment of
"lesbian" in the conversation and goals of the chat room.
Members expend an enormous amount of linguistic labor
attempting to "authenticate" new members. It is this antagonistic
relation to anonymity that I will now discuss.

Constituting an Ideal Community: Hailing "Fixed" Identities in Fluid Conditions; A Problem of Identity, Hyperbolized

The community of a given chat room is composed entirely of
its participants. Without users' words, there would simply be an
empty screen. The endeavor to realize #LesChat's idealized
community requires constant construction. In the case of this chat
room, the originators and operators desire to foster a progressive
lesbian-feminist community composed of "real" lesbian women
(ideally above age 30). Sexuality, lesbian identity, is here regarded

as a stable identity. How does a cybercommunity devoted to embodied notions of personhood achieve its goal in a geography resisting (an already problematic) authentication? In Stone's terms, operators and regular members have identity warranting as their primary goal. Identity play, for the originators and regulars of the room, is a source of irritation and trouble. Without (troublesome) body signification, regulars have developed alternative means of securing membership.

Members maintain sincere dedication to the confirmation enterprise. In several interviews, I suggested the possibility that any number of the operators or regulars could indeed be engaging in identity play. A few interviewees said that they were engaging in a form of drag but it didn't matter in their particular cases.[3] Generally, most respondents were aware of this likelihood but claimed with certainty that most regulars could be trusted. However, the same confidence is not afforded to random pedestrians.

The principal means of "sussing out" unsought visitors is a set of rules which appear in two formats. An abbreviated version is situated at the top of the screen in each user's client program. Usually this reads something like: "We say >NO= to men/ netsex/picbegging"(#LesChat, chat room logs). This text is visible to all chat room inhabitants for the duration of their visit; it is a reminder that men, netsex, and soliciting for photographs are all prohibited. The following is the more comprehensive list of rules that all new visitors are expected to read:

-LesBot- There are a few rules to help #LesChat run more smoothly:

-LesBot- 1 - Treat everyone with respect, even those who don't belong here.

-LesBot- 2 - This is a safe space for lesbians so if you are not a woman then please respect our space and find another chat room to visit.

-LesBot- 3 - All women over 18 are welcome here. If you identify as a woman and you are living as a woman then you are welcome. Period. If this doesn't totally describe you, then please talk to us.

-LesBot- 4 - If you have to have a fight with someone, please fight in private msgs or take it there as soon as possible to reduce chat room disruption. If a fight gets really out of hand all participants will be asked to leave until they cool off.

-LesBot- 5 - Please do not solicit netsex, romantic friendship, pics, etc.

-LesBot-   —Enjoy your visit!— (#LesChat, chat room logs)

This list includes the three rules from the abbreviated version, and some additional ones dictating other behavioral limitations. Defying the above guidelines is grounds for expulsion from the chat room. Uninvited visitors comprise the primary target of the rules, with an occasional nod or wink toward the regulars. Rule #1, for example, speaks to everyone, and requires respectful treatment of all. By stating, "Treat everyone with respect, even those who don't belong here," regular users are asked to abstain from bullying unwelcome visitors.

Rule #2: "This is a safe space for lesbians so if you are not a woman then please respect our space and find another chat room to visit." "Woman" (biological sex) and "lesbian" (sexuality) are conflated here. In describing the ideal lesbian community the respondents clearly state that only lesbians are allowed. However, in this rule we find that biological women are acceptable visitors in a space designed for lesbians. The anonymity of computer mediated communication precludes warranting; as the regulars scramble to circumvent this barrier, "stable" identity categories fall apart. Here (and elsewhere, see subsequent analysis of the enforcement of these rules in the warranting process of gender interrogation) the category "lesbian" loses its stability, becoming impossible to warrant, yet "woman" remains traceable. Operating through an essentialist notion of gender, the rule writers will settle for "confirming" biological sex, as sexual orientation appears to be more elusive.

Rule #3 states, "All women over 18 are welcome here. If you identify as a woman and you are living as a woman then you are welcome. Period. If this doesn't totally describe you, then please talk to us." This rule connotes a more queer definition of gender than rule #2. Queer theory's limits are broad, as the term describes any form of erotic desire or activity outside of the hetero-normative. As noted above, another crucial rereading of identity that queer offers is a radical rethinking of gender as a copy with no original. This insight detaches gender from anatomy, instead regarding it as a discursive, embodied performance. While rule #3 encourages participants to maintain queer conceptions of "wo-man" (i.e., if you are living as a woman), rule #2 (i.e., no men allowed) opts for a more rigid, essentialist, biological notion. These two rules, combined with the requirements for an ideal lesbian space, make for a complex convergence of theoretical positions. Can the political lesbian they hail be reconciled with a queer treatment of gender? Sexuality is at once stable and elusive. Gender is at once biological and performative.

Rule #4 speaks to the problem of heightened emotional exchange in the chat rooms. Intensified fervor is such a significant problem that it must be addressed in this imperative. Rule #5 prohibits solicitations for netsex (Internet sex), romantic friendships, and pictures. Other chat rooms centered on cruising and dating allow these solicitations to occur. #LesChat forbids any kind of cruising, as even the solicitation of "romantic friendship" is prohibited. This particular regulation holds true for overt flirtation, but many romantic relationships emerge despite it. When asked about the purpose of restricting amorous displays, an originator said, "ya know, it gets sleazy here. i for one am anti-sleaze so we'll have none of it" (Kate93, 1999, personal communication).

There is a constant confluence of users entering and exiting #LesChat. The entrance rituals start with an operator asking new users to access the rules by typing a specific command in their client program. If the user has read the rules and would like to stay, an additional set of activities commences for further proof of eligibility. The operators hold a public inquisition. As alluded to above, this practice entails asking the visitor a series of questions (most of which are stereotypical of "feminine" discourse) which they contend will be easy for a woman, and difficult for a man, to answer. If the person has difficulty with the questions it is believed that they are either not female, or are not successfully performing as such (according with the theoretical positions outlined above). This offense is punished; the operator will usually "kick" or "ban" the visitor from #LesChat. Both the inquisition and the kicking practices work to eradicate detected "male" visitors and interpellate the successfully performed "female" ones into ideal community members. The process advances the larger project of generating an idealized lesbian community.

The Public Gender Interrogation

In the common space of the chat room, the new visitor is asked a series of questions that (assumedly stereotypical) "male" subjects would have a difficult time addressing. The standard questions are "What is a speculum?" "What is a pap?" and "When do you ovulate?" (#LesChat, chat room logs). It is particularly fascinating that biological gender and sexuality are conflated (again), as the screening process seeks to legitimize "women" instead of self-identified lesbians. I asked the chat room originators why they chose not to screen for the latter, and the most common response is that it would be too difficult; producing lesbian-specific screening questions presents too much of a challenge. Gender is again regarded as a biologically essential category, and it is assumed that locating "women's" questions is an easier pursuit because there are issues that all (and only) women face. It is implied that sexuality is more evasive, that it seems too difficult to find issues that all (and only) lesbians face. Gender is "fixed"; sexuality is fluid.

In *The Domain-Matrix: Performing Lesbian at the End of Print Culture*, Sue-Ellen Case approaches the problem of identity screening in a lesbian bulletin board system (BBS) entitled "Sappho." Because of privacy concerns, she is unable to describe the mechanisms of screening employed on the BBS. However, she discusses the problem of not knowing who people are, and how that threatens the potential of Sappho's role as a "new cyber-community, or social body, now possible for lesbians" (Case, 1996). In a move similar to screening questions, Case suggests that members of the BBS write all postings in a private language, employing creative uses of screen space and text. Lesbian identity would be spatially encrypted in the arrangements of text on the screen. Case's analysis of Sappho, combined with the struggles in #LesChat, indicates a seemingly insurmountable impasse with regard to embodied notions of identity.

In the case of #LesChat, however, the operators have responded to awkward circumstances by inventing a dialogue which, they contend, functions successfully. Often, visitors are stumped by the questions, which according to operators, indicates that they are not women (or, I suggest, are not familiar with the terms and rituals of Western medicine). Additionally, the extraordinarily "female" tenor of the questions serves another function in the community. The "women-only" nature of the chat room is reified across the interviews; topics that are about "female" biology but are not regularly topics in the public sphere (even in "real life") are aired in the space of the chat room. The words "speculum" and "pap" performatively ordain the chat room as a "female" site. The signifiers also prepare visitors for the conditions of the chat room. These questions announce that the content of this room is female-identified, and therefore visitors are encouraged to appreciate and respect the specificity of that configuration.

Equally interesting, however, is the hailing function that the interrogation performs for the regulars. This public ritual can occur as often as five times an hour. Upon each iteration, the regulars watch and sometimes participate in the process. For example, if a visitor is obviously struggling with the questions, a regular might make a comment indicating this, urging the inquisitor (operator) to "kick" a visitor suspected to be a "man" in disguise (drag) as a woman. This ritual reifies the politics and agenda of #LesChat with each performance. The regulars are reminded that they survived the interrogation, and are therefore accepted in the environment. This ritual functions like the laughter in the WOW stage shows of the 1970s in Greenwich Village; the shared local knowledge performatively harvests coherence among people.

Clearly the anonymity of cyberspace creates a lot of trouble for the chat room operators. It gives them an insurmountable challenge and hours of word labor. Yet the very problem of authenticating visitors is, paradoxically, a community-forming agent. Operators experience a great deal of pleasure as they reiterate the goals of the chat room and suss out the bad elements. Getting rid of the bad guys is even more satisfying than detecting them.

Kicking the Unwelcome Element

When the interrogation uncovers an unsolicited visitor, operators "kick" or "ban" that individual from the chat room. As physical warranting is impossible, it is no surprise that embodied terms (and processes) such as "kicking" and "banning" come into play. These activities are decidedly material and point yet again toward the importance of the body in this computer-mediated context. The disagreeable visitor is expelled from the room indefinitely (or until the same individual dials in through a different ISP). The "kicking" is usually followed by a third-person narrative describing a fictional, fantastical kicking maneuver. (This occurs in the form of an "action command," which is a third-person narrative comment.) The actual kicking is anticlimactic; a programmed command by the operator produces an automated reply stating that the user has been kicked or banned. But the third-person narrative is a creative, mythical kicking which cleans the room of the unsolicited presence. An example of a kicking follows; "Radclyff" is the operator and "Claire" is the man in disguise who has been kicked:

> Radclyff takes a running leap up to Claire, extends her super lengthy arms, cries a shrill battle wail (much like Xena's) and uses her scepter to shove him out of the chat room into oblivion. (#LesChat, chat room logs)

Each time unwanted visitors are suspected, they are booted with equally intense fervor. These moments of extreme power exercised over the "men" by the "women" of the chat room play a significant role in identity formation within the space. Upon each reiteration, the members of the chat room are reminded of the control they have over this digital environment. I liken these dramatic and violent kickings to the treatment of a scapegoat or *pharmakos*, reiterating the digital "lesbians'" fleeting sovereignty from patriarchy. The kicking is a reminder of the instability of the space: the always-present intruder and the ceaselessly unattainable goal.

The simulation of a dramatic, violent "kicking" becomes a sarcastic embellishment of the operators' power to defend the community. As one chat room operator stated, "in the real world, lesbians are oppressed and the overstated power we show in #LesChat compensates for the oppression we encounter in our daily lives" (Scholar882, 1999, personal communication). To return again to Butler (1989), her theory posits that gender is a constant process of imitation, and with every reiteration, gender is simultaneously reified and opened up for misiteration. The repeated kicking performance serves to restate the existing social order of the chat room. However, the repeated presence of the "man in disguise" constantly challenges the "women-only" social order. Within this struggle, however, regular users experience repetitious pleasure and power.

A close look at the rituals and practices of the chat room illuminates a profusion of slippery moments. For example, while operators and regulars are (for the most part) not consciously operating through the frameworks of queer or postmodern theories, they are committed to queer-like understandings of gender (see rule #3 above) yet they maintain an ardent commitment to lesbian critique and identity. The rules and screening process indicate a conflation of biological gender and sexuality. When the relativistic Internet context meets the needs of the community, various opposing conceptions of gender and sexuality emerge.

Anonymity is a source of trouble, which becomes a source of power and pleasure, and as you will now see, an exquisite tool for micro-political tactics as well.

The Kiss-In

In a not-so-everyday occurrence, a group of simulated lesbians from #LesChat staged a kiss-in in a fundamentalist Christian chat room. They used their desire to disturb the heteronormativity of the Christian space.

The strategy of the kiss-in emerged while the participants were engaged in a text-based game of truth or dare. One chat room "regular" dared all the individuals who were present to disguise themselves and enter a fundamentalist Christian chat room to stage a kiss-in. Ten cyberactivists then proceeded to disguise themselves as heterosexual women (presumably white, given that whiteness is most often in these spaces assumedly unmarked) by changing their nicknames from those that might have been marked as lesbian (from "Sapphite" to "Kathy," for example). The intent was to fill the Christian chat room with what appeared to be god-fearing female computer users, and then, without warning, sully the pious space with an onslaught of same-sex affection. The renamed virtual lesbians entered the

Christian chat room incognito and engaged in biblical conversation, just to establish the legitimacy of their visit. Then, in third-person narrative form, they began to describe intimate and passionate kisses occurring between women. One participant described the dialogue: "We said stuff like, 'Mary leans over and kisses Rebecca on the lips passionately'" (Gina, 1998, personal communication). As the virtual fundamentalists began to realize that they were being ambushed by sinners, they systematically "kicked" and "banned" the activists from the room.

The Internet Context—How Do Anonymity and Invisibility Affect Political Work?

Generally, the kiss-in political strategy (of Act Up and Queer Nation) involves a group of lesbian, gay, bisexual, or trans-gendered activists. Most frequently in marked attire (including, for example, pink triangles and rainbow flags), the group will enter heteronormative sites like malls or bars and engage in public displays of queer affection. By bringing taboo intimacy to normative sites, the activists upset the social order of those spaces and enact critiques of the implicitly homophobic contexts therein.

The virtual kiss-in was performed without bodies, sounds, visual images, and tactile or aural cues. How does this context change the process and effect of such a pursuit? A major difference in the two contexts is the level of physical risk: "real world" kiss-ins face the risk of physical, corporeal violence from onlookers; virtual kiss-ins do not encounter the same threat. Banning activists is certainly a kind of violence, a discursive brutality that is significant but not analogous to corporeal hostility.

Because of the inability to "authenticate" any of the agents involved (including the virtual lesbians and the virtual Christians), we discover here the meeting of two imagined and dramatically performed identities. Like the lesbian chat room, the fundamentalist Christian space presumably contends that participants are telling the "truth" about their religious beliefs. There is a collective agreement in both chat rooms that all users are portraying their "real" selves. The shared consent of performed authenticity functions to officiate imagined identities.

To complicate things further, the kiss-in activists added another level of drag to the already imagined identities involved. One of the participants described the need for this transition: "If I kept my name [Sapphite] I would've been banned immediately. I had to appear normal long enough for us to start macking in front of them" (Sapphite, 1998, personal communication). They used the invisibility of cyberspace to disguise themselves as heterosexual women of unmarked (white) race so they could stage a kiss-in that would further the objectives of "stable" lesbian identity.

Since no one can know for sure if the lesbians are "really" lesbians or the Christians are "really" Christians (as if these categories are ever stable), how effective can oppositional politics be? What if one of the fundamentalist Christians is "really" a lesbian or Jewish or any number of other possibilities? If this political tactic is not being used by lesbians to disturb Christians (but really any combination of identities), does it work, and what does it mean?

This occurrence highlights the problem of oppositional identity politics. Postmodern theories (such as queer theory) criticize and deconstruct notions of the unified subject. Behind identity politics is the assumption that people are, by essence or construction, firmly situated in one personality category or another. Whether sexuality is regarded as a choice or as biologically determined, oppositional identity politics assumes that identity is fixed, solid, unchanging. While this notion is taken up by marginalized groups, in very complicated ways, it is a problem at the root of all oppression. As theories like queer suggest, in order for identity-based oppression to end, the notion of identity must be critiqued and abolished. To get beyond discrimination based on difference, the underlying binary structure needs to be dismantled. (To fight inequality then we thankfully arrive at strategic essentialism.) Notions such as queer, a mode of being that refuses identification, presents new possibilities; the turn away from oppositional politics is a call to rethink the very terms of personhood.

Examining the kiss-in in this context, we see that the oppositional politics are not attached to stable subjects. Identity politics are put to the test, as these imagined groups articulate their differences in a completely relativistic context. The Internet context renders the oppositional politics of the kiss-in even more problematic than they would be in the "real world." For, if neither side can be "verified" in the popular sense, or if the two are really permeable in the theoretical sense, how can such politics avoid reifying power imbalances based on illusory stability? This moment can be read as an example of what happens when already unstable constructs meet completely unstable conditions, in other words, when modern subjectivity faces its instability as it confronts postmodern critique or context.

The Politics of the Kiss-In

The virtual kiss-in borrows its format most specifically from the "real" kiss-ins staged by Act Up and Queer Nation starting in the 1980s (not to mention their precedents such as "sit-ins," "bed-ins," and "be-ins"). In these political events, groups sought to materially criticize heteronormativity. The critique lies in the social fact that most public spaces are dominated by hetero-centrism, which dictates that heterosexuality is the only acceptable kind of performance or existence. Kiss-ins seek to disturb these normative spaces by engaging in queer affection (i.e., girls kissing girls and boys kissing boys). The occurrences call attention to the "otherness" of these intimate acts, and implicitly and explicitly provoke embodied critiques of heteronormativity. The objective is to criticize institutions such as heterosexuality, and call attention to what they exclude. By combining lesbian and gay liberationist discourses with queer politics, the kiss-in positions normative against non-normative. The virtual kiss-in functions politically through the virtual lesbians' self-positioning as "other." They enter the fundamentalist Christian chat room anticipating their abject ejection from that space. In Julia Kristeva's *Powers of Horror* (1982), the abject is characterized as that which threatens to reveal the precarious state of normative constructed identities, and that which enables the normative construction enacted by symbolic systems. The abject is "opposed to I"; it is composed of those constituents that transgress and threaten the sanitary and decent body. The abject both threatens and enables the articulation of unified subjectivity. For Kristeva, abjection is fundamental to the maintenance of subjectivity and social order, while the condition of being abject is subversive of both formations.

What does it mean when a group of marginalized agents use their abjection in activism? Assimilationist and civil rights politics demand that the abject be regarded as subjects, no longer relegated to the margins, inducted into mainstream culture. However, the politics of the virtual kiss-in sought a different effect. The virtual lesbians sought to invoke their own abjectness in order to subvert the normativity of the fundamentalist Christian chat room. Their innovative and facetious maneuver served to disrupt the normative order for only a moment, and then to undergird its structure. The abject is at once disruptive and foundational of subjective and social orders. It is the process of abjection (banning the lesbians) that serves to reiterate the social order of the Christian space.

The concept of the abject is also useful as it illuminates how the body is referenced and invoked through the kiss-in. The camouflage of cyberspace is helpful as it allows for the ambushing of the Christian chat room. However, once the invaders are "outed" as virtual lesbians, their public queer intimacy signifies and invokes images of abject, embodied otherness. Despite identity difficulties in cyberspace, the citation of gay sexuality summons the visceral lesbian bodies into the identities before them; the linking of discursive acts and imagined lesbians invokes images of "stable" lesbian subjects.

Michel de Certeau (1984) assigned the term "tactics" to guerrilla acts performed by those with limited power: acts which seem haphazard and have as their goal antagonizing or over-turning the dominant. These tactics do not lead to revolution; rather, they are an everyday method of being a little resistant. The moment of the kiss-in was fleeting at best, and hardly functioned to overturn fundamental Christianity or the specific form of it operating in the chat room. However, the kiss-in did happen, and its linguistic guerrilla tactic briefly unsettled heteronormativity.

In the case of the kiss-in, the mediation of cyberspace does not result in a sense of fragmentation among users. Instead, virtual lesbians use their invisibility strategically—as a moment of playful activism that seeks to further the cause of lesbian oppositional politics. By using their abjection to bring the body back into the picture they summon an image of identity rooted in the body. Despite indeterminacy (and the concurrent deconstruction of identity), the unidentified work to keep the stable subject intact.

Through this illustration, we discover how social actors wrestle with challenges to identity that are otherwise largely relegated to scholarly exchange.

The kiss-in activists' use of anonymity isn't that much different (in form) from the sneaky, unsolicited "male" visitors in #LesChat. The difference from the activists' perspective is that it is done with "righteous political goals instead of sleaze" (Betsy, 1998, personal communication). Of course what is missing in that configuration is that a lot of visitors in #LesChat might be doing more banal, benign experimentation. But even this wouldn't be acceptable. The regulars accept that a few people slip through the cracks of their screening system, but clearly they do it, not just in an attempt to control the anonymity, but for pleasure as well. The interrogation, the kicking, the linguistic practices are fun and they foster a sort of queer, yet lesbian-feminist coherence.

At the beginning of this chapter, I speculated about the difficulty of determining women's everyday uses of the Internet. It certainly is a slippery enterprise. In the case of #LesChat, I find that the slipperiness of the question itself defines the condition of the chat room. The originators, operators, and regulars navigate through conflicting theories of gender and sexuality; they at once abhor, enjoy, and make use of the inability to know. Such is the spirit of this moment in which identity has a tryst with its critique.

#LesChat identity affairs are particularly interesting because the users are committed to "stable" notions of personhood. The mediated context pushes users to think through queer treatments of sexuality and gender, in spite of a driving thrust to support the political and emotional needs of electronic lesbians, a construct rooted in the body and the material world, struggling to stay coherent in the face of utter fragmentation.

More optimistic critical writing regards the Internet as a place for marginalized groups to finally gain as powerful a voice as the center.[4] This chapter has been an examination of such an effort. It indicates that identity will necessarily meet a hyperbolic form of its critique on the Web. It points to the ingenuity of those committed to "fixed" identities. In a sense, marginalized groups are perhaps better equipped than others to face the challenge. After all, people on the margins have a long history of highlighting, camouflaging, inserting, politicizing, strategizing, cohering, camping, and ironizing their material and linguistic presence.

Notes

1. Turkle, Reid, and Stone also share a sense of optimism about what might be considered the liberatory potential of virtual subjectivity. Others, and there are many of them, feel that while identity fracturing is definitely the condition of computer-mediated communication, its effects can be devastating. Mark Slouka (1995), for example, considers multiplicity an "assault" on the self, generating a new (Orwellian) degree of dependency on machines. This critique is valid, but the other voices represented here start from a position of identity critique (instead of nostalgia for wholeness) and lead to ideas that complicate the specific identity concerns in #LesChat.

2. The following synopsis of theories of lesbian identity is cursory. For the purpose and scope of this examination, I am introducing only two positions rather than exhaustively representing all positions among their many contextual discourses.

3. The originators of the chat room (all three of them) claimed to be male to female transsexuals, preoperative. They stated that they were born into the wrong bodies and that their online gender personae were "true" and would become material, biological very soon; all three claimed to be living as men otherwise, but their online interactions involved their true selves. In another paper, I'd like to explore the complexity of the operators' dedication to lesbian feminism.

4. See Howard Rheingold's *Virtual Community* (1993) and Douglas Schuler's *New Community Networks* (1996).

References

Althusser, L. (1986). Ideology and Ideological State Apparatuses. In H. Adams & L. Searle (Eds.), *Critical Theory Since 1965* (pp. 239–251). Tallahassee: Florida State University Press.

Betsy. Personal Communication, December 1998.

Butler, J. (1989). *Gender Trouble: Feminism and the Subversion of Identity.* New York: Routledge.

Case, S. E. (1996). *The Domain-Matrix: Performing Lesbian at the End of Print Culture.* Bloomington: Indiana University Press.

De Certeau, M. (1984). *The Practice of Everyday Life.* Berkeley: University of California Press.

Gina. Personal Communication, May 1998.

Jagose, A. (1996). *Queer Theory: An Introduction.* New York: New York University Press.

Kate93. Personal Communication, January 1999.

Kristeva, J. (1982). *Powers of Horror.* New York: Columbia University Press.

#LesChat. (1997–99). Internet Relay Chat logs. Undernet Server.

Radclyff. Personal Communication, November 1997.

Reid, E. M. (1991). *Electropolis.* Retrieved September 10, 2001. http://www.cross winds.net/~aluluei/electropolis.htm

Rheingold, H. (1993). *Virtual Community: Homesteading on the Electronic Frontier.* Reading, MA: Addison Wesley.

Sapphite. Personal Communication, May 1998.

Scholar882. Personal Communication, January 1999.

Schuler, D. (1996). *New Community Networks: Wired for Change.* Reading, MA: Addison Wesley.

Slouka, M. (1995). *War of the Worlds.* New York: Harper Collins.

Stein, A. (1997). *Sex and Sensibility.* Berkeley: University of California Press.

Stone, A. R. (1996). *The War of Desire and Technology at the Close of the Mechanical*

Age. Cambridge: MIT Press.

Turkle, S. (1995). *Life on the Screen: Identity in the Age of the Internet*. New York: Simon & Schuster.

Part Four

Gender, Agency, and New Media

Extending the School Day: Gender, Class, and the Incorporation of Technology in Everyday Life

S. Elizabeth Bird and Jane Jorgenson

Introduction

As widespread access to computers and the Internet continues to be touted as the route to greater equality in educational and social opportunity, the computer is now widely framed as an educational tool for the home that will give children the "edge" in an increasingly competitive world. Many of the assumptions about computers and education tend to be drawn from research in primarily affluent households, as family members become computer literate—or "computer fluent" as it is now often termed (Shields & Behrman, 2000)—steadily adding new skills to a growing array of competencies that come from regular, sustained use of the computer. Assumptions about gender and computer fluency have also been developed from the middle-class experience: We see a pattern of computer technology originating as a very "masculine" phenomenon, before being gradually "domesticated" and also appropriated by women. In the middle-class household, computers until very recently have been coded as both "masculine" and "educational," and it has often been up to men to help children gain the computer fluency they are assumed to need in order to achieve educationally.

It is not surprising, then, that the assumption has been made that low-income, working-class families would follow the same path if computers were available to them. Efforts to narrow the "digital divide" have led to a variety of experimental initiatives to provide low-income groups with household computers (e.g., Hansen, 1992), in order to enrich educational opportunities. Indeed, research does suggest that home computer ownership, rather than mere access to computers, is important in developing true computer fluency (Hoffman & Novak, 1998). Although some of these experiments confirm that computer ownership has succeeded in raising test scores in certain circumstances (Kafai & Sutton, 1999), there has been little empirical exploration of how people at the disadvantaged end of the "divide" actually use home computers or of how the technology fits into their lives. Theories of the domestication of technology would suggest that the process is complex, since these household computers are being adopted into an "already constituted social space" (Sutherland et al., 2000, p. 211), characterized by distinctive roles, relationships, and knowledges among family members.

After studying a particular "digital divide" initiative, we suggest that these established roles, relationships, and knowledges may be significantly different among working-class families, and that in particular gender plays into discourses around class and education to produce different experiences of technology. Using in-depth interviews with parents and children in a rural Florida community, we seek to understand how computer technology is incorporated into the existing complex of activities performed by mothers, and what the role of the technology might be in reproducing or challenging traditional gender relations. Even though most of our research participants tended to dismiss the idea that the computer and Internet access have led to many significant changes in their family life, their stories suggest that the reality is a little more complex. Many expressed ambivalence about the educational benefits of the computer and emphasized the psychological effort required in fulfilling program requirements. Even so, their accounts suggested that the computer also facilitates a new basis for women's engagement in technical thinking, one that, in some cases, creates tensions in the marital balance of power.

The Research Context

We have been examining the impact of "FamilyNet," a program designed by staff at an elementary school in rural Florida.[1] It uses federal Title 1 funds, earmarked for schools with large numbers of low-income students, to provide educationally at-risk children and their families with computers and instructional programs. In an attempt to "extend the school day into the home," as one of its coordinators put it, FamilyNet families receive iMac computers and an educational software package with which children, in grades 2 through 5, are able to practice reading and math skills. The package, designed to promote interactive learning and the reinforcement of material, is not designed in the school, but purchased from a national supplier of educational software. Using a connect script, the iMac dials into the family's Internet provider and logs in, then students complete a 15-minute math and a 15-minute reading module five days a week.

Students' progress is monitored by the school's parent coordinator, who runs student reports from her home every evening. Parents are expected to keep their children on task with daily at-home lessons. They understand that if their child is unable to maintain the regular study schedule, the computer may be taken back by the school. Although users have Internet access (their only financial obligation is the monthly service fee) and are provided with lists of suggested informational sites for parents and children, they are prohibited from downloading Internet files onto the iMac, and the computers do not have CD drives or printers. The educational software and Internet connection are available for use by all family members.

This research is based on interviews with 12 FamilyNet families living in a predominantly white, rural Florida community. In-depth home interviews were supplemented with observations of monthly parent meetings at the school, following the ethnographic, qualitative approaches used by researchers such as Morley (1992) and others. The initial plan was to interview entire families together, including both parents and children (all but one were two-parent families). However, fathers actually took part in only four interviews, even though several had implied they would be present. In some cases we were told upon our arrival that the father was elsewhere in the house, resting or working. This rather consistent pattern turned out to reflect a particular attitude to gender roles in the families, an issue that forms a focus of this analysis.

Although we used a set of guiding questions, interviews were open-ended and informal, and all were tape-recorded for later transcription, with parents giving permission for the use of their opinions in publication. The parents were all white (matching the demographics of the county), and ranged in ages from the mid 20s to the mid 40s, with family incomes typically ranging from $25,000 to $30,000. Our questions focused on several areas, including parents' initial expectations regarding the FamilyNet program, their perceptions of the program's efficacy, and the ways in which the completion of the 30-minute exercises fit into the family's daily routine. Children were also asked about their attitudes toward the math and reading exercises. Other questions explored the nature of family members' Internet use, the presence of other communication technologies in the home, and family members' overall sense of whether the computer and the Internet had had a significant impact on family life.

We also asked the mothers about their relationships with family and friends and about their own academic history. During the interviews and in the subsequent analysis we tried to listen to their accounts in ways that valued mothers' perspectives as insiders and yet allowed for critical insights that would enable us to situate our interpretations within a wider social context. We have recently begun a series of follow-up interviews with families already involved in the study.

The Relevance of Gender and Class

At its narrowest, our study was intended to evaluate the effectiveness of the program for our research partners. In a broader and more theoretical context, we wanted to explore the dynamics of family life, and the way the technology program was incorporated into these dynamics (see, e.g., Silverstone, Hirsch, & Morley, 1992). Our preliminary results suggest that much of the existing research does not adequately explain the different experiences of working-class life, particularly the dynamics of gender relationships and role definitions.

Cassidy (2001) provides a thorough discussion of the way computer technology has been until recently gendered as "male." Turkle (1988) characterizes women as being "computationally reticent" and fearful of the new technology. Other researchers have documented ways in which women and men interacted differently online, with women adopting a more collaborative, inclusive communication style that contrasted with the more aggressive, argumentative style that had come to characterize much Internet discourse (Balsamo, 1994; Bird, 1999; Warnick, 1999). As Cassidy puts it, "American fathers brought work home from the office, balanced checkbooks, tinkered with the machine as hobbyists, and played combative games alone or with their sons" (p. 49), and the computer was essentially a "masculine subdivision" of a feminine domain, the home (Morley, 1992). Cassidy then points out that in the early 1990s, the industry needed to expand the customer base for the personal computer. Advertising developed an ideal image of female consumers as "post-feminists"—upper middle-class women who have both fulfilling careers and families, and for whom the computer can be a crucial tool. Through technology, working women can tie together the demands of a career (not merely a "job"), household responsibilities, and childrearing.

Striking in both the established "masculine" discourse and the newer "feminine" one is the picture of an affluent, urban family. For instance, Cassidy (2001) examines magazines that discuss where women should keep their computers. Implicit in the advice is the assumption of wealth, as in an article she quotes in *Family PC*: "Choose a main floor location for your home office to make it easier to hop in and out of your domestic and business roles as needed. ... When child care and business hours overlap, play soft music for your baby to sing and dance to as you work on light business tasks" (quoted on p. 57).

Although this idyllic picture is certainly advertising hype, it does to a significant extent match the reality of computer ownership and use in the United States. Rainie and Kohut (2001) point out that women are now online in equal numbers with men, although they do not necessarily pursue the same activities as men. Both in Britain and the United States, men still tend to spend longer periods on their computers, probably reflecting more leisure time (e.g., Anderson et al., 1999). But whether male or female, the activities reflect the interests of the middle class—hobbies, banking, financial information, travel information, shopping. And that of course is hardly surprising. Only 18% of Americans with less than a high school education have Internet access, compared with 74% of those with a college degree (Pastore, 2000).

The consequence of that is that we now know quite a lot about the way computer technology has been appropriated in the middle-class household—a definitely "male" technology has been gradually adapted into a technology that is used in different ways by all members of the family for a wide variety of purposes.

On the other hand, we know very little about the relatively small numbers of Internet users who are not members of the affluent middle class, and for whom the image of working on "light business tasks" while a baby happily dances and sings is completely alien, if not patently absurd. The families we are working with are among that minority. As Reed (2000) points out, media technologies do not have a fixed meaning: "Rather, it is necessary to look at the formation and organization of their uses and to the social practices, conflicts, negotiations of power, and authority they illuminate and with which they engage" (p. 162). Our analysis is an attempt to look at how this technology has entered the social world of our informants, producing different articulations of gender, class, and discourses around education.

A Mother's Responsibility

In the first place, among members of the group we studied, computer technology is not defined as "male." In almost all the families we interviewed, if any parent had experience with computers, it was the mother. In the group as a whole, women almost invariably had a higher level of education than men, many of whom had not graduated from high school. At the same time, women who had used computers had rarely become truly "fluent," having likely used them primarily for such tasks as word processing in an office job. We did not find any families that felt comfortable with all dimensions of computer use, and men in particular were often indifferent to computers. Construction workers, landscapers, or day laborers do not "bring home work from the office" or "tinker" with their computers. In fact, they have very little interest in computers at all, and find them irrelevant to their lives.

The fathers do have an often vaguely defined interest in their children's education. They do want their children to do well at school, and they do share their wives' belief in the computer's ability to help the children. Thus, husband and wife Jeff and Kathy discuss the power of the computer as an educational tool, with Kathy stating, "It's amazing the stuff they have on computers, I'm telling you. ... It teaches Spanish on the computer, I mean it's unlimited, it's endless." Jeff agrees: "Yeah, it's, it's a plethora of knowledge." Yet the men often do not have the skills (or interest) to contribute much to the educational process. A few minutes later, Jeff says that he does very little with the computer: "I'd like to start ... paying bills over the Internet ... but other than that I really don't use the stupid thing." Furthermore, unlike the situation in many middle-class families, education in the group we studied is clearly coded as a task for women; since the computers appear in the home as educational tools, they also tend to be considered as within the female sphere. Research confirms that across all socioeconomic groups, the task of mediating between family and public institutions such as schools has traditionally fallen to women (Reay, 1995, 1999; Ribbens, 1994). Reay's studies of class differences in parental involvement in children's education underscore the burdens shouldered by women, especially working-class women, not only in producing a fed, clothed, and "properly resourced" child for the classroom but also of monitoring the home-school relationship. Reay's findings suggest that working-class fathers tend to be only peripherally engaged in such tasks. These tasks, by definition, tend to be part of what "being a mother" is all about.

For instance, summing up her weekly contribution as a teacher's helper in her son's school, Anita said, "I put in as many volunteer hours as I can. That's my job. I'm Robert's mom, I'm Cory's mom, and, you know, I do things that moms do." The way she says this suggests that she believes the meaning is obvious. The mothers who participated in this study assume they will play an educational role in their children's lives. Routinely, they help with homework and monitor academic performance, but in some cases, their efforts go farther. One mother maintained a "math wall" in her kitchen on which she tacked up large cut-outs of fractions and pie charts as a way of reinforcing arithmetic concepts. Another described how she provided academic enrichment during summer vacations in the form of daily workbook exercises. Mothers took pains to expand their children's learning opportunities outside school by coordinating after-school activities; nearly all the FamilyNet children took part in extracurricular activities ranging from karate and baseball to Boy Scouts and sign language.

In the rural, white, working-class world of these participants, motherhood is constructed as an intensive, full-time job in which the active promotion of children's educational success is a key component. In this context, it is not surprising that mothers (and fathers) generally welcomed the opportunity to take part in FamilyNet. They saw the instructional programs as providing "a head start, a good foundation," in the words of one mother. "It's like having your own personal tutor," and "it's a godsend," others told us. Several simply said they felt lucky to be included. Some perceived the computers as crucial in preparing children for a technologically rich future, beyond their immediate value in supporting school learning and improving grades, and facilitating computer use was an important task of a mother. As Carol said, "everything's going to be computerized you know. So you, you really need to know something about computers 'cause when their generation grows up the computers that we have now are going to be obsolete ... so they need to know it early and be able to grow with it."

In characterizing the computer as "a powerful thing of the future" and the child who knows how to use it as having "an in-demand skill," parents depict the home computer as a vehicle for the attainment of the educational and cultural capital that will ensure a child's future security. Yet as our conversations with parents unfolded, it became apparent that the mothers' optimism about the program's benefits for children was sometimes at odds with their descriptions of the difficult, even stressful conditions surrounding its use. Clearly the FamilyNet program has presented certain dilemmas for mothers. One dilemma centers on the explicit mission of FamilyNet to "extend the school day," as the coordinators describe it. Since the mothers are dealing with domestic chores, taking care of other children, and in many cases, doing paid work, it is hard for them to provide the exclusive focus on their children's educational needs that the program seems to require. Time shortages limit the extent to which they are available to supervise and help the child complete the 30 minutes a day online, and fathers rarely help. As Cassidy points out, even for middle-class women, the introduction of new technologies, intended to help, may actually place extra burdens on women, who now have a new duty to add to their many others: "Fanciful rhetoric covers over the inevitable strains generated by new duties and practices" (p. 52).

Still, the benefits of maternal availability were generally taken for granted, and the effort devoted by adults to helping with the math and reading exercises was seen as distinguishing successful from unsuccessful FamilyNet parents. Thus Mary, reflecting on why some of the families in the program might have been unable to complete the daily exercises (and were therefore required to return their computers), said: "You know what I think it is—I think a lot of the other [parents] don't want to be bothered with it. ... Nowadays a lot of parents, just my experience with Cub Scouts, they don't even want to be bothered ... if they can get away from their kids for an hour they do it. You know you have to be there to be able to help them." And although Mary referred to "parents," it was clear from her context and from her own experience that she really meant "mothers."

Such comments, emphasizing the child's needs for supervision and "moral support," tend to obscure the emotional claims made on the mothers whose children take part in such programs. Because the decision to embark on the FamilyNet program is so firmly entrenched in a notion of its benefits, most of the participants were reluctant to discuss their reservations. But several mothers' comments point indirectly toward the psychological effort required when children are uncooperative. We heard these comments: "The hardest part is just getting him to do it"; "At first he liked it but now it's like pulling teeth"; "If he's stressed out, the whole exercise would be blown"; "If she's not in the mood [to do the exercises], she's not in the mood. If I feel she's not going to use it [the computer] properly and not use it the way she's expected to use it, then so be it, we'll take it away"; "One of the conditions is that he has to do it, and if it becomes a big fight,

I'm not going to fight with him every night." Helen was particularly frank in describing the emotional work involved in getting and keeping her 10-year-old twins on task every day. She spoke of having to squeeze the exercises into an already busy schedule, saying: "No matter how hard I try to set aside a time when we're all calm, it never happens." By the end of the first year in the program, she felt that the family had become "burned out." "It's really strange," she concluded, "how that machine in there causes a lot of negativity in this house."

The practice of parental involvement in these pressurized circumstances is experienced, to varying degrees, as difficult and stressful. Such feelings make sense given that parents are faced with competing discourses with regard to the meaning of the technology. For instance, while the educational benefits are taken for granted, many mothers also spoke about their fear of the Internet as holding many dangers for children, or of computers taking too much time and keeping kids away from more healthy, outdoor activities.

So while participants took the position that any problems they had were balanced by the benefits of the program, conflicted feelings still came through. Several expressed concerns about the possibility that academic advancement was being achieved at the expense of the child's emotional well-being. Thus Maureen gave the program credit for her son's improved reading scores but was ambivalent about the increased academic pressure: "I always had a belief and I'm not sure if it was true or not, I didn't want to push him ... the trend was to get reading with your infants and reading with your toddlers. I thought to myself, I had a nice childhood. I had a great education ... anyway I thought let him be a kid, let him enjoy what childhood is about, he's got plenty of time for school. But then I got worried, when he wasn't with the other kids. ... I think the world is going a little quick with all this technology." Similarly, Kathy worried that computers might discourage a child's active outdoor play: "When I was a kid all we ever did was go run around, ride bikes, play ball. All these kids nowadays want to do is sit in front of either the computer or TV." Sometimes parents expressed discomfort with particular properties of the technology. One mother found the nightly computing of the child's scores by the FamilyNet coordinator "intrusive." For Helen it was the fast pace of the programmed exercises that frustrated her child: "No matter how much time they've given him, he's very slow at it. So, it's like it makes him feel horrible because he's not reading fast enough."

Gender Conflicts

Although most families seemed to accept the fundamental tenet that education=computer=mother's responsibility, in several families we saw strains emerging around the gendered construction of education, with regard to the FamilyNet computer. Several women, for instance, have been trying to persuade their husbands to advance their own educations, by taking advantage of the opportunity to study for the G.E.D. using the FamilyNet system, an initiative the school is also coordinating. Although the possibility of finding a better job was mentioned as a reason for this, a primary point seemed to be that seeing a father study would motivate the children. Fathers, however, were not willing to become the role models the women wanted. Some mothers believed that technology was a way out of the life they were living themselves, while they regarded their husbands as "obstinate" or "stubborn" because they would not go along. One husband (not present at our interview), a mason with an eighth-grade education, had begun pretesting for a G.E.D. program, at his wife Mary's urging: "Well, I was hoping that he'll go for something in computers. You know, go to technical school or something ... I mean he's 33 years old and his back hurts him now." However, his enthusiasm was in doubt. His fourth-grade son commented about his father's attitude: "He's like 'I'm not gonna stay here and read 10 stories' ... or 'I don't want to play the stupid [spelling] games.'" Another mother commented, "I want him to get a GED. ... It's not a goal of his, it's more a goal of mine, so motivating him ... is not that easy. ... He doesn't feel he needs it because of the line of work he has, it doesn't matter whether he graduated from high school or not."

Wives did accept that their husbands' work often required long hours away from home: several fathers worked in construction some distance away, or spent long hours as self-employed manual workers. So women took responsibility for dealing with the tensions generated by the computer in homes where men were more "computationally reticent." As Frances put it, "the guys around here are less interested; I guess it depends on the kind of man." Indeed, in various ways women described men as marginal to family life at home. Frances, for instance, characterized her husband as "an outside kind of guy" and "a redneck" who "mostly sits out in the shed with his buddies." Fathers may be proud of their children's accomplishments in an abstract sense, but they seem to be insulated from daily demands on their time and energy, and are not motivated to explore the computer much, except for the occasional game. Stan, the grandfather of a participating child, was using the program to study for his G.E.D., but even after months working on the computer, he had never attempted to use it for anything else, including email: "I wasn't that much interested in the Internet or whatever else is on there. I understand you can get quite a bit."

Maureen was grateful that her husband sometimes supervises their son's daily online lesson, but expects little more. He was a largely silent presence during the interview; at one point she looked at him and commented: "He watches [the son] do his project, his lessons, but that's as far as it goes. He wouldn't really know how to turn it on, right, Dave?" Anita expressed disappointment that her husband used the computer in a very limited way, when she had hoped he might develop his interest in games to do more: "I've never seen my husband pick up a book, he just doesn't read. But he does go on the computer, so I had hopes ... but mostly he plays his fantasy baseball. He picks his players, and I don't even know if he knows how it works. ... I don't really know if he understands the whole, what everything is. What is open to you with it, you know ... or he's just not interested in it."

Similarly, fathers were only marginally involved with school; we observed that very few fathers ever attended the monthly parent meetings. Those who did attend tended to sit on the periphery of the group, perhaps minding an infant, but not actively participating. In contrast, Reay (1999) presents a picture of middle-class fathers as much more involved in their children's education, both at home and at school. She argues that working-class fathers remain peripheral, in part because of teachers' perceptions that they are less competent than their middle-class counterparts in supporting their children's education.

Thus, in keeping with the idea of home and school as feminine spheres, it was mothers who took primary responsibility for their children's success in the program and when a child's progress was slow, mothers may have felt they were especially to blame. Thus Helen attributed her children's ongoing resistance to doing the exercises and their lack of general interest in the computer to her own discomfort with computer technology: "You see, I'm not gung-ho about this and I'm sure that's influenced them somewhat. ... I'm passing that on to the children."

Computer Fluency

Thus women saw the program and the larger area of computer fluency as a road to educational success. They seem to have thoroughly accepted the belief that "a working mother could guarantee her children's success simply by purchasing a computer," as Cassidy puts it (2000, p. 51). In that respect, working class mothers are reinforcing a view that is widely held across all strata of American society—people believe that computers will bring educational benefits, and cite education as a primary reason for acquiring one (Pastore, 2001). As Chen (2000) writes, "'equality of digital opportunity' is fast becoming synonymous with 'equality of educational opportunity'" (p. 168).

Yet while there are growing numbers of studies that suggest an educational advantage associated with computer ownership (Kafai & Sutton, 1999), there is also evidence that the benefits are not felt equally. For instance, Attewelle and Battle (1999) found that ownership of a home computer does correlate with higher test scores in math and reading. But children from higher socioeconomic status homes achieve significantly larger educational gains, suggesting that "pre-existing forms of social inequality may modify the frequency of home computer use, and/or the ways computers are used, and hence affect the educational benefits derived from home computing" (p. 1).

That seems to be the crux of the problem with the families we came to know. Cassidy describes the romanticized advertising for the Encarta encyclopedia, in which a father fondly discusses Jean-Paul Sartre and existentialism with his children as he tucks them into bed, after they have perused the encyclopedia as a family.

While this picture probably does not reflect the everyday experience of any family, it does point to a fundamental fact. Affluent families simply have the cultural capital (Bourdieu, 1984) to aid their children's educational development. It is easier for them to conduct a literature search for a research paper, not just because they are more familiar with computers: they may know some basic terminology, names of sources to start with, or even more basically, appropriate questions to ask. For instance, Carol told of helping her son with a science fair project in which he invented an extension to an oven mitt, "and I was trying to find out who invented the oven mitt. ... I asked Jeeves and they gave me a whole bunch of listings of different kinds of oven mitts and stuff, but nobody could tell me who invented the oven mitt."

Indeed, the families we met did not seem to find the Internet a particularly welcoming place. Like women across all social strata, many had embraced email, finding this an effective and pleasurable way to keep in touch with family or reconnect with old friends. But when it came to exploring the Internet, the women in our study varied widely in the extent to which they sought out educational and recreational applications for themselves and their children. A few mothers played an active part in facilitating their child's exploration of the Internet as an educational resource. Frances, for instance, found the computer "really useful. I mean, you don't even have to go to the library anymore. They've got everything on there." Frances successfully helped her daughter research a science fair project on the Internet and explored a variety of entertainment sites with her including Walt Disney and the Back Street Boys. She also discovered a wide range of personal uses for the Internet, including emailing high school friends in her hometown, and in anticipation of a possible move back to the northeast she began looking up information about school districts in the area.

Few other families shared her experience. Helen, for example, looked up various sites she thought her twins would enjoy ("animal sites, Ricky Martin, Crocodile Hunter") but became frustrated by her children's lack of curiosity: "They have no interest so why should I?" She has used the computer herself to check sports scores, but gets impatient: "It takes you forever to find what you're looking for and by the time you find it, who cares anymore?"

Many of the women don't have the time to surf, and many don't really know where to start when faced with a research project. They have not found many compelling reasons to stay on the net to gain the fluency they need; many lack credit cards, so they do not shop, manage finances, or plan extensive travel online. As the Internet rapidly becomes a site of consumption, the nonaffluent consumer is not desirable. The women in our study, therefore, focused very intently on having their children complete the assigned study plan, and were being rewarded by higher scores. But they were much less certain about how to really use the computer to tap into the rich educational resources they knew were out there. Jeff said directly what many of the women also seemed to feel. Although he had used the computer quite frequently when it first arrived, he had become frustrated: "I've hit walls every time I want to try and do anything." This seemed to be a fairly common pattern among the families we interviewed, echoing a point made by Katz and Aspden (1998), who found that low-income families were the most likely to experience a drop off in Internet use over time.

It may be, then, that the relative lack of social and cultural capital experienced by these families places a severe limit on women's ambitions to create the transformed educational experience they want for their children. Indeed, computers may eventually be seen as yet another way in which those who are already advantaged increase the gap between them and those with markedly less capital.

Conclusion

Hardt (1998), points out that American media studies have long failed adequately to take into account the realities of class in a society that prefers to see itself as "classless." He suggests that working-class people are much more likely to be alienated from dominant perspectives on the world. "Consequently, communication studies remains informed by progressive notions of change that adhere to ideological and political constructions of a social reality in the context of middle-class expectations" (p. 51). We believe that the discourse on computer and Internet use has indeed reflected middle-class experience, including middle-class definitions of both gender relations and educational success, and we suggest that these definitions do not necessarily hold true in different contexts.

In examining the use of computers in education, Robinson (1998) concludes that the most significant "digital divide" is not in access to the technology but in children's abilities to use higher-order thinking skills to navigate it effectively. As she explains, people "need computer skills that are not only technical, but also social and cognitive" (p. 149), and it is here that children from low-income families are often at a disadvantage, lacking the kind of parental expertise that enables them to become truly computer fluent. Some fathers in our study were aware of this, but mothers, who want very much for their children to succeed, often seemed especially conscious that they were unable to offer the kind of support they felt their children needed. Furthermore, our findings suggest that technology can have a potentially disruptive effect on existing family dynamics. For instance, women apparently believe more firmly in the possibilities of the technology to provide educational advancement for both their children and their husbands, while husbands resist their wives' pressure both to engage the technology for their own education and to become more actively involved in their children's learning. Indeed, the men in the study implicitly and explicitly raised important questions about the taken-for-granted notion that computer fluency is something to which everyone should aspire. One man, for instance, pointed out that he lived in a rural area and worked outdoors because he preferred to be away from the pace and technology of urban life. While he did not use this terminology, his view might well be seen as resistance to a bourgeois, paternalistic norm that tells people like him (a self-described "red-neck") how to live their lives.

Our study is necessarily preliminary, and we cannot draw sweeping conclusions from such a limited sample. However, we believe it points to some significant issues. First, we suggest that the still-pervasive rhetoric of computer technology as the "great equalizer" (Wolf, 1998) needs serious interrogation. Many still suggest that simple economics will take care of technological inequalities, as cheap computers saturate the household market, much as televisions did (Compaine, 2001). Forgotten is the point that television is an essentially passive medium, with a finite capacity. Computer technology is uniquely interactive, demanding increasing levels of skill and competency from its users, if its virtually limitless capacity is to be used. Our study was conducted among families who believe in the rhetoric. They are convinced that computers will bring great benefits to their children, and they have more training in how to use them than families who buy independently. Mothers have made a commitment to being active partners in their children's education, and extensive research shows how important that commitment is (Baker et al., 1999; Samaras & Wilson, 1999; Schneider & Coleman, 1993). Yet most still have a sense of frustration about their inability to become part of the great new world of digital competence. Every family regarded television as a much more important form of technology for the family; we asked families whether they would rather give up the computer or their TVs, and all found the question absurd. As Sutherland et al. (2000) write, "home computer use amongst young people is far from a simple and uniform phenomenon" (p. 211) but develops in "a complex interplay between familial discourses and technological characteristics of the computer" (p. 211).

Hardt (1998) recommends that media scholars should be "working with the complexity of communication over time and within the social, economic, and cultural frames of lived experience, by incorporating ethnographies of consumption into social and cultural histories of participation" (p. 60). Our intent here was to contribute an example of an "ethnography of consumption" that adds some depth to the more macro-level assessments of computer use. We suggest that without a more subtle understanding of the way class and gender articulate in everyday experience, we cannot hope to be able to assess the real impact of computer technology in any society.

Notes

We acknowledge the support of the University of South Florida Collaborative on Children and Families, which funded the research upon which this chapter is based.

1. The name of the program has been changed to protect confidentiality. All participants quoted are also identified by pseudonyms.

References

Anderson, B., A. McWilliam, H. Lacohee, E. Clucas, & J. Gershuny. (1999). Family life in the digital home: Domestic telecommunications at the end of the twentieth century. *BT Technology 17*(1), 85–97.

Attewelle, Paul, & Juan Battle. (1999). Home computers and school performance. *The Information Society, 15,* 1–10.

Baker, Amy J. L, Susan Kessler-Sklar, Chaya S. Piotrkowski, & Faith Lamb Parker. (1999). Kindergarten and first-grade teachers' reported knowledge of parents' involvement in their children's education. *The Elementary School Journal, 99*(4), 367–381.

Balsamo, Anne. (1994). Feminism for the incurably informed. In M. Dery (Ed.), *Flame wars: The discourse of cyberculture* (pp. 125–156). Raleigh, NC: Duke University Press.

Bird, S. Elizabeth. (1999). Chatting on Cynthia's porch: Building community in an Internet fan culture. *Southern Communication Journal, 65*(1), 49–65.

Bourdieu, Pierre. (1984). *Distinction: A social critique of the judgment of taste.* Cambridge, MA: Harvard University Press.

Cassidy, Marsha F. (2001). Cyberspace meets domestic space: Personal computers, women's work, and the gendered territories of the family home. *Critical Studies in Media Communication, 18*(1), 44–65.

Chen, Milton. (2000). Commentary. *Future of Children, 10*(2), 168–171.

Compaine, Benjamin M. (2001). The digital divide as myth or reality? Paper presented at the Fifty-first Annual Conference of the International Communication Association, May 24–28, Washington, D. C.

Hansen, E. (1992). The BUDDY project. *T.H.E. Journal, 20,* 61–65.

Hardt, Hanno. (1998). *Interactions: Critical studies in communication, media, and journalism.* New York: Rowman & Littlefield.

Kafai, Yasmin B., & Sharon Sutton. (1999). Elementary school students' computer and Internet use at home: Current trends and issues. *Journal of Educational Computing Research, 21*(3), 345–362.

Katz, James E., and Philip Aspden. (1998). Internet dropouts in the USA: The invisible group. *Telecommunications Policy 22*(4/5), 327–339.

Morley, David. (1992). *Television audiences and cultural studies.* New York: Routledge.

Novak, T. P. & D. L. Hoffman. (1998). Bridging the Digital Divide: The impact of race on computer access and Internet use. Accessed online at http://ecommerce.vanderbilt.edu/research/papers/html/manuscripts/race/science.html

Pastore, Michael. (2000). Lower-income households moving online. Accessed online at: http://cyberatlas.internet.com/big_picture/demographics

Pastore, Michael. (2001). Parents see Net as education aid. Accessed online at: http://cyberatlas.internet.com/markets/education/print/0,,5951_328051,00.html

Rainie, Lee, & Andrew Kohut. (2001). Tracking online life: How women use the Internet to cultivate relationships with family and friends. Report: The Pew Internet and American Life Project. Accessed at http://www.pewinternet.org

Reay, Diane. (1995). A silent majority? Mothers in parental involvement. *Women's Studies International Forum, 18*(3), 337–348.

Reay, Diane. (1999). Linguistic capital and home-school relationships: Mothers' interactions with their children's primary school teachers. *Acta Sociologica, 42,* 160–168.

Reed, Lori. (2000). Domesticating the personal computer: The mainstreaming of a new technology and the cultural management of a widespread technophobia. *Critical Studies in Media Communication, 17*(2), 159–185.

Ribbens, Jane. (1994). *Mothers and their children: A feminist sociology of childrearing.* London: Sage.

Robinson, Paulette. (1998). Equity and access to computer technology for grades K-12. In Bosah Ebo (ed.). *Cyberghetto or cybertopia: Race, class, and gender on the Internet* (pp. 137–154). Westport, CT: Praeger.

Samaras, Anastasia P. & Josephine C. Wilson. (1999). Am I invited: Perspectives of family involvement with technology in inner city schools. *Urban Education, 34*(4), 499–530.

Schneider, B., & J. S. Coleman. (Eds). (1993). *Parents, their children, and schools.* Boulder, CO: Westview.

Shields, Margie K., & Richard E. Behrman. (2000). Children and computer technology: Analysis and recommendations. *Future of Children, 10*(2), 2–24.

Silverstone, Roger, E. Hirsch, & David Morley. (1992). Information and communication technologies and the moral economy of the household. In R. Silverstone and E. Hirsch (Eds.). *Consuming technologies: Media and information in domestic spaces* (pp. 15–31). New York: Routledge.

Sutherland, Rosamund, Keri Facer, Ruth Furlong, & John Furlong. (2000). A new environment for education: The computer in the home. *Computers and Education, 34,* 195–212.

Turkle, Sherry. (1988). Computational reticence: Why women fear the intimate machine. In C. Kramarae (Ed.), *Technology and women's voices: Keeping in touch* (pp. 41–61). New York: Routledge.

Warnick, Barbara. (1999). Masculinizing the feminine: Inviting women on line ca. 1997. *Critical Studies in Mass Communication, 16,* 1–19.

Wolf, Alecia. (1998). Exposing the great equalizer: Demythologizing Internet equity. In Bosah Ebo (ed.). *Cyberghetto or cybertopia: Race, class, and gender on the Internet* (pp. 15–32). Westport, CT: Praeger.

Chapter 12

Gendered Agency in Information Society: On Located Politics of Technology

Marja Vehviläinen

Introduction

Gender is one of the important relations to be addressed in technologically mediated agency. Culturally, information and communication technologies are male-dominated worlds (Herring, 1996; Spender, 1995; Wakeford, 2000). Although both women and men use computers and the Internet easily, women tend to define themselves as nonexperts (Henwood et al., 2000). It is young men who are the first users of the newest technologies (Nurmela, 1997). There seems to be a commonly shared understanding in Western societies that it is (some) men who have the core expertise in technology generally and in information and communication technologies (ICT) particularly. There is a nexus between (male) experts and technology, as Judy Wajcman (1991, p. 165) puts it. This undermines women's agency within the technologically mediated society.

Feminist researchers have discussed gendered agency and citizenship. Ruth Lister (1997) points out that citizenship has two sides: the rights of the citizen that are universal to all, and the particular social practices that consist of the local and situated activity of people, organized in various social relations of gender, class, ethnicity, age, and place. People, for example, act in a segregated world where women work in the fields of care and men in the fields of technology. Related to this segregation, women's lower salaries are based on contracts between labor unions and employers. These practices shape agency and intervene in people's possibilities of using their universal rights. Equal access to information technology is a universal right in Nordic societies, and certainly important, but people's actual agency and citizenship go beyond the right of equal access to the practices and relations embedded in agency and citizenship as well as to people's subjectivity.

Lister's political agency bridges two fundamentally different approaches to understanding agency in the debates about gender and technology research and politics. The first one, related to universal rights, is often referred to as a liberal approach. Since women have a lesser role in the development of technology than men, liberal feminists have designed programs to help women "catch up" in technology in order to create equal access to it. As Rosalind Gill and Keith Grint (1995, p. 6) explain by quoting Syvia Walby (1990, p. 4), liberal feminism sees technology as neutral: "women and men are seen as both equal and, at some fundamental level, the same, sharing a basic humanity and rationality ... [G]ender is seen not in terms of social structure but as 'the summation of numerous small-scale deprivations.'"

The second approach relates to what Flis Henwood and her colleagues (2000, p. 114) call a social constructionist approach. Like Lister, it stresses the crucial role of gendered practices of agency, including gendered orders of skills and technology and is "less concerned with getting women in to the technology than with understanding why and how women are so often excluded and why technology has come to be perceived as masculine. ... In contrast to liberal discourse, in the social constructionist literature, 'skill' is not a neutral term. ... Gender is constructed in relation to technology and technical skills" (p. 114). Gender, agency, and technology are thus seen as social constructions which are shaped through people's concrete everyday practices.

In the spirit of Lister, I am particularly interested here in the bridging of and the dialogue between the two approaches, and I explore the ways liberal politics intertwine with the located and situated, the socially constructed agency found in the practices of certain women's information technology groups. However, there are strong tensions between the approaches, as Henwood and others argue. In order to achieve a productive dialogue the approaches must be combined in some way. The universal version of equal access to technology must become more situated and better account for agency. Agency here refers to human activity, including conscious political activity at work, at home and, for example, in neighborhood centers and other semi-public sites. The focus is on activity that relates to new information and communication technologies and especially to women's own situated and located definitions of technology.

The located and situated intertwine with partially technologically mediated social orders. As suggested in Donna Haraway's (1991) theory of cyborg subjectivity, the agency of people binds the bodily and located together with the machines of global economies. The located is by no means distinct from the global, and this also holds true for located politics.

Arturo Escobar (1999, pp. 36–37) raises the question of located politics in the context of cyberspatial technologies. Global technologies have a tendency to erode the sense of place and local practices, detaching women from their localities and emphasizing sameness and equal access instead. Escobar develops agency as that which balances the local, social, and global. This entails conflicting demands: "(1) to maintain the value of rootedness and place; the importance of the face-to-face interaction for the creation of cultures; the viability of local times; the organicity of certain relations to the natural; and yet (2) to affirm the transformative potential of places and the need to transform them (places have their particular forms of domination and even terror); finally (3) to advance both processes through a critical engagement with cyber culture."

Here I explore located agency and located politics of technology in the context of a Nordic welfare state and the development of an information society which runs according to the liberal politics of equal access. I share Escobar's emphasis on the located and look at the politics that start from the everyday practices of women's ICT groups. Women have widely used small groups as a method to share and articulate their own local knowledges (Blum, 1991; Bono & Kemp, 1991). Like Henwood and Lister, I see the importance of the gendering of social order in these practices: As Ecobar says, the local practices contain relations of power which need to be explicated. Furthermore, I briefly take up Escobar's third point concerning the critical engagement with cyberspace.

The North Karelian women's information technology group project started as a grassroots activity in a neighborhood center (Vehviläinen, 2001) and later expanded into a broad educational program administered by a college-level institute for vocational education (Vehviläinen, 2000). I have, together with Sari Tuuva and Johanna Uotinen, followed the project from 1997 to 2000. On three different occasions we interviewed a significant number (one-third) of the participants, as well as all the teachers and developers of the project, and we attended meetings and collected documents and newspaper clippings about the project.

I start by describing the Finnish and North Karelian contexts and the two phases of the women's information technology project. In both phases the women's groups aimed to bridge differences between located and liberal approaches to constructing knowledge of technology. The two phases provide concrete and different settings for my study. I use these settings first as a starting point to examine the construction of located agency. This is accomplished by relating these project experiences to texts about information society strategies as well as to the institutional practices that supported the women's groups. I map the social and textual practices found, including the social stratifications embedded within them (Smith, 1990). Overcoming the differences between located and liberal politics is difficult and I examine the disadvantages that the women faced. I end by discussing the practices that empower located politics of technology.

The Finnish and North Karelian Setting

The Finnish economy has since the mid 1990s developed in resonance with the Nokia mobile phone industry. Equal access to information and communication technologies has been a governmental goal expressed, for example, in national strategy documents, and people do indeed use mobile phones, computers, and the Internet in large numbers (Nurmela, 1997). Slightly more women than men have used computers in their workplaces since the 1980s (Lehto & Sutela, 1999), and in most parts of Finland schools have good computing facilities.

Although "equal access to computers" as stated in governmental policies is generally provided, equal access is most commonly seen as a universal right available to individuals regardless of gender, class, and region. There is a strong paradoxical rhetoric which argues that equality between women and men is an already existing fact—in spite of the exceptionally deep segregation in the labor market and in domestic work and the enduring wage gap between women and men (Rantalaiho & Heiskanen, 1997). Recently the same rhetoric has found its way to information and communication technologies, although few women are involved in the design of new technologies and there is no reason to conclude that the culture of new technologies is "less male" in Finland than in other places.[1] There has been little discussion of the gendered bias in information technology and there have been very few political initiatives in relation to women and technology. The women's information groups discussed here, for example, did not have prior Finnish examples to refer to and struggled in amorphous terrain with relatively undeveloped terms and concepts (compared, e.g., to the UK or even the other Nordic countries).[2]

The study discussed in this chapter took place between 1997 and 2000 in the North Karelia province, on the eastern border of Finland, next to the state of Karelia in Russia. It is a region of high unemployment (20–30%) and long distances. The regional authorities there aimed to develop information technology in order to transform the region's peripheral position into a local and unique—both culturally and geographically—entry point into the global nets. Furthermore, as a region of a Nordic welfare state, North Karelia aimed to take care of its inhabitants and invite them all to take part in societal development. A number of ongoing development projects focused on the problematics of citizenship in the regional information society. Many of the projects were partially funded by European Union (EU) structural funds for peripheral areas. The funding agents which distributed EU funds locally used the regional "local agency" strategy as (one of) their reference(s) when they prioritized projects to be supported.

Local (Liberal) Politics of Technology: Information Technology in a Women's Group

The first women's ICT group gathered in a neighborhood center in a suburb of the regional capital. Those involved ranged from busy working women to students and mothers engaged in part-time work. Living near the suburb was all they had in common. They approached information technology from the starting point of their everyday lives and aimed to develop their own understanding of it. So, for example, during the summer they picked berries in the huge North Karelia forests and their first computer experiment was the making of labels for canning bottles. In December they produced Christmas cards and they built their own home pages. They used the Internet to search for information on child care and cooking as well as on their work.

Thirty-six-year-old Sari, mother of three young children, was an active member of the group. She said in an interview:

> I want to be at home as long as the children are small. I work (sell cosmetics, study for a new occupation) while the children sleep. ... In the group I have learnt how to do letters, registers, and time schedules for my work with the computer. We have a computer at home, bought by my husband, for example, for games for the girls. I did not, however, first see how I could use it myself but it was first in the group that I learned to see my needs. ... I was asked: What are you doing there? Have you used computers? I had not been using, and then other women also felt that they could join us although they had no experience. ... First we made canning labels. Each woman was able to say what she wanted to be done. The group first met every fortnight. ... In the group we speak about other things, too.

The group worked in a neighborhood center which was supported by a welfare network of local residents and experts including social workers, city planners, youth workers, and others. The network had cooperative discussions about the well-being of the neighborhood and, for example, took care of the center and arranged for equipment to be used by local residents. The social workers supported the residents by discussing, encouraging, and giving advice on their self-help and practical arrangements—but they never arranged things *for* people. They used the services of the welfare state to facilitate people's grass-roots activity and local agency. They were partially financed by the European Union but they were also employed by a Nordic welfare state. The women's information technology group was initiated by an active woman living in the area who brought women together and developed goals for learning information technology (IT) based on the women's starting points. The welfare network did not start or run the group, but as soon as it was established the network lent a hand and provided better equipment and computer support for the group. It protected the group and strengthened the ground upon which the group acted. The network provided equal access but it did this in a situated manner, very much in the spirit of Lister.

The group gained media attention and provided a model for further development and involvement of North Karelian women. It was an ideal example of the North Karelian regional information society strategy for the years 1999–2006, *By Joint Work Party to the Information Society*:

> The information society is about to come—but who sets the terms? Its development is often discussed with enthusiasm, but it is still society that faces the challenges of a new environment brought by technological development. ... People themselves influence the kind of information society they act in, and the kind of acting they do. Technology is enabling but also shaped by people. Information society is not only a sector of experts but a natural and useful part of people's everyday leisure and work. (p. 1)

> Information society is the whole of interacting communities, built together by North Karelians, where information technology is used for one's own needs. (p. 5)

> North Karelia has all the prerequisites to act as a laboratory in which technology has been developed and experimented with in actual situations for the needs of users, toward the achievement of a true information society. (p. 17)

The North Karelian strategy emphasized the citizens' perspective and active agency as necessary to develop and shape an information society. It was understood that individuals needed to start from their situated locations, rather than simply learn skills for using technology as liberal politics implies. The North Karelian regional strategy supported situated citizenship and the agency of the women's information technology group.

The women's group started from everyday practices and this

made the group important. It allowed the women to share neighborhood experiences and allowed them to approach information technology from their own starting points. The group, although temporary and gathered for a specific purpose, catalyzed the women's agency. In the group, women were active in integrating information technology into their own lives and specific situations.

Liberal Policy With Some Locatedness

In the second phase, the North Karelian Institute for Vocational Education took up the idea of women's information technology groups and ran a similar project in 1998 and 1999 supported by European Union structural funding. Six groups of 10–12 women gathered together with female teachers in rural areas as well as in the regional capital for one and a half years. The women participants were also invited to the institute for day-long workshops that were presented by male teachers.

In the second phase the teaching consisted of basic skills in information technology and the women students took standard exams in basic computing to earn "ICT passports." The women's information technology groups were only one of the numerous projects at the institute. The hierarchical relations typical to large public organizations intertwined with the women's information technology project and altered the educational goals to the teaching of basic skills, with these skills understood as neutral.

Group responses to this approach varied, and resulted in more and less successful outcomes. In some groups women began to talk among themselves and to help each other. In those groups information technology was actively considered in the context of the women's lives. Basic skills were taught in a standard manner, but the women started to evaluate the content by commenting on it to each other. The commenting was not systematically supported but some teachers knew they should leave room for the women's own reflections. Even within hierarchical practices there was some space for situated definitions and women's agency.

The women who took part in the second phase were not aware of the "everyday" starting point of the first group. They were offered a free information technology training course which was organized in women's groups close to their homes. They used the opportunity tailored specifically to them, as one of the participants put it: "Already the [course] title indicated that it was meant for rural women, and of course this was the first sign that it suits me better than any other course. It was a call just for me" (Tuuva & Uotinen, 1999).

The participants who were able to follow the instruction were usually content to study with other women and with a woman teacher. They passed their exams and many of them bought a computer or new programs and the project helped install them. The women integrated information technology with their everyday lives but there was a difference compared to the first group. Women's grassroots activity in information technology had turned into information technology education based on liberal politics.

The development of the Finnish information society has been coordinated through a number of strategy documents. Among the strategies, the Finnish National Fund for Research and Development strategy *Quality of Life, Knowledge and Competitiveness* (1998) aims to be a national—common to all—strategy for the Finnish Information Society. It defines the space of agency and aims "to provide equal opportunities for acquisition and management of information and for the development of knowledge" and "to strengthen democracy and opportunities for social influence" (p. 10). The equal opportunities are provided by making services and basic skills available to everybody and by providing easy-to-use products. Now "each individual, business and organization has responsibility for developing their know-how and availing themselves of the opportunities offered" (p. 11).

An information society is built by individuals who take the initiative on their own regardless of situated and social relations. Some groups are mentioned in the context of basic skills, such as the elderly and the displaced, and these groups are taken care of. The Finnish society defines itself as a welfare state which looks after those who are in need of aid. Yet the active agents who build and shape the society are all individuals. They are citizens in terms of liberal theory, citizens who have a universal right to equal access and who are able to make their own decisions without regard to their daily practices or gender and class relations. The only social difference recognized is the difference in the basic skills of technology and information use. This is a gendered difference, but it is not recognized in the strategy.

In the information society, basic skills in information and communication technologies are to be arranged for everyone and thus for women as well as men. If women want to study the skills in groups, the strategy suggests funding for groups. The situated active agency of women which acknowledges social differences gets, however, no support from the strategy.

Although the education institute started its women's information technology project by referring to regional strategy formulations of local agency, it later turned to the national strategy. The institute educated women through standard ICT training packages and the training was top-down, a method which cannot support active agency. Instead, the women studied basic skills as individuals and they faced "their opportunities" as individuals. Although the teaching was done in small women's groups, the groups served only as a form of organizing students. If the first women's group was an ideal type of located politics, which intertwined with the liberal, the second-phase groups were an ideal type of liberal politics which had adopted a few elements of located politics.

The Liberal Takes Over the Located Politics

Liberal feminist politics have been compared to other types of feminist politics and this comparison is also made in gender and technology research. Cynthia Cockburn (1985) claimed relatively early that equal opportunity is not enough and feminist politics need to take into account gendering relations and practices. This debate is no less important in the context of the information society. Liberal politics is relevant and all individuals need to have equal access to information and technologies. There are, however, different versions of liberal politics, and liberal politics can also be disadvantageous to women.

For example, in the second-phase groups, there was one woman, let us call her Irma, who did not know how to type. She was a very active woman and she took responsibility for many others. Her lack of typing skills, however, made it impossible for her to continue: "I am not able to learn as fast as the people who have used computers for many years, and I am all new. (The course should be for beginners?) Yes, it was, but now we follow the speed of those who are a bit more advanced, and it is natural that they feel as if they need to drag somebody along, that they are not able to proceed fast enough, and I cannot continue together with them. I must be able to proceed slower, or drop out." And she dropped out. The project meant for all women displaced her.

The liberal approach ignores social differences and claims that only the attitude of each individual matters (Henwood et al., 2000). Irma's case shows strikingly that the understanding of equal opportunity in liberal politics does not work. It makes active people feel guilty and incapable of following instruction meant for everybody. It cannot be the responsibility of each individual to reach the universal opportunity; opportunities should be situated as well.

Furthermore, the liberal-politics way of teaching information technology undermined the women's knowledge and agency. In the first group, the women together built an alternative information technology. They studied and developed information technology from the starting point of their lives as women who inhabited a particular neighborhood in North Karelia. They built both the practices and the contents of information technology, a space for their gendered being and acting, for their gendered local agency. When other information technology (read: men's) groups in the neighborhood center examined programs and nets as such, without locating them, women made labels for jam bottles and other items specifically related to their lives. They built situated knowledge and technology instead of objectified knowledge and neutral technology. In this way they truly challenged the realm of male expertise and made their own mark.

Women in the second stage of the project also worked in small groups with women teachers. They, however, studied the basic skills in information technology like everybody else involved in the institute. These women's groups did not challenge the content of information technology. The liberal approach ignored the women's situated and local knowledge and discussed only universal and "neutral" technology.

The liberal approach tends to encourage the uncritical use of new technologies. When a national strategy proudly boasts of the high numbers of technology users in the country, as it does in Finland, it becomes the responsibility of each citizen to use the technical opportunities provided by society. Citizens do use the newest technologies as soon as they become available. But in the located politics of technology it is possible to evaluate technology from the starting point of each group's concrete setting. In the liberal approach to education there is no room for such evaluative practices. People learn new technical skills efficiently but do not situate their use.

However, the critical evaluation of technology remained rather limited in the first group as well as in the second-phase groups. The first group learned about technologies in their everyday setting, and this challenged conventional practices of technology. The group did not, however, articulate or critique the gendered relations and masculine cultures of technology. For such a critical evaluation of technology they would have needed support. Instead they worked among themselves and saw technology as basic tools available in the neighborhood center. Critical evaluation of technology from the starting point of located practices is difficult and it is here that the welfare network supporting the neighborhood center could have taken a more active role. They could have provided means to help the women to deconstruct gendered relations of technology and to achieve a balance between their own starting point and new technologies.

Gender relations in the second-phase groups were shaped in an unexpected and contradictory manner. Sometimes the women's groups and their teachers gathered together in the institute for workshop days. They were then taught by male teachers. In this way the institute perpetuated the idea that there are certain areas in information technology education that cannot be taught by women and must be left to male teachers. This suggested to the women that expertise in information technology is highly gendered: There are areas where women can teach but there are other areas where women teachers are of no use. There is a place beyond the reach of women where only men can be experts. This was not brought up in interviews with the women and it probably was not discussed among the participants themselves. It reflects stereotypical Western understandings of gender and technology relations; it passed unnoticed and was taken as self-evident (only one teacher took up this point in an interview).

It strengthened rather than challenged the existing gender bias. So in the second phase the women's information technology group project allied itself with counter-feminist rather than feminist politics.

There is a contentious relation between liberal and located politics of technology as revealed in these women's information technology groups. The liberal politics easily engulfed located concerns. Liberal politics is embedded in the rhetoric of the welfare state and information society development, and thus is familiar to people. In the project, the rhetoric and the politics related to it were not discussed or made explicit, and this resulted in a lessening of women's agency. Most women learned standard skills and thus developed some agency, but they could have done it far more effectively if they had been able to begin with their own experiences. This located approach would also have benefited from more explicit conceptual efforts and articulations of the gendered construction of agency embedded in institutions, technologies, and everyday life settings.

There are possibilities for better integration of the two political approaches. Liberal equal access is valuable and all efforts should be made to defend it. Equality, however, should be understood as a situated and located relation. Otherwise the "equal" does not extend to all equally. Some people drop out and situated knowledge is lost, and unwanted differences are strengthened instead of being discarded. All citizens should have equal access to better developed practices for critical evaluation of technologies.

Located Politics in a Liberal Society?

The welfare state, organizational practices, and gender relations are social and material orders that contribute to located agency in a technologically mediated society. Other relations, such as class, age, place, and relations between the transnational, national, and regional, also play a part in shaping located agency.

A citizens' information society should not give "equal access" only to individual (lonely hero) citizens; the citizens' perspective should be located in a broader societal and institutional context. The citizens' perspective, including their own articulations, experiences, situations, and definitions, is embedded in institutional and textual practices which do or do not support it. Institutional support is important for all, but it is especially important to those who deviate from the (liberal) ideal, in a Western information society, of the white, middle-class, well-educated man. Different and contradictory figures, such as the woman who cannot type, should find room in the courses developed in terms of "equal access." The welfare network that supported the neighborhood center of the first group is an important model. The members of the network assessed residents' interests and needs and then succeeded in giving support and space to the people's agency. This is far from a self-evident process. Even the grassroots activity eventually mimicked the forms and practices used by the traditional educational institute.

The first women's group respected the women's situations. Its members did not challenge the male gender, technology, and expertise nexus in a particularly explicit way. They rather chose an affirmative path that focused on their own voices and developed ICT of their own. The women's groups in the second-phase project, on the contrary, gathered in the spirit of a universal, equal, and liberal citizenship. ICT was understood as neutral and the same for everybody. The understanding of gender in the project was limited to social interaction: It was "nice" and safe for women to study ICT in women's groups. Yet gender was deeply present in the practices of the project. In some areas the women teachers were not regarded as competent experts and were replaced by men. The project strengthened mainstream gender divisions between men as experts and women as users.

The project experience suggests that relationships of gender and technology need to be articulated openly. If they are not articulated, the deep bond between male expertise and technology may continue to appear self-evident, and the project may—paradoxically—turn against its own goals and limit agency instead of encouraging it. Gender intertwines with other social relations in women's practices, and articulation work is necessarily situated.

The women's group as such turned out to be good for women's learning. In all cases the participants said that they liked to study in a women's group. They felt that they were able to ask questions better than in mixed groups. A women's study group is a forum for empowerment and encourages redefinition of the relations of gender and expertise in information technology. In women's groups the women studied at their own level while in mixed groups they felt incompetent, which certainly hinders learning.

Women's ICT groups may look very similar in newspaper pictures, but there may be significant differences in their practices and goals. Women's groups that create situated beginnings result in voices different from those groups that follow universal liberal politics and study the standard "driving skills" of ICT. In the former, women begin to understand that ICT has been presented in terms of male expertise. In order to create voices of their own, women need to connect technology to their own experiences, which means struggle and work. Starting points need to be defined and articulated and women's groups can help with this. One's own starting points are constructed in complex social relations (e.g., relating to career prospects or money available) that often intertwine with gender. Groups that begin from women's situations and everyday starting points have room for societal differences and can make technology situated. There is room for differences between women as well as for communal agency which situates structural and cultural relations within individual choices.

Notes

1. I have studied this paradox in another article. It seems that the Finnish economic dependence on the ICT industry, the use of liberal politics in information society development, and the tendency toward technical nationalism together create a context for a paradoxical discourse of equality in new technology.

2. The first group started through the initiative of an active woman living in the area who had earlier participated in national-level equality politics. She knew about women's technology groups in other countries.

References

By Joint Work Party to the Information Society: The Information Society Strategy and Action of North Karelia 1999–2006. (1999). Joensuu: The Regional Council of North Karelia.

Blum, Linda M. (1991). *Between Feminism and Labor: The Significance of the Comparable Worth Movement*. Berkeley: University of California Press.

Bono, Paola, & Kemp, Sandra, (Eds.). (1991). *Italian Feminist Thought*. Oxford: Basil Blackwell.

Cockburn, Cynthia. (1985). *Machinery of Dominance: Women, Men and Technical Know-How*. London: Pluto Press.

Escobar, Arturo. (1999). Gender, Place and Networks: A Political Ecology of Cyberculture. In Wendy Harcourt (Ed.), *Women @ Internet: Creating New Cultures in Cyberspace* (pp. 31–54). London: Zed Books.

Gill, Rosalind, & Grint, Keith. (1995). The Gender-Technology Relation: Contemporary Theory and Research. In Keith Grint, & Rosalind Gill (Eds.), *The Gender-Technology Relation: Contemporary Theory and Research* (pp. 1–28). London: Taylor & Francis.

Haraway, Donna. (1991). *Simians, Cyborgs, and Women: The Reinvention of Nature*. New York: Routledge.

Henwood, Flis, Plumeridge, Sarah, & Stepulevage, Linda. (2000). A Tale of Two Cultures? Gender and Inequality in Computer Education. In Sally Wyatt, Flis Henwood, Nod Miller, & Peter Senker (Eds.), *Technology and In/equality: Questioning the Information Society* (pp. 111–128). London: Routledge.

Herring Susan. (1996). Gender and Democracy in Computer-Mediated Communication. In Rob Kling (Ed.), *Computerization and Controversy: Value Conflicts and Social Choices* (pp. 476–489). London: Academic Press.

Lehto, Anna-Maija, & Sutela, Hanna. (1999). Gender Equality in Working Life. Helsinki: Statistics Finland, *Labour Market*, 22, 155.

Lister, Ruth. (1997). *Citizenship; Feminist Perspectives*. London: Macmillan.

Nurmela, Juha. (1997). *Suomalaiset ja uusi tietotekniikka (Finns and the New Information Technology, in Finnish)*. Helsinki: Tilastokeskus.

Quality of Life, Knowledge and Competitiveness: Premises and Objectives for Strategic Development of the Finnish Information Society (1998). Helsinki: Finnish National Fund for Research and Development, Sitra.

Rantalaiho, Liisa, & Heiskanen, Tuula. (1997). *Gendered Practices in Working Life.* London: Macmillan.

Smith, Dorothy E. (1990). *The Conceptual Practices of Power: A Feminist Sociology of Knowledge.* Toronto: University of Toronto Press.

Spender, Dale. (1995). *Nattering on the Net: Women, Power and Cyberspace.* Melbourne: Spinifex.

Tuuva, Sari & Uotinen, Johanna. (1999). Tiedon valtateiltä kinttupoluille (From Information Highways to Paths, in Finnish). In Päivi Eriksson, & Marja Vehviläinen (eds.), *Tietoyhteiskunta seisakkeella: teknologia, strategiat ja paikalliset tulkinnat* (pp. 203–214). Jyväskylä: SoPhi.

Vehviläinen, Marja. (2000). Institutional Support and the Gendering Local Agency in Information Society. Paper presented at 4S/EASST Conference, Vienna, Austria, September 2000.

Vehviläinen, Marja. (2001). Gender and Citizenship in the Information Society: Women's Information Technology Groups in North Karelia. In Alison Adam & Eileen Green (Eds.), *Virtual gender* (pp. 225–240). London: Routledge.

Wajcman, Judy. (1991). *Feminism Confronts Technology.* Cambridge: Polity Press.

Wakeford, Nina. (2000). Gender and the Landscapes of Computing in an Internet Café. In Gill Kirkup, Linda Janes & Kathryn Woodward (Eds.), *The Gendered Cyborg: A Reader* (pp. 291–304). London: Routledge.

Walby, Sylvia. (1990). *Theorising Patriarchy.* Oxford: Blackwell.

Chapter 13

Interactive Television in the Everyday Lives of Young Couples

Liesbet van Zoonen and Chris Aalberts

Introduction

Television as we know it is on its deathbed, at least if we want to believe the industry's predictions about the digital future. Digitization makes the integration of television and the Internet possible by combining the audiovisual appeal of television and the interactivity of the Internet into a powerful new medium. In part this medium is already with us. Cable and satellite operators throughout the world are offering an abundance of new general and thematic channels to subscribe to; live soccer and feature films have been used to create popular demand for these services, which have been introduced with varying rates of success (see, for example, PBS, 2001; Swedlow, 2000). In addition, various forms of "delay-television" have been introduced—the best known examples being TiVo and Replay TV—enabling viewers to escape the schedules of broadcasters and watch programs at their own time and pace (Lewis, 2000). New television sets feature electronic program guides (Swedlow, 2000) and intelligent agent systems that learn from viewing preferences and behavior, and will assist viewers in compiling their own television evenings (Lewis, 2000). True interaction is predicted for the future: Requesting additional information from news or sports broadcasts, participating in television debates or quiz and game shows, and browsing through the pages of TV-order catalogs will all be possible (e.g., Heuvelman & Peeters, 1999).

Discourse about interactive television is for the most part technocentric. Technology is seen as central to the new media ventures (Kim, 2001), making possible an abundance of services and applications. The industry expects these new applications of television and Internet technology to transform individual viewers' preferences and behavior to such an extent that television as the social and cultural phenomenon that we know today will disappear. It is mostly interactivity through selection that makes individualization and rationalization the key words which characterize television culture in the future. Reaction and conversation could also make television a more individualized experience. Unlike the social, collective, and relatively passive experience that television offers at this moment—watching with family and friends, exchanging likes and dislikes the day after—television of the future is forecast to be part of an active, individual lifestyle, geared to fulfilling specific personal needs. That is at least what the industry, constituted by the converging communication sectors of software houses, broadcasters, advertisers, cable operators, and others, predicts:

> What is still a broadcast, passive, linear, entertainment viewing experience for millions of people around the world, television is now becoming an on-demand, participatory, non-linear, infotainment, advertising targeted, broadband, two-way communications platform. When fully realized on a mass scale ... our current experience of television will drastically transform. For the first time, possibly, TV can become something a viewer can control and use for information and communication. (Swedlow, 2000)

Visions of interactive television have all the features of technological determinism and are part of a technocentric discourse that offers no space for the particular contexts in which technologies are to be taken up and used (McOmber, 1999). The complex articulations of habits, rituals, interactions, needs, instrumental ends, expressive goals, and lifestyles of which television is made up are completely ignored in favor of a belief in technology as an all-powerful motor of social and cultural change. But interactive television is not so much a technical project as a cultural project (Kim, 2001). In technical terms the integration of television and the Internet is accomplished with specification and standardization as the main hurdles to be overcome in the future (not easy ones for that matter). Technological sophistication, however, does not predict what forms its domestication in the household, as Silverstone and Hirsch (1992) have termed it, will take. The nature of the household has changed considerably in the past decades. We have seen a change from its main function of constituting the private sphere to its becoming a place where work and leisure now continuously intermix (Frissen, 1992). We have also witnessed a fragmentation of forms: Single households, living-together households, living-apart-together households, single parent households, and other forms of households have been added to the nuclear family. These ways of living together necessitate continuous negotiations and agreements between partners, between parents and children, and among children. As many a research project has shown, information and communication technologies are deeply implicated in these negotiations as their use is the result of particular rules and rituals in the household, while at the same time the technologies influence and change the rules (Silverstone & Hirsch, 1992).

The question of whether and how interactive television will acquire "meaning" (in terms of usage, relevance, and psychological investment) in particular configurations of everyday life is therefore central to its future success. This is the issue we will take up in this chapter. Our purpose is to provide an alternative to the industrial-future rhetoric by contrasting the technological possibilities of interactive television with the actual and everyday uses of its enabling technologies—television and the Internet. Existing research and an exploratory interview study conducted among young Dutch couples provide our data.

Before we proceed, however, we need a clearer understanding of "interactive television." Our cursory list of specific applications of interactive television does not provide a clear definition of the concept. The main issue concerns the definition of "interactivity." In general, interactive television seems to reflect possibilities that are already available on the Internet (Elberse, 1998). This is a familiar view because interactive television is said to be a combination of television and the Internet. We use the distinctions made by Heuvelman and Peeters (1999) between three forms of interactivity that are relevant to television:

♦ Conversation: an exchange of messages that tries to come close to the conversational ideal, like chatting with other television viewers.

♦ Reaction: the reactions of television viewers to questions posed on interactive television, like answering questions in game shows.

♦ Selection: the selection of programs at a personally convenient time.

Since the second and third forms of interactivity are part of present reality to some extent, and because they dominate industrial visions about interactive television, we will focus on these two in the present chapter.

Framework

Most information on interactive television comes from market research. Since the 1970s the Western industrialized world has seen a number of experiments with interactive television (Elberse, 1998; Kim, 2001) which have invariably been accompanied by research for marketing purposes studying potential commercial venues and the most profitable target groups. While such research inevitably produces an optimistic press release, such as "Majority of Network TV Viewers Are Ready for Interactive Programming" (Techtrends, 2000), it does not allow the delivery of data and methods to the public domain of science. The accumulated press releases show contradictory results—as Internet marketing research does in general—predicting both great and gloomy futures for specific applications at the same time (van Zoonen, 2001). In addition, marketing research suffers from its institutional epistemology (Ang, 1991), producing relevant data for strategic commercial decisions but little information about the everyday variegated use patterns that often exceed the limits of easily identifiable consumption patterns. In addition, its focus is on individual uses of interactive television, and it pays little attention to the particular context in which new applications will be used.

While market research on interactive television suffers from these problems, scientific research on interactive television is scarce. Elberse (1998) shows that Dutch consumers are attracted to interactive news applications, preferring them to traditional television news. The study shows that consumers think it is more important to determine the time the program is watched than to select news items themselves (Elberse, 1998). An experiment with video-on-demand in Norway shows that trial participants developed a metaphorical background into which they could fit the video-on-demand service. Many participants see this service as that of an extended video recorder (Ling, Nilsen, & Granhaug, 1999).

Existing research on the question of which meanings interactive television will acquire in everyday life in the future does not get us very far. By and large interactive television is positioned as a medium for use in the domestic context. Morrison and Krugman (2001) show that there are two main clusters of media in the home, one around television and one around the computer, which both carry technological and social symbolism. These clusters are identified as logical groupings of technologies in which a main technology (computer or television) is the anchor for associated technologies like the VCR and Internet. As interactive television is expected to be a combination of these two clusters, research about the television cluster and the computer cluster is most relevant for an understanding of the coming uses and meanings of interactive television. Following the expectancy value theory of media use (Palmgreen & Rayburn, 1994), we assume that audience expectations of interactive television will be rooted in their experience with its enabling technologies: television/VCR on the one hand, and PC/Internet on the other. Being a combination of these clusters, interactive television is most likely to be informed by their existing patterns of use, their expected rewards, and their relevance in the household. It is less likely that interactive television will produce a whole new situation, although it is precisely such a novelty that is suggested by the marketing efforts around interactive television and the digital future in general.

Methodology

We use two kinds of sources to construct our forecast:

♦ Research literature on the everyday uses of television, VCR, PC, and Internet, which constitutes a well-elaborated empirical field within media studies;

♦ A specifically designed exploratory study carried out among young Dutch heterosexual couples which focuses on their understandings, expectations, and appreciations of interactive television.

We interviewed 20 heterosexual couples between 20 and 30 years of age who live together and don't have children.[1] We chose to focus on a relatively young generation, assuming that they would be comfortable with digital technologies. Much of the new information and communication technologies are aimed at young target groups—men and women alike—who have grown up with various kinds of media, who have relatively high spending power, much leisure time, and no family responsibilities (Tapscott, 1997). A second reason to focus on young couples is that they may not be rigidly caught up in traditional gender relations. This new generation often claims not to be affected by "old-fashioned" gender relations and is deeply convinced of its capacity to make its own choices and to avoid discrimination, at least in the Dutch cultural context (Cels, 1999). Nevertheless, the social relations we found were somewhat traditional with 80% of the men in these relations working full-time, as opposed to 60% of the women. The other respondents were either working part-time or still engaged in their studies. All the couples interviewed had a television and a PC with an Internet connection in the house.

The interviews took place in June 2000 and were semi-structured.[2] The first topic of the interview was everyday life: What do an ordinary day, a week, and a weekend look like? Next the different appliances and technologies in the house were discussed: Where are they located, who uses them most, and can the appliance be typified in terms of gender? Television and the Internet were addressed in more detail, discussing the use of the television, the remote control, VCR, and Internet applications including email and Internet searching. Finally, the future of television was introduced, with the interviews focusing especially on the possibility to watch programs on demand at a personally convenient time, and on the option to request additional information about news, sports, or leisure. The interviews were transcribed and examined using a thematic analysis guided by the topics and sequence of the interviews. Before we turn to the meaning of interactive television in everyday life, we will discuss television and the computer/Internet, which we consider the main building blocks of interactive television.

Television and VCR

Existing research about the everyday uses of television has shown that its use patterns are deeply gendered. In the traditional nuclear family, the home is a site of leisure for men, who see it as clearly marked by a temporal and spatial distance from the workplace, whereas for women it is a place of work inhabited by a husband and children who require continual emotional, physical, and material care. This gender pattern resounds in the use and interpretation of television. In general, the husband (or the eldest son) decides what will be watched, a decision that is not so much the result of an open discussion but "already taken for granted." This pattern is only slightly disrupted in families with female breadwinners. In the traditional situation, women do not often consult the TV guide, nor do they take much initiative in watching television. They do not seem to care much about what is on, with the exception of their favorite serials. Still, they watch as much as their husbands and children do, only in a different way. While the husbands watch attentively, in silence, and without interrupting the flow, their wives perform a host of domestic duties and leisure activities like ironing, sewing, or reading a book while they are watching television. They also comment more often on what they see on television, using it as an occasion to make and maintain contact between family members (van Zoonen, 1994, pp. 115–116). With respect to the VCR, Gray (1992) found that women in traditional families perceived it as a complex technology toward which they felt a lack of competence. That might account for their relatively infrequent use of the VCR; however, as Gray convincingly shows, there is also a degree of calculated ignorance "whereby women resisted becoming involved in the VCR simply to avoid yet another domestic servicing function" (Gray, 1992, p. 248). In addition, women's display of technological ignorance (re)constructs male superiority in the household, a strategy consciously used by a number of Gray's respondents. More than the television, then, the VCR is constructed as male territory in most traditional households, the result of male desire to acquire one. It is a technological device that proves male competence but which also carves out a new area of family responsibility for men.

In our interviews it appeared, similarly, that the use of information and communication technologies (ICTs) could be typified in terms of the gender relations revolving around them. They were, however, not as unequivocally traditional as the research literature suggests. In general, four gendered use cultures emerged: a traditional one in which the man in the household determined the use of ICTs with the woman following his lead; a reversed one in which the woman appeared to be dominant in using ICTs; a deliberative culture in which the partners negotiated about ICT use and what it meant for them as a couple; and an individualized one in which each partner had his or her own appliance. These cultures, however, were not the same for each specific ICT. In other words, within one and the same household different use cultures occurred around television/VCR and around PC/Internet.

Contrary to public debate and "common sense" in the Netherlands, our interviews show that the traditional gender culture around television which has been abundantly identified in the literature, occurs among young couples as well:

> Man: We both watch television quite often. But Ingeborg watches somewhat more in the afternoon whereas I usually watch a bit more in the evening. But when we watch together, I usually determine what to watch and I have the remote with me. Fortunately we have a rather similar taste.

> Woman: Yes, that is more or less correct. But he really does control the remote. As soon as we sit down he grabs it and keeps it all night, ha ha ha. But fortunately I can zap once in a while as well. (Interview no. 20)

Nevertheless, it is not self-evident that holding the remote control also means having complete power over watching television: In a number of households women appear to tell men what do to with the remote:

> Woman: He does zap, but he lets me finish my movie. If I say: hello there, I am watching this, he will zap through the channels a bit more to see whether he will go to the other set to watch something. (Interview no. 22)

It is rare, however, that women take physical possession of the remote. In the few cases, traditional gender culture appears to be reversed, mainly as a result of the fact that the woman in the household watches television most often and appreciates it the most. The men prefer to do something else.

Whether the man or the woman physically holds the remote control, the favorite rhetoric of most couples is that they deliberate about what to watch. Thus they do not interpret their television culture as driven by the preferences of one of the partners, but consider it as something they share, thus making it part of their experience as a couple and much less involved with their individual needs and preferences.

> Woman: When we are watching together, he will take into account what I would really like to see. The other way around, that he really wants to watch something does not occur very often, but then I will take that into account. When we are zapping and I go like: Yak, I hate that, then we will zap along. Or when he says I like that, then we'll watch. (Interview no. 3)

Hypothetically, this deliberative culture around television contains a considerable source of conflict. While in the traditional and the reversed culture television has become a relatively uncontested territory for one of the partners, in the deliberative culture the partners share their investment in television and need to arrive at a common preference and evaluation. This appears to have become part of a rather easy daily give and take that rarely produces real conflicts. In the odd situation a program is recorded, but in general the VCR is not used very often.

> Woman: I don't find it very important what we watch, but if I really would like to see something else, then I just go to the set in the bedroom. (Interview no. 23)

A second television set is an increasingly common option that seems to forebode the individualized television culture that interactive television assumes. Nevertheless, for most couples the second set does not provide a real alternative because it is usually an older set located in a bedroom or other uncomfortable setting. But most importantly, the partners in these households consider a second television to be not *gezellig*, a Dutch term indicating a sense of togetherness, shared experience, fun and everyday conversation. Very rarely is a television program considered important or interesting enough for one person to withdraw into an individual viewing situation, thus undermining the *gezelligheid* of being together or doing things together in the living room.

Our interview data thus suggest more variety in domestic relations around television than is usually discussed in the literature. Whereas a traditional gender culture around the use of television was certainly found, the reversed case was also present. But both traditional and reversed use cultures were part of a discourse of deliberation suggesting that television is predominantly part of a shared understanding of the couples, affirming their sense of togetherness rather than constructing an instrument of power for one of the partners. Among the couples who deliberated daily about what to watch, the role of television as an instrument in relationship management, so to speak, is even clearer. Watching together is greatly preferred to watching individually, although in most households this is physically possible because of the presence of a second television set. The sense of togetherness seems totally opposed to the discourse of interactive television, which predicts that this new medium will be an individualized experience.

Personal Computer and Internet

The personal computer and the Internet are other building blocks of interactive television. Haddon (1992) has shown in great detail how the rules and rituals of particular households inform their use and interpretation of personal computers. Cranmer (2000) builds on this approach, adding the use of the Internet to her research design. She observed how 12 British families used the PC and Internet, and found these tools to be the domain of fathers and sons. Female members of the household labeled the computer activities of the men as "technical," whereas they named their own use of the PC and Internet as "merely" word processing or emailing. Similar family relations were found in an international comparison by Pasquier et al. (1998) of French, Flemish, Italian, and Swedish families: Father-son relations develop around the PC, brother-brother relations around computer and video games, whereas mother-daughter relations revolve around television. Like the TV and VCR, then, the PC and the Internet are implicated in fairly traditional gender patterns.

In our interviews, the PC and access to the Internet hold a rather different place in the household and in the relation between

partners than television does. Whereas television is—predictably—used as a means of enjoying leisure, the PC and the
Internet are associated with work and school. PC and Internet use
have in many cases turned households into extensions of the
workplace, producing a convergence of private and public
spheres, or rather a colonization of the private sphere by public
activities. The use of the PC and the Internet is embedded in the
same four cultures that were identified with television. However,
the PC and Internet cultures are more traditional and have a more
pronounced gender profile.

In a traditional use culture, the PC and Internet are considered
male territory in the household. The man is the one who uses
them most often, shows most interest in them, and performs as an
expert. Sometimes this results in the PC and Internet being "no-
go" areas for the female partner:

> Man: I am actually the only one who uses the computer. Maria would
> like to send an email once in a while, but we do that together. She will
> tell me what to write and I will then send it. She has become a bit more
> interested since we have the Internet connection and wants me to email
> and look for information on our holiday destination or so.

> Woman: I don't understand much of it yet. I think if I had a better idea
> of how it works, I would use it more often. Now I always need his help
> to email and stuff. That is because he works with computers and I don't.
> (Interview no. 20)

Whereas the couples concerned recognized their patterns as
traditional, they did not seem to experience them as problematic
but considered them as one possible way of doing things, as their
own specific choice, in other words. The problems in these situations occurred when the male partner withdrew to the PC,
closing himself off from the female partner:

> Woman: Some time ago we did not have any kind of agreement about
> the computer. We had a row every time he was behind the computer
> preventing us from doing things together. (Interview no. 15)

With other couples such deliberations were less conflictual and
part of a more egalitarian and sharing use of the PC and Internet:

> Woman: I like the Internet the most, when it comes to using the PC. You
> too, don't you Marco?

Man: Yeah, and email as well.

Woman: To look up things about your holiday, or about interiors or gardening and stuff.

Man: I do pretty much the same, sometimes even a bit of random clicking and surfing. ... But the novelty has worn off somewhat for both of us and we don't use it that often anymore. (Interview no. 1)

In such deliberative cultures, using and talking about PC and Internet use construct a sense of togetherness between the partners ("we don't use it that often anymore"), instead of delineating a male domain as in traditional cultures. When the partners have conflicting interests in using the PC, the one with a "useful" purpose (by and large defined in terms of study or work) has priority; random surfing or gaming will just have to wait. In the particular context of Dutch gender and work relations, this way of prioritizing is primarily beneficial to male partners (who are the primary breadwinners in Dutch society and in our group of respondents):

Woman: His reason for use is more important than mine, I just want to go on the Internet a bit. So I put up with that and will do something else. (Interview no. 12)

In some more equal social situations, buying an extra PC or laptop or bringing one in from work pragmatically avoids conflicts of interests. The use culture then changes from one of deliberation to one of individualization:

Man: Titia is working on her thesis and when she needs the PC, I will take one home from work. (Interview no. 7)

In an individualized use culture, gender changes from a factor that decides the use of ICT in interaction between the partners into a factor that distinguishes a particular individual relation to ICT.

In two extraordinary cases, women were dominant in using the PC and Internet; it was their terrain in the household. However, this was made possible because the male partners had jobs that put them behind a PC all day. They did not want to extend that into their leisure time, which made the domestic PC and Internet available to the female partners:

> Man: I work with computers all day, then I am not going to stare at that screen again when I come home.

> Woman: And I am writing my thesis at the moment, I need the PC desperately for that. (Interview no. 6)

It is tempting to conclude that in three of the four use cultures we found around the PC/Internet, male agency drives the specific articulations of gender: In the traditional culture he claims the PC and Internet as his domain and the reversed culture becomes possible only because he consciously leaves the terrain open. In addition, in the deliberative culture, deliberation disappears as soon as one of the partners claims the PC for work or study. In the particularities of the Dutch context, this usually benefits the male partner. The male grip on PC and Internet use only seems to disappear in individualized use cultures where both partners have their own appliances. Although such a conclusion is partially valid, it is incomplete in its denial of the active role women play in the male coding of the PC and Internet. Turkle (1995), for instance, has shown how women use their distance from computer technology to construct their identity as "real" women because computer love and knowledge are not seen to accord with prevailing notions of femininity. We have already referred to Gray (1992), who showed how women's "calculated ignorance" was part of a gender strategy that brought them advantages rather than exclusion and discrimination. Turkle's and Gray's modifications reveal the complex and contradictory nature of articulations of gender and ICTs in domestic contexts.

Interactive Television

As core building blocks, television as we know it, VCRs, PCs, and the Internet will import highly gendered predispositions and expectations into interactive television. Existing research suggests that traditional gender patterns will prevail in interactive television use, with women keeping their distance from it much as they do at present with VCRs, PCs, and the Internet, and to a lesser extent television. However, most research is conducted in the context of the nuclear family and has little to say about the new kinds of households, such as young couples without children that are so typical of current Western societies.

The use cultures we found around television/VCR and around PC/Internet were rather diverse in gender terms, varying in degrees of tradition and deliberation. However, when the interviews turned to the future interactive possibilities of digital television, a highly traditional pattern emerged in the conversations. When asked whether they could envisage interactive television, almost all male respondents said they could, whereas considerably fewer women did so. When we explained in more detail what kinds of applications were to be expected, focusing on the possibility of watching programs at a personally convenient time and the possibility of requesting additional information, a similar difference emerged: By and large, men evaluated the possibilities more favorably than women. Men, at this point, also took the lead in the interview situations:

> Man: It would be rather convenient, to watch the news when you want to and not have to wait another hour for it. (Interview no. 15)

Another man who claimed to like such possibilities adds an important disclaimer:

> Man: You might just say, yeah, now I have the time, now I'll watch that. On the other hand, at this moment, if I've missed something, I'll just say, too bad, better next time. Or I just wait for the news to start. (Interview no. 6)

Amidst all the positive evaluations, such skepticism is common and extends to what individual respondents feel are the intrinsic values of television:

> Man: You know, I don't think we will get more time to spend, and in addition I would hate it if I could not just simply lie on the couch anymore, zap through the channels, and be surprised about what is going on, instead of tailoring it all to my predictable preferences. (Interview no. 11)

One of the few women who comments on the future possibilities is concerned with the individualization that is predicted. At the level of her household she fears that the *gezelligheid* of watching TV together would be endangered. Taking her concerns to a social level, she does not like the idea that television as a collective experience will disappear:

> Woman: Such developments tend to frighten me a little bit. It will be quite different if you can decide what you want to watch and when you want it. The experience of watching television might change. You don't watch with the rest of the Netherlands anymore. ... I actually like the idea that other people are watching the same thing. (Interview no. 7)

More generally, most respondents recognized the tensions involved in trying to bring the Internet and television together. They contrast the passive entertainment provided by television with the active, instrumental use of the Internet:

> Woman: Television is something to turn on and let go. So many channels, let all the bullshit flow! And now they want us to think about that and make choices? I don't feel like that at all. (Interview no. 16)

Another respondent put it a bit more gently:

> Man: The nice thing about television is that it entertains you, that you can watch it passively. If it becomes interactive, you have to make choices again whereas now I really appreciate that it is offered to me and that I only have to watch. (Interview no. 1)

Conclusion

Interactive television is predicted to produce an individualized and tailormade form of leisure and entertainment. Most couples we interviewed are highly skeptical about this new kind of television because what they like at present about television are precisely those qualities that interactive television is thought to break down, making the experience active instead of passive, individual instead of collective, instrumental instead of coincidental. Yet there is an even more fundamental problem in the background. The way television/VCR and PC/Internet are used in the households of young couples is very much at odds with the qualities predicted for interactive television, as the interviews have shown. In many of the households we visited, the partners use television to construct a sense of togetherness, a shared experience and—if the relationship survives in the long run—a shared history. While they hardly reflect upon it, they do take serious trouble to use television as an instrument in the management of their relationship. Conflict about what to watch is avoided through a variety of partly unconscious strategies. The widely available option of watching a particular individual program preference on the second set is often avoided because it is considered not *gezellig*. Unlike most research, which reports different patterns of male domination over television watching, our data on these young couples suggest a more equal, deliberative culture around the television. PC and Internet use is organized differently, although here too we found many households in which the computer and the Internet were used in deliberation and were made part of the common culture of the couple. In addition, the desire for togetherness is seen in the explicit conflicts that arise around computer use when one of the partners withdraws into PC and Internet use at the cost of spending time together. Such a withdrawal is only tolerated when it occurs for purposes of work or study. Leisure and being at home are expected to be formed into a shared experience—that is what we learn from our interviews; they are the instruments couples use to construct and reconstruct their sense of togetherness. Whereas this is a discourse maintained most eloquently by the women in our interviews, it is supported—although less vocally—by most men. Paradoxically, then, the individualization predicted to be a highly desirable asset of interactive television will only work with these young heterosexual couples if it can be "collectivized," that is, if it can be turned into a medium of shared meanings and relevance.

Notes

1. The interviews are part of a larger project that examines the articulation of particular living situations and the uses and meanings of ICTs. Interviews with singles and young couples with children will be part of future data gathering.

2. The interviews were conducted by MA students of the University of Amsterdam in the context of a teaching assignment.

References

Ang, I. (1991). *Desperately Seeking the Audience*. London: Routledge.

Cels, S. (1999). *Grrls! Jonge Vrouwen in de Jaren Negentig (Grrls, Young Women in the Nineties)*. Amsterdam: Prometheus.

Cranmer, S. (2000). *Family Uses of the Internet*. Paper presented at the Crossroads in Cultural Studies Conference, Culture, Communication and Society, Institute of Education, Birmingham.

Elberse, A. J. T. (1998). Consumer Acceptance of Interactive News in the Netherlands. *Harvard International Journal of Press and Politics, 3*(4), 62–83.

Frissen, V. (1992). Trapped in Electronic Cages? Gender and New Information Technologies in the Public and Private Domain. An Overview. *Media, Culture and Society, 14*(1), 31–50.

Gray, A. (1992). *Video Playtime: The Gendering of a Leisure Technology*. London: Routledge.

Haddon, L. (1992). Explaining ICT—Consumption: The Case of the Home Computer. In R. Silverstone & E. Hirsch (Eds.), *Consuming Technologies: Media and Information in Domestic Spaces* (pp. 82–96). London: Routledge.

Heuvelman, A., & Peeters, A. (1999). Interactieve Televisie: Toekomstmuziek of Toekomstige Realiteit? (Interactive Television: Castles in the Air or Prospective Reality?). *Tijdschrift voor Communicatiewetenschap (Dutch Journal of Communicationscience), 27*(1), 81–91.

Kim, P. (2001). New Media, Old Ideas: The Organizing Ideology of Interactive TV. *Journal of Communication Inquiry, 25*(1), 72–88.

Lewis, M. (2000). *Boom Box*: New York Times Magazine. Available: http://www.nytimes.com/library/magazine/home/20000813mag-boombox.html. Retrieved June 6, 2001.

Ling, R., Nilsen, S., & Granhaug, S. (1999). The Domestication of Video-on-demand. Folk Understanding of a New Technology. *New Media and Society, 1*(1), 83–100.

McOmber, J. B. (1999). Technological Autonomy and Three Definitions of Technology. *Journal of Communication, 49*(3), 137–153.

Morrison, M., & Krugman, D. M. (2001). A Look At Mass and Computer Mediated Technologies: Understanding the Roles of Television and Computers in the Home. *Journal of Broadcasting and Electronic Media, 45*(1), 135–161.

Palmgreen, P., & Rayburn, J. D. (1994). An Expectancy Value Approach to Media Gratifications. In K. E. Rosengren, L. A. Wenner, & P. Palmgreen (Eds.), *Media Gratifications Research: Current Perspectives* (pp. 61–72). Beverly Hills, CA: Sage.

Pasquier, D., Buzzi, C., d'Haenens, L., & Sjöberg, U. (1998). Family Lifestyles and Media Use Patterns. An Analysis of Domestic Media Reception Among Flemish, French, Italian and Swedish Children and Teenagers. *European Journal of Communication, 13*, 503–520.

PBS. (2001). *Digital TV: A Cringley Crash Course*: Available: http://www.pbs.org/opb/crashcourse/enhanced_tv/experiments.html. Retrieved on April 2, 2001.

Silverstone, R., & Hirsch, E. (1992). *Consuming Technologies: Media and Information in Domestic Places*. London: Routledge.

Swedlow, T. (2000). *2000: Interactive Enhanced Television: A Historical and Critical Perspective*: [Online] Available: http://www.itvt.com/etvwhitepaper.html. Retrieved on April 3, 2001.

Tapscott, D. (1997). *Growing up Digital: The Rise of the Net Generation*. New York: McGraw-Hill.

Techtrends. (2000). *TechTrends Press Releases: Majority of Network TV Viewers Are Ready for Interactive TV Programming, According to TechTrends*. Available: http://www.techtrends.net. Retrieved on June 6, 2001.

Turkle, S. (1995). *Life on the Screen: Identity in the Age of the Internet*. New York: Simon & Schuster.

van Zoonen, L. (1994). *Feminist Media Studies*. London: Sage.

van Zoonen, L. (2001). Feminist Internet Studies. *Feminist Media Studies, 1*(1), 67–72.

About the Contributors

Chris Aalberts is a PhD candidate at the Amsterdam School of Communications Research at the University of Amsterdam. His research interests include new media technologies and the meaning of youth culture and popular culture for young people's political understandings.

S. Elizabeth Bird is professor in the Department of Anthropology at the University of South Florida. She is the author of *For Enquiring Minds: A Cultural Study of Supermarket Tabloids* (University of Tennessee Press, 1992), editor of *Dressing in Feathers: The Construction of the Indian in American Popular Culture* (Westview Press, 1996), and author of more than 30 articles and book chapters on media and cultural studies.

Mia Consalvo is an assistant professor in the School of Telecommunications at Ohio University. Her research interests include gender, popular culture, and new media. In addition to her research on women and the Internet, she is investigating new theoretical approaches to studying computer and video games.

Leda Cooks is an associate professor in the Department of Communication at the University of Massachusetts at Amherst. Her current research focuses on identity, collective memory, and (Central and Native American) nationalism, desire, and resistance in the classroom; and on the intersections of community service learning and critical pedagogy.

Johanna Dorer is an associate professor in the Institute for Journalism and Communication Science at the University of Vienna in Austria. Her research areas include feminist media studies, new media technologies, and cultural studies. She has published extensively on these topics.

Karen E. Gustafson is a doctoral student in the Radio-Television-Film Department at the University of Texas at Austin. She is currently an assistant instructor in the department and is also active in the university's Women's Studies program. In her dissertation, she is examining the relationship between mainstream and specialized discourses of the Internet in the 1990s, and contemporary shifts in federal policy.

Jane Jorgenson is assistant professor in the Department of Communication at the University of South Florida. Her research focuses on family communication, with particular attention to relationships between families and other social systems such as schools and work organizations. Her work has appeared in *Communication Theory*, the *Journal of Applied Communication Research*, and the *Electronic Journal of Communication*.

Virpi Oksman is a researcher at the Information Society Research Centre at the University of Tampere, Finland. She has been involved in a number of projects in which she has conducted extensive research into the relationship of children and teenagers to new and traditional media in the contexts of everyday life. She has also studied young people's attitudes toward technologies such as the mobile phone, the Internet, and computer games. Currently Oksman is a researcher for an international project called Wireless Kids. The project studies childrens' and teenagers' use of the mobile phone and other new media in five countries.

Kate O'Riordan is a lecturer in Media Studies for Continuing Education at the University of Sussex, UK. She is also a PhD candidate at the University of Brighton. Her research and teaching interests are in the dynamics of information technology and culture with a particular focus on gender and sexuality. She also looks at technological change and convergence in relation to the Internet and mobile telephony.

Susanna Paasonen is a researcher at the department of Media Studies, University of Turku, Finland, where she recently finished her PhD on the popularization and gendering of the Internet and genealogies of popular cyberdiscourse. In addition to numerous articles, she has published a monograph and edited three books on media studies and feminist theory.

Mari Castañeda Paredes is an assistant professor in the Department of Communication at the University of Massachusetts at Amherst. Her current research focuses on the ongoing political-economic development of the digital television industry in the USA and abroad, the property creation of transnational Spanish-language Internet web portals, and the impact of regulatory policy in the technical and commercial convergence between television and the Internet.

Jamie M. Poster is a doctoral student in Modern Studies at the University of Wisconsin-Milwaukee. She earned her MA in the Communication, Culture, and Technology program at Georgetown University. Currently, she is conducting research on the similarities and differences between the film spectator, the television viewer, and the web surfer.

Noemi Sadowska has experienced the various consequences of the objectifying misrepresentation of women within the media. As a designer, she became aware of the ongoing discourse and repositioning of ideologies concerning women's portrayal. As a result, she has used her creative/professional design and research skills to address the ways in which women are gendered and depicted within the Internet publishing industry. Sadowska has received a Bachelor of Fine Arts degree and a Bachelor of Design degree (from Nova Scotia College of Art and Design in Canada) and a Master of Art in Design Futures from Goldsmiths College, University of London. Her work experience includes a practicum at Le Moniteur Architectur, France, and a post as a visual communication designer at Designgruppe Transparent, Germany.

Erica Scharrer is an assistant professor in the Department of Communication at the University of Massachusetts at Amherst. She studies media messages and media impact, especially pertaining to gender roles and violence. She is second author (with George Comstock) of *Television: What's On, Who's Watching, and What It Means* (Academic Press, 1999), and her articles have appeared in *Women and Politics*, the *Journal of Broadcasting and Electronic Media*, and *Media Psychology*.

Jennifer M. Tiernan is an assistant professor in the Gaylord College of Journalism and Mass Communication at the University of Oklahoma. Her current research focuses on the snapshot photographs created by US soldiers and support staff during the Vietnam War. She is also interested in the uses and implications of the Internet and new media technologies.

Liesbet van Zoonen is professor at the University of Amsterdam and professor at the University of Maastricht. Her research expertise covers two areas: One is concerned with the everyday uses of the Internet, the other with the relations between popular culture and citizenship. She is an internationally recognized expert in the area of gender and media studies and has published various books in this field and a large number of articles in international journals. Her book, *Feminist Media Studies* (Sage, 1994), is used in academic curricula around the world.

Marja Vehviläinen is a professor in Human-Machine and Gender Studies at the Technical University of Luleå, Department of Human Work Sciences, Sweden. Her background is in social sciences and women's studies as well as in information systems. She has researched gender and information technology in various settings, most recently in the context of citizenship, the information society, and the history of computing in Finland.

Index

General Editor: Steve Jones

Digital Formations is the new source for critical, well-written books about digital technologies and modern life. Books in this series will break new ground by emphasizing multiple methodological and theoretical approaches to deeply probe the formation and reformation of lived experience as it is refracted through digital interaction. Each volume in *Digital Formations* will push forward our understanding of the intersections—and corresponding implications—between the digital technologies and everyday life. This series will examine broad issues in realms such as digital culture, electronic commerce, law, politics and governance, gender, the Internet, race, art, health and medicine, and education. The series will emphasize critical studies in the context of emergent and existing digital technologies.

For additional information about this series or for the submission of manuscripts, please contact:

Acquisitions Department
Peter Lang Publishing
275 Seventh Avenue 28th Floor
New York, NY 10001

To order other books in this series, please contact our Customer Service Department:

(800) 770-LANG (within the U.S.)
(212) 647-7706 (outside the U.S.)
(212) 647-7707 FAX

or browse online by series:

WWW.PETERLANGUSA.COM